# Trumped-up Aid and the Challenge of Global Poverty

Tony Vaux

Published by: Tony Vaux

ISBN: 978-1975737009

For further background to this book, publications and information about the author please refer to the Human Security website

www.humansecurity.org.uk

Correspondence for the author may be addressed to vauxt@aol.com

I would like to thank Matthew Bywater for drawing my attention to parts of the literature I had missed, Torquil MacLeod who guided me into epublishing and Andrew Ward who maintains the Human Security website

# CONTENTS

# WHAT IS THE CHALLENGE OF GLOBAL POVERTY?

If you take the view, as I do, that the fundamental purpose of aid is to help the poorest people, the results have been disappointing. It is true that in the last three decades, very large numbers of extremely poor people have escaped from poverty. The UN Secretary General reported in 2015 that- *'Globally, the number of people living in extreme poverty has declined by more than half, falling from 1.9 billion in 1990 to 836 million in 2015'*[1] but generally this is not because of aid. A growing global economy and the efforts of specific governments, notably China, have been by far the main causes of progress.

It is also important to note that the number of people left in extreme poverty is still very large. The World Bank and others recognise that further progress will be much more difficult.[2] This is partly at least because global inequality is increasing.[3] Inequality has the insidious effect of giving extremely rich people greater power over political systems and rich people tend to serve their own interests. They may even be able to block the progress of very poor people, as they do in India. At the same time, increasing inequality makes the persistence of extreme poverty more worrying. But throwing money at the problem

---

[1]   UN (2015)
[2]   World Bank (2015)
[3]   World Bank (2016)

1

through the aid system is not the answer. It has not worked in the past and will not do so now.

Some very recent trends increase the likelihood that the poorest people will be forgotten. Nations and peoples seem to be increasingly drawn towards self-interest rather than global interest. Nationalist slogans such as 'America First' undermine the moral basis not only for aid but also for any kind of intervention on behalf of the world's poorest people. This makes it an appropriate time to take stock and consider what can be done without relying on any assumptions of continuity with the past.

Aid might look like a good solution to the challenge of global poverty but it is not. This is not because of the reasons commonly cited, such as corruption and waste, but because aid undermines the responsibilities of nation states and the capacities of civil society. In the UK, the pledge to allocate 0.7% of GDP for aid may look like generosity but can also be viewed as a sign of increasing self-interest because aid is being used, more and more, to support the political, security and trading interests of donor countries. More aid can mean more bias of national governments away from their own people towards alignments with the West. Politicians in the UK may favour aid because they need huge amounts of aid money are needed to patch up the follies of Western dabbling in Iraq, Afghanistan and Syria. As the UK breaks its partnership in Europe it seeks to use aid to make new partnerships elsewhere. In the USA the aid budget is simply being cut. In this political maelstrom there is a strong likelihood that poor people will lose out.

My experience of over forty years convinces me that it is time to bypass the aid system and seek out new radical solutions to the challenge of global poverty.

We must come to terms with the fact that the dramatic reduction in extreme poverty seen over the last thirty years has occurred in countries that do not receive significant amounts of aid. China and a small group of countries, many of them in East Asia, have successfully linked economic progress to social development. Another group of countries, notably India, has reduced poverty through economic development, but by failing to address social development effectively, achieved only patchy results. Powerful lobbies in India have opposed further progress towards poverty eradication. Many of the world's remaining poor people live in Sub-Saharan Africa where economic development and relatively stable governance could have positive effects in the future but this depends on what their governments do, not on aid. Answers are likely to come from the UN General Assembly rather than from the aid system.

The global level of extreme poverty is likely to remain fixed around current levels unless there is a new approach. This is acknowledged by the World Bank and others which recognise that the eradication of poverty will not come about through 'more of the same'.[4] A key purpose of this book is to explore what role the aid system has in this process and what might be the alternatives.

The basic problem of the aid system is that it has become institutionalised, inward-looking and self-serving. It has provided an excuse for governments not to tackle the root causes of problems but simply deal with the symptoms. Many of our aid institutions go back to a period of optimism and idealism following the end of World War II and the founding of the UN. Over a period of seventy years it is not surprising to find that they have become very big, very concerned with becoming bigger and averse to challenging the hands that feed them. They are also averse to challenging national governments and tend to increase the power of elite groups rather than poor people.

There may have been a time when the governments in poorer countries genuinely needed support and lacked the means to address problems of poverty and distress. But this is surely not the case in India or in many African countries where conspicuous wealth is starkly evident. The problem is no longer lack of means but lack of political will. By continuing in a 'helping hand' mode the aid system perpetuates poverty. Today, even in the case of humanitarian disasters, the governments of poorer countries should be taking the lead, preparing for such events and setting aside the means to address them. So long as the aid system promises to take on this responsibility, governments will devote their energies to other things. The same is true at community level; if the international aid system is always ready to step in, local effort and a sense of community responsibility will be undermined.

The aid system serves itself. Its interest lies in exaggerating its own role and giving the impression that without aid there would be no response to poverty and disasters. Aid agencies control their own

---

4    World Bank (2015) and World Bank (2016)

news stories and enlist well-meaning journalists on short assignments, sponsored by the agency, to add to their calls for more money. Celebrities now play a similar role, earning credit for themselves and money for the agencies. In a highly competitive aid environment each agency claims greater successes than the other. Advocates of aid often claim to be 'saving lives' (or 'saving children's lives') but in my experience this is rarely the case. In disasters it is neighbours, family and local people who save lives, and life-saving improvements in child health require the commitment of national governments to make them effective and sustainable. The aid system does not achieve these things but it is quick to take the credit. This perpetuates a mistaken notion of the helplessness of peoples and governments in poorer countries.

Deeper changes involving political change may be necessary for the elimination of poverty in poor countries but these changes are generally beyond the remit and power of aid. They need to come from the political discourse of that country. Instead aid tends to reinforce existing elite groups, making them less responsible to poor people and goading elite opponents into desperate measures in the hope of gaining control of the aid pot.

As a result, the Western public remains woefully ill-informed about the potential for change in poor countries and about the dangers and difficulties of aid. The interests of the agencies work against critical analysis and in the rare cases when serious studies are undertaken, they are either suppressed within the agencies or appear years after the event when public interest has moved elsewhere.

This process goes right back to the beginnings of the modern aid phenomenon when TV first brought startling images of global suffering into the sitting-rooms of Western peoples. I was sixteen in 1966 when images of starving children in Biafra appeared on TV and in the newspapers. Those skeletal, wide-eyed miniatures were an outrage. I felt that this should not happen in the modern world. A few years later, haunted by those images (and disillusioned after a year in international banking) I left my office behind the Bank of England and went to work for Oxfam. At the time I had a romantic vision of becoming a fork-lift truck driver in the warehouse, doing anything so long as I could believe in the cause, but I lacked practical skills and was taken on as a copywriter. So began my career in aid.

Many years later, I came to learn that those images from Biafra had been selected by a public relations company. They did not depict the general situation but showed exceptional cases of malnourished children in hospitals. The images were used deliberately in order to promote Western political support for Biafran secession from Nigeria. Oxfam was taken in and agreed to airlift relief goods into Biafra on planes that also carried weapons for the Biafran separatists. Years later it became clear that aid had prolonged a pointless and unnecessary war.[5]

By the time I learnt the truth about Biafra, nearly twenty years after the event, from colleagues who finally and reluctantly agreed to share the truth, I had spent six years living in India and was working for Oxfam in Calcutta (now Kolkata). I was grappling with other complexities of aid and had become used to seeing failure as often as success. I had learnt the impossibility of ever understanding the infinite gradations and forms of poverty but I had found out that aid very often missed the poorest people or had unintended negative effects. I learnt that the destitute people of Calcutta had fled from worse destitution in Bihar and so I went to Bihar, the poorest State of India. I was taken to meet a community of landless labourers who were so poor that they lived off snails –a particular degradation for Hindus. I began to discuss with a local organisation what might be done to help these desperate people. Perhaps they might be helped to grow a few vegetables around their houses or gain a plot of land, I wondered. Then among them I saw an old woman crawl out from an assembly that I thought was just a heap of discarded stalks. It was her home and she lived alone, dependent on the labourers who themselves depended on the whims of agents in the service of landlords. The woman was a widow with no family and she depended on the charity of others who struggled to feed their own families. She was slowly but surely dying and was shunned by others because she was a widow and might bring bad luck.

But just as I came to the conclusion that she must represent the worst possible poverty I heard that labourers from a nearby community had been deliberately blinded by landowners because they had asked for an increase in their wages. The widow and the community in which she lived expressed gratitude that they had not met such a fate. I began to see that poverty, however extreme, is not as bad as the threat of losing even the little that poor people had –the risk of violence and

---

5    Black (1992) pp118-131

death. I learnt that poverty walks hand in hand with violence. Over the years I came to see that poverty is not just about physical needs but also about fear and insecurity. This led me to the concept of human security as an expression of what poor people aspire to—'freedom from want' and 'freedom from fear'.

In order to help the snail-eating community in Bihar, a group of local Gandhian social workers put forward a proposal and I prepared the necessary forms for an Oxfam 'project'. But before I could send it off to Oxford for sanction, a group of young people came to my house in Calcutta, hundreds of miles away, and told me that they were aware of what I was doing and they were troubled by it. They also wanted to help the poor people of Bihar but their approach was different. They were organising political action in the area to challenge the landowners who had blinded the labourers. The only way forward, they said, was through mass organisation of poor people in order to change the balance of political power in the State. They objected to what Oxfam was doing because it confused the issues and made some people feel that they need not take part in the wider struggle.

Since then I have better recognised that poverty arises from a power struggle in which some people have lost out. Extreme poverty is an injustice that can only be defended by force. Poor people are well aware of this injustice. They face oppression rather than neglect; charity is not always the right answer. In India the system is reinforced by caste. In much of sub-Saharan Africa, tribal patronage systems lead to inclusion and exclusion. In Haiti and parts of Latin America, the basis for exclusion is an elite class system. And so on for each country. Throwing money at the problem does not usually help. Even well-designed projects cannot reach the enormity of the problem. Money is likely to make matters worse.

Two decades later I returned to Bihar to make a study of violence in India for the UK's Department for International Development (DFID). I found that Bihar had indeed changed. People from the labouring classes now dominated the political balance and had forced landlords to give way on land reform. Poor people were claiming land for themselves. Education and health services were improving rapidly. Blindings were a thing of the past. The police were now more responsive to poor people instead of simply protecting landlords. My political questioners seemed to have been proved right. I was confronted with the limitations of aid.

So it is no surprise to find that the big steps in reducing extreme poverty have been taken by national governments, especially China and India, with little effect from aid. It is also telling that the big steps in relation to global health have been led by philanthropists, notably the Gates Foundation, in relation to the common diseases affecting poor people. In Eastern Europe the big steps in promoting democracy and government accountability have been taken by George Soros through his Open Society Institute rather than by the aid system. The aid system is divided against itself by internal competition. It cannot take on visionary, focused effort.

This indicates that it is time to look at the aid system in a wider context of change coming about from different sources. The biggest factor is the increasing role and capacity of national governments and their desire to take the lead. By the 1990s aid agencies had begun to realise that their efforts to promote ideas that were not genuinely accepted by national governments always proved futile. The increasing assertiveness of national governments also arises because Western aid has been heavily tainted by its co-option in highly controversial Western 'projects' notably the interventions in Iraq and Afghanistan. Elsewhere aid has been caught up in various kinds of 'soft diplomacy' and even in attempts to reduce migration to the West. The 9/11 event and subsequent 'securitization' of aid encouraged national governments to assert a desire to control aid processes. The Paris Declaration of 2005 put national governments in charge of aid —at least in theory. Since then the Global War on Terror has continued to distort aid planning, and added to the suspicion of national governments that they are being manipulated around hidden agendas.

This makes a fundamental rethink of aid necessary, and a reappraisal of the roles and responsibilities relating to the task of eradicating extreme poverty. The root problem with the aid system is that aid agencies decide what is needed. They may listen to poor people and national governments but ultimately they retain the decision-making capacity. They can choose to spend their resources on this or that, in this country or another, this village or the next one without any accountability for their strategic decisions. They may be prepared to allow dialogue on small details but they keep the big decisions to themselves. They can do this because the system is made up of innumerable elements. A poor person cannot hold any single agency to account because that agency may say they are not involved 'in that sector' or 'in that region'.

The challenge of global poverty is essentially to reverse this top-down polarity and put the decisions and resources into the hands of people in need, their civil society representatives and their governments and develop clear lines of accountability. The aid system simply muddles everything up, or to be more exact the aid system is the main obstacle. A simple and practical way of putting poor people in control of aid would be to divide up the aid money and give it to poor people but aid agencies realise that they would lose control and without control there would be no reason for their existence. So they endlessly oppose the simple steps that would give poor people power over them and in the process belittle and undermine poor people.

In recent years, national governments in poorer countries have begun to implement cash distribution programmes to ensure that people cannot be poorer than a certain minimal level. This is a much surer way to tackle extreme poverty than is offered by the aid system and it works well even in times of disaster. Some aid agencies have reluctantly begun to concede that the best form of assistance is to hand out cash. The success of this approach has been demonstrated time and again over more than twenty years but agencies still argue against it and call for more research. The reality is that they just do not want to be put out of business.

They realise that once cash distribution is accepted as a norm the question will come that it must be fair and include all those in need. The argument for selective projects will disappear because a situation in which each agency hands out different amounts of cash to different people will cause trouble. Government will step forward to take control away from the agencies. So aid agencies have a strong interest in calling into question not only the ability of poor people to use money effectively but also the ability of national governments to manage such programmes. This is where the aid system stands today —unable to declare its own demise.

Aid agencies like to argue that they strengthen local civil society but the opposite is more often the case. 'Foreign funding' provides an easy excuse for national governments to close down local Non-Government Organisations (NGOs) and the flow of cash into organisations based on principle and voluntarism is often disastrous. Civil society can bring about important changes in the political landscape but foreign funding is more likely to undermine than support such efforts. Aid agencies like to portray the work of local civil society as if it was in some way the result of their support [6] but this is very rarely the case.

The role of aid has been pernicious in turning idealistic groups based on voluntary effort into contractors who do what aid agencies want rather than what they want to do themselves based on their principles and interaction with local people. The spirit of voluntarism in poor countries has been deeply undermined by the effects of aid.

Is the aid system capable of reforming itself? The answer must be negative. The trend over the last decades has been to exacerbate the problems of central control and dependence. UN organisations and international charities such as Oxfam are increasingly dependent on Western government donors and those donors have become more assertive. This is not simply a matter of the 'securitization' agenda following 9/11 (the dominance of Western security interests over any other factor determining aid choices) but also reflects a trend towards greater 'public accountability'. This means that donor departments must set objectives and then keep to them as rigidly as they can. They are measured, if at all, against their ability to meet those objectives. There is very little room in the system to respond to proposals that arise spontaneously from poor people and their representative organisations. There is little possibility of adapting to changing circumstances even if it is something as big as war. Fierce competition between aid agencies ensures that there is no real critique of donor governments. The agency that raises problems simply gets dropped off the funding list. The same applies to civil society in poorer countries. Comply with the funders or fail.

Aid staff today rarely stay in country for more than a couple of years -four years is considered quite exceptional. This not only results in limited local understanding but also puts pressure on individual managers to demonstrate results within hopelessly unrealistic timescales. Naturally they look for the 'low hanging fruit' (a common expression in DFID). This would not matter so much if there was also a strategy to reach the fruits that are inaccessible, representing the really tough problems that keep poor people poor. Aid is largely a

---

[6]  See for example Green (2008) published by and for Oxfam

matter of quick fixes for relatively unimportant problems. Sloppy and short-term forms of aid can easily increase inequalities and bolster systems of patronage that may perpetuate inequalities. The rich get richer and extremely poor people remain at the same level, just about surviving. If they were poorer they would be dead. This is why aid has done so little to reduce extreme poverty.

Because there is no single purpose or strategy for aid it is easily manipulated by both recipients and givers. People in recipient societies compete for the benefits and it is often the better-off who get the most. Having made impressive pledges to the Western public, the givers of aid use ambiguities about its purpose and uncertainties about the definition of poverty to use aid for purposes that suit themselves. Depending on the direction of criticism, aid can be justified as a contribution to national and international security, trade, diplomatic relations and many other potential uses.

This confusion of aims means that the aid system itself is confused. This might not be such a serious issue if the poorest people benefited along the way but this is not the case. As aid comes under increasing attack from Western politicians who want to put themselves or their nation first, it is time to try to sort this out. We may not have to put the poorest first but we must not forget them entirely.

The practice of using aid for a wide range of self-interested purposes is nothing new but it is now spoken about more openly and in more positive terms. Presidents and Ministers openly justify aid as serving the interests of their own country. The UK government has begun to justify aid as a means to promote trade deals in advance of Brexit. President Trump has ruled out government support for any organisation that provides information or services relating to abortion. The ban on abortion may cause the very poor women and girls to lose a remedy against the threat of sexual violence. But the effects of these policies on poor people around the world were not taken into account.

Today's aid agencies do not take the risk of challenging the politicians and donor departments that provide their resources. They have become dependent and are 'too big to fail'. They cannot challenge Trump if it means a risk of losing American support. UK aid agencies are muted in their criticisms, for example, of arms sales to Saudi Arabia which result in humanitarian disaster in Yemen. The role of raising such issues in public has fallen to newspapers and specialist campaigning groups that do not depend on government finance. The UN is directly dependent on a small group of Western countries for its funding. The biggest charities are linked together in international chains: defying Trump is likely to affect the entire international network. As a result our larger international agencies do not speak out against injustice caused by Western action. Instead their default position has been to praise their government for providing aid money and keep quiet about arms sales, human rights and controversial issues such as military intervention.

Aid has gained support by being all things to all men and particularly by claiming to be helpful to women and children. It has served as a 'force multiplier' for Western ventures in Iraq and Afghanistan and is now being used to promote good relations with countries considering trade deals with the West. This may not matter unless we also lose sight of the fundamental objective of eliminating extreme poverty.

This book represents my personal attempt, having retired from the aid system, to look at the challenge of global poverty in a new way rather than through the prism of aid. The early chapters trace the founding of the aid system after World War II and how it has been affected or transformed by the Cold War and the effects of neo-liberalism as the dominant Western ideology. The book explores the way in which aid institutions tend to atrophy from principle and risk-taking towards pragmatism and caution as they grow bigger and richer.

Using my experience as a conflict analyst for DFID, I explore the relationship between aid and the patronage systems that co-exist with democracy in many countries, especially in Africa. In a case study focused on Nepal I explore what aid can do when the circumstances are exceptionally favourable. Later chapters focus on the effects of the Global War on Terror, the term coined by President George W Bush to describe the US-led responses to the 9/11 event. The final chapters describe the increasing assertiveness of national governments, concluding that this is the time to set aside the aid system and focus our concerns on supporting national governments in a narrowed-down effort to abolish extreme poverty.

My argument is that it is time to move from a Western-led aid system to a pattern of global governance in which very poor people take greater control of the issue of poverty. Aid may have a role in supporting national governments that take on the task of assisting poor people to overcome poverty. This is not necessarily an argument that all other functions of aid must be dropped. It can be used to support the Global War on Terror or trade deals. But we must not lose sight of the aim of abolishing extreme poverty.

On a recent visit to Kenya, the UK Secretary of State for international development, Priti Patel, praised a DFID project that has helped to build a container port. She noted that this would open the way for the UK to discuss a trade deal with Kenya after Brexit.[7] But she also met women who were receiving cash top-ups through their mobile phones and getting help to start up or run small businesses. The former type of aid will appeal to those who applaud self-interest as the basis for aid while the latter could easily provide a basis for much bigger schemes, targeted more precisely towards the poorest people.

The spread of mobile phones among poor people also offers a possibility to address the problem of violence. Phones can be used among poor people to warn each other of threats and to call for help. Women and girls with phones may be much better able to resist violent attacks. Phones can also provide warnings of disaster and provide information about health issues.

By putting cash directly into the hands of poor people, most of the paraphernalia of aid can be jettisoned. Instead of aid managers researching projects, consultants designing them and contractors putting them into effect, poor people can make their own choices and it is pretty obvious (even without the current weight of research evidence) that poor people know best about their own needs.

Ideally national governments should not only take the lead but also commit the necessary resources. In most cases they could well afford to do so. But in extreme cases other countries, regionally and internationally, may wish to help. The aid system may still have a role to play but it will be a supporting one. It is time for poor people and poor countries to take back control.

---

7    BBC News report downloaded 17 November 2016 from *http://www.bbc. co.uk/news/uk-politics-37758164*

# CHAPTER ONE

# GLOBAL SECURITY SINCE WORLD WAR II

It may take a cataclysm for altruism to supersede selfishness in the global order but World War II created the unique circumstances not only for a demand to 'make the world a better place' but the willingness of national politicians to put global interests first. The UN Charter signed on 26th June 1945 remains a potent statement of the challenges facing the world today-

> 'We the peoples of the United Nations determined-
> To save succeeding generations from the scourge of war, which twice in our lifetime has brought untold suffering to mankind, and
> To reaffirm faith in fundamental human rights, in the dignity and worth of the human person, in the equal rights of men and women and of nations large and small, and
> To establish conditions under which justice and respect for the obligations arising from treaties and other sources of international law can be maintained, and
> To promote social progress and better standards of life in larger freedom.'[8]

---

[8]  United Nations: Charter of the United Nations at http://www.un.org/en/charter-united-nations/

The failure of the League of Nations to prevent the outbreak of World War II arose largely because the big powers did not engage with it. The UN Charter gave a mandate for robust action to promote global security but decisions had to be endorsed by the Security Council consisting of China, France, USSR, USA and UK (with ten other members elected from the General Assembly but without the right of veto). This arrangement has served to engage the superpowers in the UN but also led to a proliferation of client states that can use the protection of a superpower to avoid censure. Human rights violations and wars have in effect been signed off by Security Council members. Censure is limited by the veto. A better solution has yet to be found but the institution of the Security Council is under increasing pressure. The new US president, Donald Trump, has made it clear that he will not be constrained by it.

The UN Charter includes provision for the 'pacific settlement of disputes' under Chapter VI and, where such a settlement has been reached, the UN has been called upon to provide peace-keeping forces recruited from member states and wearing the blue berets of the UN. Under Chapter VII, *'action with respect to threats to the peace, breaches of the peace and acts of aggression'* may be authorised, including military interventions, but this provision has been used much more sparingly and members of the Security Council have tried to block the use of it by others, as in the case of Iraq. The Global War on Terror following the 9/11 event may have given the Security Council a reason for unity but the practice in Syria suggests that the old pattern of rivalry between superpowers still leads to inconsistency rather than united action based on global interests.

The high-minded commitments of the Charter encouraged the aspirations of colonies to independence, especially those that had provided soldiers in World War II. Decolonization was the dominant process of the following twenty years. In the case of India there was untimely haste leading to the disastrous process of partition. Some colonial powers, such as Portugal in Mozambique held out for as long as they could against independence movements. That phase is now over but it created divisions that, exacerbated by the Cold War, persist in many parts of the world. Artificial boundaries created during the colonial period still cause instability, notably in the Arabian peninsula. The attempt to maintain order in countries that do not make sense as specific entities, leads towards dictatorship. Many of the new wars, especially in the Middle East are attempts to overthrow home-grown dictators. Although the UN Charter has done much to create a global order for security, the colonial period and Cold War created many of the challenges. As this becomes more and more evident, people in countries wracked by war come to question a world order created and maintained by the West. But for most of the intervening period, the USA and Western allies ('the international community') upheld the global order including human rights and the defence of minorities. This phase now seems to be coming to an end, with President Trump declaring friendship with some of the world's worst human rights abusers, and placing trade deals above all other considerations.[9]

One of the reasons for this retreat from moral leadership may be that direct intervention in other countries is costly, can make matters worse and leaves 'the international community' with the impossible task of building a new state. Hence the trend back towards narrower national interests.

Another legacy of World War II was the determination to make war a less ghastly process. Steps taken include The Hague Congress in 1948 which led to a reinterpretation of the rules of war and the updated Geneva Conventions of 1949 which give better protection for civilians and extend international law to include civil wars. The formation of the Council of Europe in 1949 (which in turn created the European Union under the Treaty of Rome in 1957) was originally intended to prevent future war in Europe. It is an example of the atrophy of these instruments that today it is widely viewed as an economic instrument or even as a mechanism of control by European bureaucrats. The longstanding issue of a homeland for Jews was settled in 1947 with the creation of Israel. This allayed some of the guilt associated with the Holocaust and the UN also put into place a Genocide Convention in 1948 intended to prevent any repetition of the Holocaust by committing states to intervene.[10] But the creation of Israel led to hostilities between Israelis and Palestinians that continue to have a profound effect on stability in

---

[9]  Such as Duterte of the Philippines and the royals of Saudi Arabia. See *Goodbye to Values* The Economist June 3 2017 pp62-3

[10]  UN Convention on the Prevention and Punishment of the Crime of Genocide

the Middle East and bring into question the legitimacy of the USA as an unbiased leader on global issues.

Perhaps the most ambitious of all the post-war commitments was the 1948 Universal Declaration of Human Rights which set out in detail what had been sketchily envisaged in the Charter. This became a bone of contention between systems of government that give great weight to individual freedom and those that give greater priority to the well-being of the state. This division, reflected in aid flows, has tended to make the philosophy of international aid recognisably 'Western'. At the height of its role as the world's moral leader, human rights was a major factor in international relations. This led some of the world's worst abusers to take control of the UN's human rights institutions. The USA itself has long faced criticism for its use of the death penalty and high rate of incarceration. Today it seems that the USA may withdraw completely from the UN's Human Rights Council.[11]

Even before the main elements of international principle and governance were in place, there were disasters for which the UN seemed to have no answer. The partition of India was followed by civil war in Israel in 1947-8. But the most serious development was the continued division of Germany and the slide into the Cold War. This shaped the international agenda for the following three decades, pitting state-centred socialism against capitalism and individual human rights. The conflict of ideologies took place not only between East and West but also within Western countries in the form of debates about socialism versus capitalism but by the 1980s neo-liberalism ('The Washington Consensus') had become the dominant approach of Western countries. This perpetuated divisions even after the end of the Cold War with the collapse of the USSR in 1989.

During the Cold War, the involvement of the USA and USSR in decolonisation processes fuelled wars and instability in many countries especially in Africa where the exploitation of tribal identities made this process particularly pernicious. While most of the rest of the world made huge economic and social advances, Africa lagged behind. The lasting effect of outside intervention has been to boost tribalism. Only very recently have leaders emerged with sufficient stability to tackle such problems and foster economic development.

---

[11]   *The UN and Human Rights* The Economist 3 June 2017 p63

Both the USA and the USSR took direct action to destabilise their immediate neighbours in order to prevent them from turning to the rival power or using their position as a bargaining tool. Many of the Central American countries as well as Cuba and Haiti in the Caribbean suffered from this process. Russia continues to destabilise the countries of its 'near abroad'. During these processes Western countries used aid as a sophisticated tool that could be used to reward allies, promote human rights and support neo-liberalism. Aid became a Western project because other countries including Russia, China and Japan used it with much less subtlety, and generally on a smaller scale, to arm client states and as a form of 'soft diplomacy' to gain influence for political or trading purposes. The institutions of the aid system including the UN and the World Bank were largely controlled and financed by 'the West' especially the USA.

Another important part of the post-war global dispensation was The UN Convention Relating to the Status of Refugees in 1951 which committed member states of the UN to protect and care for refugees who fled from their own country because of a genuine fear of persecution or violence. In Africa's proxy wars, the Convention, supported by the aid system, could ensure that there was a safe haven to which refugees could flee and where aid from the office of the UN High Commissioner for Refugees (UNHCR) would be made available. This introduced some of the dangerous dynamics of aid that were to emerge in the subsequent decades. In effect the West took over responsibility for refugees from national governments. Secondly, willingness to pay for refugee welfare became a substitute for action to address the causes of their displacement. As a result, refugee camps became permanent.

Western aid penetrated far into the governance of smaller states. In many countries the 'development' budget was almost entirely funded by Western aid. This was expected to lead to improvements in governance but instead it allowed patronage systems to expand and flourish. Aid money could be directed by political leaders towards their political preferences. Aid bolstered dictators who had no need for support from their people because they were supported by aid. With the spread of global media and increasing influence of Western charities, responsibility for disasters was taken away from governments and given to the aid system. Here too the effect was to isolate leaders from public responsibility. Even in times of national disaster, when a leader might be expected to make extraordinary efforts, the responsibility shifted to groups of foreign aid workers who pushed aside local people in their efforts to achieve profile and raise more funds.

The preamble to the UN Charter set out four ways of expressing Humanity or Humanitarian concern- peace, human rights, international principles and the composite of social and economic progress. At the time these were viewed as interconnected and interlocking but as the aid system developed the term Humanitarianism was used in a much more limited sense to denote short-term relief in relation to disasters. This arose because aid came under criticism for engaging in all kinds of projects, many of them clear failures. By commandeering the term 'humanitarian' for short-term disaster response, the aid system narrowed the basis of Humanity in order to highlight an aspect of aid that few critics would be willing to challenge. The response to any question about aid was 'we are saving lives'.

Humanitarian relief was put forward as being above question. The Western public that paid for aid, directly or indirectly, was led to believe that most aid was of this type. As the aid system became bigger and bigger it was able to create a false stereotype of itself, focusing on the few situations in which life-saving might be possible and belittling the efforts of local people and national governments.

This stereotype drew attention away from the underlying causes of disasters and the reasons why natural hazards caused such terrible suffering among poorer people. Aid agencies were careful to play down any political elements that might deter public support. Wars and oppression were airbrushed out of the experience of poverty. The problem was presented simply as lack of money and money would solve all the problems. Charities that attempted to 'educate' the public about the complexity of poverty found that they were upstaged by those peddling stark images of starving children. The realities of human suffering and its causes were not pleasant subjects. The agency that presented a simple picture, a simple solution and a 'heartfelt' message of gratitude got the money.

The Cold War created an unusual situation in which the superpowers were prepared to leave aid agencies to take their course with very little interference. Up to the end of the USSR in 1989 it might be possible to argue that there was a significant altruistic element to aid. Aid agencies moved in a neutral space created by the stand-off between superpowers. From a US point of view Western aid was useful to support friendly regimes and to wean other states away from the USSR. The USSR was unwilling to provide aid itself and found it convenient to allow Western agencies to mitigate the crises caused by wars and disasters. This created the kind of stability and well-being that both superpowers liked to see in their client states. These unusual circumstances led to a brief but fruitful 'Golden Age' of humanitarianism in which agencies could practically ignore borders (hence the rise of the *sans frontieres*' charities) and deliver aid wherever it was needed. Agencies could afford the luxury of developing elaborate principles of impartiality and neutrality as if they were dictating the terms of humanitarianism rather than simply being used as a convenient tool.

The illusion came to an end quite quickly. In 1989 the Berlin Wall came down and the Cold War was replaced by a period in which Western governments were no longer afraid of a backlash from the USSR. Neo-liberalism could be promoted without restraint (see next Chapter) and there could be military interventions without fear of sparking superpower conflict. Unfortunately the first attempt to use this new power, the US military intervention in Somalia in 1991, was particularly disastrous and has cast a long shadow that continues to inhibit efforts to stop wars and atrocities.

I had visited Somalia myself at the end of 1990 and seen people literally dying of starvation.[12] I was one of those urging Oxfam to join calls for military intervention but I was shocked by the way the intervention (or rather 'invasion') was conducted. The landings around Mogadiscio were stage-managed as if the soldiers were making a Hollywood film. The soldiers were clearly the goodies and by implication the Somalis were the baddies. The Somalis naturally resented this and regarded the exercise as an invasion by foreigners.

Fighting broke out between Americans and Somalis. The Somalis captured, publicly humiliated and then executed American soldiers. Those images horrified American viewers and inhibited further military interventions. The fault was on the American side for mis-managing the intervention but the blame fell on Somalis for obstructing those who came to help.

---

[12]  See Vaux (2001) Chapter Six

Unfortunately the following years produced a series of situations in which military intervention was not only justified but enjoined by international law. Worst of all was the failure to stop the 1994 genocide in Rwanda which should have evoked an automatic military response under the terms of the 1948 Genocide Convention. The shadow of Somalia led to inaction and the Genocide was finally brought to an end by an African force invading from Uganda.

In the early 1990s my work for Oxfam was focused on the collapse of Yugoslavia and in particular the war in Bosnia that lasted from 1993 to 1995. I travelled to Bosnia's besieged capital, Sarajevo, and for a day experienced the fear that its citizens experienced for three years. Shells were lobbed into the city casually by Bosnian Serb forces on the hills above. Sniper fire claimed victims every day. From time to time large numbers of civilians in Sarajevo were killed by a single mortar.

Again I urged Oxfam to call for military intervention but Oxfam itself was wary following the disaster in Somalia. Moreover, the political situation in the UK was not conducive. The war had been precipitated by over-hasty European acceptance of the break-up of Yugoslavia and recognition of the separate entities that emerged as Slovenia and Croatia. The state of Yugoslavia objected and this led to war, centred on Bosnia. The West had precipitated the war but the easiest course was to blame the Serbs. There was no appetite in Europe for military action. Politicians warned that the Balkans was full of 'ancient hatreds' and Serb forces could only be defeated by thousands or even hundreds of thousands of 'boots on the ground'.

The USA had been less complicit in the political disaster that led to the break-up of Yugoslavia and, as the atrocities became evident, offered to provide weapons for the Bosnian forces but European governments did not want to allow direct American intervention in Europe. They wanted to find a European solution but were not prepared to engage in military action. They allowed European forces to operate as a UN peacekeeping force, wearing UN blue helmets. This gave a semblance of military action but very little risk of direct combat.

The UN Protection Force (UNPROFOR) deployed in Bosnia was mandated to protect aid operations but not to confront military forces or take part in military actions. The result was that the 'blue helmets' stood by taking notes when Sarajevo was shelled and, as I found out to my great alarm, disappeared out of sight as soon as aid workers were threatened. Nevertheless the British element of the UN peacekeeping force appeared regularly on TV giving the false impression that they were somehow restraining the warring militias.

This situation continued for two years despite reports of atrocities issued by the International Committee of the Red Cross (ICRC) and from the many journalists based in Bosnia. The massacre of more than eight thousand Bosnian men and boys while seeking the protection of UNPROFOR in Srebrenica caused a public outcry. The UK government, which had previously argued that it was impossible to stop the war without 'boots on the ground', now allowed the USA to conduct airstrikes against the Serb artillery. The siege of Sarajevo ended within days and the war stopped. A peace agreement was signed at the American airbase at Dayton, Ohio, at the end of 1995. The same peace could have been imposed two or three years earlier and thousands of lives saved.

The story of 'humanitarian intervention' is remarkably inconsistent. Public opinion plays a powerful role because these interventions are voluntary in the sense that, even if enjoined by international law, no single country can be held accountable. As a result each intervention (or non-intervention) is a reaction to the last event. Strenuous efforts are made by Western governments to 'spin' the truth to suit what they have decided as a matter of expediency. If they wish to limit Western involvement to 'blue helmets' then warnings about the dangers of 'boots on the ground' are given prominence. A spurious peace agreement can be invented, as in Bosnia, and the press invited to film pointless peace-keeping forces in ways that give an impression of purpose. As the pendulum swings from one extreme to another, the lack of any fundamental global standard or norm relating to 'humanitarian intervention' has become a critical issue.

Success in ending the Bosnia War encouraged a gung-ho approach to Serbia's ill-treatment of its southern province, Kosovo. The humiliation of the Yugoslav wars had given rise to thuggish nationalist groups in Serbia which took revenge on ethnic Albanian people in Kosovo. Political discrimination and human rights violations had continued for many years but a particularly vicious attack, resulting in around thirty deaths, prompted Western countries to support the secession of Kosovo. Increased oppression by Serb forces led to a mass evacuation of the Albanian (Kosovar) population and this was followed by a full NATO intervention including airstrikes against the Serbian capital, Belgrade. Massive financial resources applied to the tiny new state of Kosovo gave a semblance of achievement but only because the post-war investment was gigantic. Meanwhile the Western public had developed a taste for the spectacular displays of precision bombing that had characterized the NATO onslaught against Belgrade. The relative success of interventions in the Balkans, and guilt at not having intervened earlier, gave the impetus for disastrous engagements in Afghanistan and Iraq.

In fact the bombings were not so precise. One of Oxfam's staff living in Belgrade a few hundred meters from a government office was injured by a bomb that came through the roof of her residential block. She could easily have been killed and Oxfam had evidence that many civilians had been killed in the NATO attacks. Oxfam also knew that, having cast Serbia as the enemy, Western donor governments were ignoring its humanitarian needs. The largest permanent movement of people during the Yugoslav wars was the ejection of more than 200,000 Serbs from Croatia. Although few of them had ever lived in Serbia they were forced to come to live there, largely without international assistance. Oxfam could not raise funds even for the most acute humanitarian needs of Serb people.

Staff in Belgrade wanted Oxfam to draw attention both to the civilian deaths and the denial of aid. Despite much debate Oxfam was afraid to appear pro-Serb in a situation in which the UK was generally pro-Kosovo. Any comment or criticism might be taken as unpatriotic. Oxfam depended heavily for support on the UK public and on the UK government. In the past this had not been much of a problem because the UK was not directly involved in the various wars and other crises that Oxfam responded to. Oxfam could provide public policy analysis of the rights and wrongs of wars in Africa without any fear of repercussions but criticising the providers of Oxfam's means of existence was a different matter.

Calling for changes in the policies and laws of other countries was easy but charity law constrained Oxfam from calling for changes in UK government policy or action unless there was a direct consequence relating to Oxfam's mandate for the relief of poverty and distress. This had led to serious problems when Oxfam openly opposed apartheid in South Africa. It could only do so by arguing that apartheid caused poverty. Similarly in 1985, Oxfam had been warned by the Charity Commissioners not to add its name to the Campaign Against the Arms Trade on the basis that the sale of weapons could not be directly linked to poverty or humanitarian distress.[13]

Oxfam came to realise that its stance as a fearless commentator on international events had been lost. Kosovo was only a tiny part of Oxfam's global operations but the relationship with the UK public and government was much more important. In the end the issue was that Oxfam had become too big to fail. It could not risk its global programmes in order to make a point about Kosovo. After much debate, Oxfam simply kept quiet. This is not a reflection on Oxfam, which is still one of the boldest of international charities, but a reflection on the nature of many aid organisations as charities limited by law and also on the institutionalisation of the aid system. A small campaigning organisation can take whatever risks it chooses but the big international charities can no longer take such risks. And yet the public looks to such charities for truthful analysis, unaware that institutional factors cause considerable 'spin'. This limitation has become all the more significant as the Global War on Terror spread its influence across many different countries after the 9/11 event.

The momentum from relatively successful 'humanitarian interventions' in Kosovo (and Sierra Leone in 2000) opened the way for military ventures that had no significant humanitarian basis and lacking the scale of resources needed for making good the damage. Following the 9/11 events, the military interventions in Afghanistan and Iraq took place in much bigger and more complex countries with considerably greater challenges of state- building. Furthermore the focus on terrorism took attention and resources away from the crucial task of state-building in the military aftermath.[14] In both cases 'mission creep' (or over-confidence) led to greater destruction of existing governance than had been necessary or intended. In Afghanistan the attack on Al Qaeda in the mountains spread into a nationwide war against the Taliban and took on overtones of a war against Islam. Without a proper UN mandate, the USA and UK invaded Iraq in order to destroy weapons of mass destruction (and more vaguely to prevent

---

[13]   Black (1992) p270
[14]   Stewart and Knaus (2011)

terrorism) but ended up by bringing about a 'regime change' in which not only was Saddam Hussain removed but the entire structure of governance destroyed. The notion of 'humanitarian intervention' may never recover from these dreadful mistakes.

The aid system, including the UN and private agencies, was dragged along on the coat-tails of the leading Western governments. Impartiality and neutrality made no sense in the new context but the agencies could not refuse to participate. It was seen as a patriotic duty or at the least, a charity that distanced itself from the interventions could be regarded as disloyal. Moreover, the media were focused on nothing else. If a charity wanted to be in the public eye it had to be in Afghanistan and Iraq. Although Iraq had not been poor before the invasion, the war had caused poverty and humanitarian needs. Afghanistan was poor already and became poorer. There might be greater needs in other countries but aid agencies had to follow the money.

Aid programmes in Afghanistan and Iraq did not cost them much because they could easily raise funds from their government. Although some agencies protested about the loss of neutrality and impartiality they were tied to Western funding and they could not avoid being placed directly under the control of military authorities. This made them a direct target for attacks by insurgents. The ICRC and Medecins Sans Frontieres (MSF) were better placed to maintain their financial independence but became just as much a target for attack as the other agencies.

A crisis of confidence led the aid system to turn, belatedly perhaps, towards the people they sought to help and espouse 'accountability' as a counterweight to political and military direction. Greater efforts were made to consult with local people and try to reflect their views but this coincided with increasing dependence on donor governments. From the late 1990s the scale of global 'humanitarian' aid increased rapidly whereas the level of development aid remained relatively constant. Agencies came to depend almost entirely on donor governments and public appeals for their humanitarian work. They also expanded in order to take up large development projects as contractors for government but in order to do this they usually had to contribute 10% or 20% from their own resources. This tied up their 'unrestricted' funding and made them unresponsive to requests coming from local people and organisations. The aid system became more and more 'top-down'.

At the same time the aid departments of governments came under greater pressure to comply with national security and political policies. Even the money for humanitarian aid was now heavily politicised. Aid agencies might not even be aware of the strategies that resulted in allocations between different causes. They could see that aid to Afghanistan and Iraq was disproportionate to aid to other countries but there was nothing they could do because winning these wars had become the top political priority. There was no room for dialogue.

Over the following decade, the wars in Afghanistan and Iraq became increasingly unpopular with the Western public. As a result, there was little support for military action in Syria, even though the use of chemical weapons contravened international law and 'crossed a line' designated by President Obama. Despite calls for action by the Prime Minister, David Cameron, the UK Parliament voted against any intervention. The arguments were the same as at the time of the Bosnia War —'boots on the ground' would be needed. But as in Bosnia, this proved not to be the case. When President Trump ordered precision air-strikes against the Syrian military, the regime was sufficiently shocked (or so it seems at the time of writing) to desist from using chemical weapons. But by then, Western inaction had left the way open for Russian intervention and the Syria crisis became embroiled in geopolitics.

The problem with 'humanitarian interventions', or lack of them, is that they depend too heavily on public opinion, which is generally ill-informed, and the domestic politics of Western countries. There is no standard of the kind envisaged in the UN Charter and Genocide Convention. Even the bottom line of UN support for such interventions has been disregarded as when the USA and UK invaded Iraq. The West itself has destroyed the old order created after World War II.

The Global War on Terror is at the root of much of this decay. Even though its effects are far less than traffic accidents or random attacks by gunmen, a specific form of Islamic terrorism has become the top priority for Western states. Issues of humanitarian intervention and global poverty are seen, in the West, through this lens. The way is open for other powers to topple the West. Russia has been able to exploit this obsession to reassert its role in the Middle East. From a humanitarian perspective this is undesirable because Russia shows little concern for the human consequences of its actions. China is asserting a role not only as a regional leader but as the world's leader on climate change following President Trump's retreat from the issue. For those of us concerned with Humanity, the question is what this new world order will bring in relation to the challenge of global poverty.

The West has intervened in the wrong places and ignored those where intervention was the only real answer to a humanitarian crisis. South Sudan presents a cogent example. This terrible but pointless war between the country's two political leaders could easily be ended by the threat of Western military action. The war has led to a humanitarian catastrophe on a scale comparable with Syria and in some ways worse because the people were much poorer to begin with. But the West has done very little to bring about peace. The issue is simply not a political priority. There is no significant risk of Islamic extremism, little economic importance and migrants from South Sudan rarely manage to reach Europe or claim refugee status. Instead, just as in Bosnia, 'blue helmets' occasionally venture out of their well- protected barracks and disappear at the first sign of trouble.

Aid agencies continue to operate in South Sudan and some might regard their staff as heroes.[15] But closer analysis, as I found during an evaluation of the international response in 2015, shows that they can achieve very little. In most areas aid can only be delivered in tiny amounts by airlifts and then it is often too dangerous for staff to stay to oversee distributions. There is little to stop militias from coming along after the delivery and taking everything for themselves. On the few roads that remain open there are checkpoints manned by militias demanding payments. On the road from Juba to Bentiu in the north there are reported to be eight hundred checkpoints. Is the aid helping the people to survive or helping the militias to continue the war?

Despite this, aid agencies continue to put out appeals and run very expensive operations. These operations have little practical result but the cost of them shows up in the 'bottom line' of aid agency accounts and may seem to show that the agency is 'doing well'. Chief Executives monitor their 'market share' against other charities and could not afford to miss out on South Sudan or to focus on calling for an end to war rather than running programmes.

Humanitarian operations in South Sudan bring colossal income to aid agencies (over $1 billion a year) and most of the money comes from

---

[15]    More on this in Chapter Seven

donor governments that have the ability to end the war by more robust intervention. The pendulum may still be in the wrong place, swinging away from the disasters of interventions in Afghanistan and Iraq, but more than a decade has elapsed and aid agencies could do much more to bring about an end to war rather than perpetuate humanitarian contracting. In South Sudan the cost of the peace-keeping mission (UNMISS) was also over $1billion annually. The mission had been deployed after the Comprehensive Peace Agreement (CPA) in South Sudan in 2005 and during the years of relative peace it deployed patrols outside its compounds, although rarely very far. But when violence erupted into full-scale war in January 2014 the UNMISS forces retreated behind the barbed wire and left the aid operation to its own devices. At the time of my visit in 2015, the mission was almost entirely occupied with improving its own accommodation. In June 2016, UNMISS troops stood by and watched as civilians were massacred in Juba.

This is by no means an isolated case of the failure of UN peace-keeping operations. A few years earlier I had the opportunity to study the UN peacekeeping mission in (northern) Sudan (UNMIS) and found that- *'UNMIS may be criticized for remaining too much within its own barbed wire protection... Monitoring of actual and potential conflicts has been irregular and lacking in vigour. Typically UNMIS patrols arrive on site long after the event, likely problems are not identified in advance and relations with local people are extremely limited.'*[16]

Humanitarian action can provide an excuse not to tackle difficult political and military questions. UN 'peace-keeping' forces provide yet another excuse. They achieve very little and cost huge amounts of money that would be better given directly to poor people.

Nevertheless they are popular with Western governments that want to avoid putting their own 'boots on the ground' and they are popular with the poorer countries that provide the troops. The payments for 'blue helmets' can be a substantial source of finance and this keeps the military happy —a serious consideration in countries such as Bangladesh, Nepal and Pakistan. 'Peacekeeping' also gives the UN a role in the world as well as substantial income. The arrangement suits everyone except those who suffer from wars —but they have no voice.

---

[16]  Vaux, Pantuliano and Srinivasan (2008) p18

There have been attempts to put the issue of humanitarian intervention on a more regular footing. In 2005 the UN General Assembly adopted the notion of 'Responsibility to Protect' (R2P) at the UN World Summit. Some member states feared that R2P would be used to justify unwarranted interference by Western countries but in the end they did not object. The speedy passage of the resolution through the General Assembly was unexpected. R2P marks a considerable extension of the 1948 Genocide Convention, covering a much wider range of violence and human rights violations. It was intended to include situations of 'ethnic cleansing' which had become the subject of much concern during the Yugoslavia wars because they did not seem to fall within the scope of the Genocide Convention.

Under R2P states can be held accountable to the UN for the welfare of their people and- *The international community has a responsibility to use appropriate diplomatic, humanitarian and other means to protect populations from these crimes. If a State is manifestly failing to protect its populations, the international community must be prepared to take collective action to protect populations, in accordance with the Charter of the United Nations.'*[17] However, R2P was hedged around with various conditions and although it has not resulted in any specific military interventions it now forms part of the framework for global security arrangements and an indirect threat to tyrants not to go too far in oppressing their own people. As the USA steps back from the role of global leader more space may be created for regional powers to assert R2P but the case of South Sudan illustrates a problem with this —regional powers tend to assert their own interest and may actually prefer instability rather than allow a rival regional power to gain supremacy. This is one of the main reasons why regional efforts to promote peace in South Sudan have failed.

An even more troubling example comes from Russia which has consistently tended to deliberately weaken and destabilize its neighbours, causing new problems rather than resolving them. The peacekeeping role has been used rather cleverly by Russia to reassert and maintain control of neighbouring countries that were once part of the USSR (the 'near abroad').[18] Soon after the breakup of the USSR, Abkhazia and South Ossetia broke away from Georgia. By imposing a

---

[17] http://www.un.org/en/preventgenocide/adviser/responsibility.shtml
[18] More on this in Chapter Ten

military stalemate and taking on a 'peacekeeping' role, Russia has been able to put its military forces into Georgia and use them to consolidate control of the secessionist Georgian territories and also as a threat to counteract Georgia's hopes of joining the EU and NATO.

On the Western side, UN peace-keeping missions have also become more tightly integrated with political strategy and also closely linked to humanitarian operations. The UN now combines all three functions under the name of 'Integrated Missions'. The UN Department for Political Affairs (DPA), Department of Humanitarian Affairs (DHA) and the Department for Peacekeeping Operations (DPKO) are expected to work together under the leadership of a single dynamic supremo ('Humanitarian Coordinator').

This arrangement brings problems for aid agencies if they have any remaining aspirations to impartiality and neutrality. High level UN decisions about aid strategy now reflect military and political considerations. Western donors have endorsed this arrangement by insisting that any agency receiving funds must take part in and comply with UN coordination. There is ample scope for aid strategy to be influenced by political and military considerations without the agencies even being aware of it. Coordination is just as likely to be focused around military objectives as political ones.

Peace-keeping forces often attend gatherings of aid workers and have access to their reports. They may ask for specific information which they can use for military purposes. Such collusion, or the appearance of it, can put aid agencies at greater risk of attack. They cannot claim to be independent of the UN and the UN is often viewed with suspicion by one side or the other (or both). Far from making their work safer, peacekeeping missions increase the risks for aid agencies. Thus the arrangements that caused such disquiet for aid agencies working under open military direction in Afghanistan and Iraq have now been institutionalised by the UN and spread to other countries.

This arrangement might have worked better before the end of the Cold War. The Global War on Terror has made it a politicised or even militarized approach. It has been introduced at a time when attitudes towards aid staff are commonly hostile, precisely because they are perceived as tools of Western interests and hidden agendas. The security of UN staff is now such a big consideration (following attacks on the UN most notably in Iraq) that they are only rarely allowed to leave their compounds and often operate from remote locations. For many years, operations in Somalia have been run from Nairobi. UN staff lack the opportunity to learn and hold dialogue with local people. The same problem of declining security and isolation from the people affects other aid agencies.

The result is a reduced effectiveness of aid and a vicious circle in which aid workers gradually become the enemy. A 'bubble' of discussions about coordination taking place in a protected compound in the capital city. Local people become less likely to provide aid workers with advice and information partly because they are excluded from discussions and partly because of lack of trust.

Because aid money is either channelled through the UN or premised on coordination through the UN, other aid agencies lose the ability to question the wider strategy. In the case of South Sudan, agencies caught up in endless debates about coordination avoided the question whether enough was being done by the UN and others to bring about peace. The UN itself was content to run gigantic relief operations that achieved very little except to swell their accounts and let the international community bypass its responsibilities. It was always possible for an agency to find a small local success story to put out to the world as if it was typical of the international response as a whole. In reality, South Sudan was off the political radar and its only chance of escaping from the nightmare of unending war was military intervention. But calls for intervention lacked urgency because the aid agencies claimed that they were relieving suffering by humanitarian means.

The most shocking conclusion, however, is that the international order itself now lacks credibility. A purely humanitarian intervention by the USA under Donald Trump is impossible to imagine. This is a catastrophe with regard to the world order built up after World War II but it does perhaps open the way for a completely new world order in which power is more evenly spread.

Arguably the way forward now is to dismantle the architecture that has arisen over the last seventy years and this includes the Western aid system. Aid has become so deeply politicised that in many parts of the world it has lost all respect as an independent process. Its only supporters are in the West where misunderstandings spread by aid agencies over many years continue to promote a false stereotype. Until the 9/11 event, aid agencies still managed to project aid as a politically neutral process intended to relieve poverty and distress. They were careful to present their work in non-political terms. Faced with criticism, agencies would refer to 'saving lives' in 'natural' disasters as something beyond criticism or scrutiny. This helped the aid system to continue expanding but by hiding the truth aid agencies have made themselves vulnerable to criticism. The reality that they portray is false and could be challenged if global power seeps away from Western governments, that find the aid myth useful, towards countries that regard it with outright suspicion and determine to 'take back control'.

The part of the myth that may cause most offence to national governments is the claim that aid is not political. The disasters in Ethiopia that gave such a boost to aid agencies in the 1980s were not caused by famine arising from rain failure but by war. The reason why people in Haiti are killed by hurricanes and earthquakes is that they live in dangerous places because of poverty and get no notice from their governments to move to safer places whereas people in the USA will be far away by the time a hurricane destroys their homes. The humanitarian landscape is highly political and so every intervention has political consequences. Attempts to influence the policies of national governments (a common part of aid practice) reflect the role of political opposition and are often interpreted as such.

Over the last decades, European charities have tended to be more critical of their governments while US organisations have taken a patriotic or 'Wilsonian' position. This may be about to change. European organisations, particularly those in the UK, are so tightly shackled to the government and sympathetic towards it that they do not speak out while those in the USA may find it necessary to explore the widening rift between government positions and humanitarian principle.

In any case the tension between running humanitarian programmes and speaking out about the underlying political and security issues is becoming greater. Organisations such as Oxfam and Save the Children that depend heavily on grants from the UK government will find it increasingly difficult to speak out and may lose credibility even if they do so. Already we can see that on issues such as UK arms sales to Saudi Arabia (which result in civilian deaths and humanitarian disaster in Yemen) it is the press and free-wheeling campaigning groups such as Avaaz and 38 degrees that make the running. As in the case of

Syria, the big international charities simply praise the valuable work being done by DFID rather than propose unpopular measures that might address the root causes of the problems. Speaking out is also becoming more difficult because, in the name of national security, the UK government has imposed tighter limits on lobbying and may make them tighter still.[19]

This reflects a long-term process of assimilation and integration. The international charities and UN agencies were much more independent in the years following World War II, especially during the Cold War. Funding from Western donors was tied to poverty reduction and humanitarian action rather than to political purposes. There was greater recognition for the value of aid as an expression of moral concern. In the UK aid agencies fiercely defended the independence of DFID and its predecessors from political direction by other parts of the UK government. When the Global War on Terror pushed security interests to the top of the government's agenda, DFID was co-opted into 'joined up' government. In spite of a rearguard defence by its formidable Secretary of State, Clare Short, DFID's work in conflict areas and fragile states (and anything related to terrorism) was rolled up with the work of the FCO and Ministry of Defence (MOD). DFID's substantial budgets relating to conflict now came under the control of the FCO and MOD. The management of the resulting fund (called the Global Conflict Prevention Fund) became a 'shared' responsibility. In practice the FCO and MOD called the shots because they were in a better position to use the argument of 'national security' (which trumped all others). The resources that DFID put into the 'Pool' were far greater than those contributed by the FCO and MOD and so it was in effect a transfer of resources designated for poverty reduction to foreign policy and military objectives. This would have been a positive move if poverty reduction had remained the central objective, supported by political and military dimensions, but the change was the other way round. Poverty reduction became a tool for achieving political and military objectives as in the cases of Afghanistan and Iraq.

International charities could no longer assume that funds received from DFID (under the Pool arrangement at least) were free from foreign

---

[19]   The Transparency of Lobbying, Non-Party Campaigning and Trade Union Administration Act

policy and military objectives. In using funding from the UK government directed for specific purposes they could not truthfully claim to be following the fundamental Red Cross principle of Independence and because of that they could not claim Neutrality or Impartiality. They were in denial of the Red Cross Code which all such agencies had signed and which states that *we shall endeavour not to act as instruments of government foreign policy*.

From a government perspective the aid budget was more useful than ever because it could be used for a range of activities relating to security concerns. Even Conservative governments (usually sceptical about aid) proved willing to protect the aid budget. Despite the financial crisis in 2008, David Cameron's Conservative government committed the UK to meet the UN target of spending 0.7% of GDP on aid for the first time. This has recently been reaffirmed by Prime Minister Theresa May despite all the pressures on government services from 'austerity measures' and the complication of Brexit.

The International Committee of the Red Cross (ICRC) based in Switzerland now presents practically the only example of an independent organisation within the aid system.[20] It insists that governments cannot tie their funding to specific projects or uses. This has enabled the ICRC to use the principle of Independence as the basis for continued claims to Impartiality and Neutrality. No doubt there are many charities and organisations that would like to do the same but they lose out because they are highly competitive. Each fears that the other will get a special deal from their government and so they prefer no deal at all. But if they are to salvage their credibility they will have to find a way of restoring the principle of Independence. Otherwise their role is simply one of a contractor supplying services to the state.

The situation continues to evolve. Although security and the Global War on Terror remain the dominant Western concerns, issues relating to migration and trade agreements are also high priorities. The indications, in the UK at least, are that aid budgets may be preserved as a 'slush fund' that can be used 'in the national interest'. The public can be persuaded to support a budget that they think is about saving lives and can be shielded from knowing that aid is just as likely to be used

---

[20]  The only other agency that could make such a claim is MSF France which is heavily funded by a relatively well informed French public

to support trade deals with abusers of human rights. The international charities can be paid (or forced) to keep silent.

None of this would matter a great deal if we could be sure that the effort to reduce extreme poverty and distress would not be lost in the atrophy of the aid system. Those of us concerned with this issue will need to focus on it as a single and central aim that is worth preserving whatever else happens. But it is not at all clear that this aim is going to be achieved through the existing aid system or even that Western people have any special obligation. It is now a matter for concerned people all over the world.

# CHAPTER TWO
# POVERTY REDUCTION SINCE WORLD WAR II

The international order laid down after World War II was in two parts. The main focus of the UN Charter and subsequent international agreements was on norms and security arrangements to prevent human rights violations and wars, as described in the previous Chapter. The other part of the arrangements was concerned with economic development. This embraced issues of trade and aid, but the key question was about economic ideology and this quickly transposed, because of the Cold War context, into communism versus capitalism. At the end of World War II communism may have seemed just as successful as capitalism. It had lifted millions of people in the USSR out of poverty, emerged victorious in the war and created conditions of security and stability. There were advantages and disadvantages on each side and over the following decades the two economic systems fought it out over third countries (The Third World). Both sides used military support but aid in the form recognised today was mainly a Western prerogative and the aid system developed as a tool of capitalism and later neo-liberalism.

The success of the Marshall Plan for the reconstruction of Europe after World War II encouraged the view that money could solve problems of development –the question was simply how much. This led to a false optimism about the effects of aid and a persistent notion that it is quantity rather than quality that counts. The economies of Europe were not started but re-started. Cash triggered the potential of pre-existing skills, behaviours and systems of governance. Everyone knew what to do. But when similar approaches were applied in 'undeveloped' countries the problem was that the skills, behaviours and systems of governance to support Western-style economic growth were lacking. Those that existed might be quite different and produce quite different results in response to an injection of cash. The reconstruction of Western industrial economies was a different process from constructing new ones in the world's least developed countries. Problems were underestimated, timescales were rushed and many of the early development schemes failed.

Aid money became a temptation for post-colonial leaders faced with the problem of securing support as they set about creating democracies and Western norms of governance in societies that had different histories and had long been ruled by foreign powers. Colonialism had distorted and damaged their economies, trade and social arrangements. Societies had been deliberately divided following the 'divide and rule' principle. Ethnicities had been manipulated and exaggerated. Chiefs with little power in pre-colonial days had been appointed as despots and encouraged to surround themselves with a panoply of tribal symbols. They turned towards old patterns of patrimonialism or patronage in order to elevate their status and retain power. Money for aid projects was a big attraction to those seeking to challenge the post-colonial rulers. Seeing a chance to grab the riches of development, they staged rebellions and wars. Africa, most of all, was a victim of the simplistic money-led forms of development sponsored by the aid system in the post-colonial period.

Although practically all countries embraced democracy as a mark of rejected colonialism, in many countries loyalties remained focused on local or tribal leaders and voting took place on the basis of homogenous blocks rather than individual opinion. 'One man one vote' was not an accurate description of the way democracy worked in many countries. A person was more likely to use their vote to express loyalty to a patron than to select between different policies or modes of governance. The state remained a distant concept associated with taxation and oppression. Those in power found it expedient to use the state apparatus to reward their followers and punish opponents rather than focus on national development. The pressures on post-colonial leaders were overwhelming. Not only elite rivals but also military leaders wanted to share in the rewards of development. Even those leaders who started out with good intentions had little option but to become dictators and manipulators. Resources that could have been used to promote human development had to be handed out as patronage in the form of jobs and contracts for clients and supporters.

The Western notion of promoting economic development through free enterprise and a vibrant private sector failed because the colonial period had wiped out what existed before and there was too little time to develop new businesses before the rivalries and militarizations of the Cold War led to disaster. Locked into tense power struggles, elite political groups had no interest in opening up markets to their rivals. There was no 'free enterprise' in the Western sense, no independence of the civil service and very little democracy. Whereas the Marshall Plan restored Europe to what it had been earlier, the money that poured into post-colonial systems of government made countries more unstable and prone to collapse into violence. Elite groups became entrenched and rivals realised that the only way to take power was by force, and this usually meant gaining the support of the rival superpower or from regional neighbours hostile to the government in power.

Aid became tied into the competing ideologies of the Cold War. Democracy, light government and free enterprise were the hallmarks of the West in opposition to the dominant socialist governments based on a single political party and state management. The USSR provided dams and power stations to its clients and helped friendly governments keep control. The question whether one system worked better than the other, or was more appropriate in one place than another, was not up for debate because aid was a tool of superpower rivalry. The formal system of governance depended on which superpower was in the ascendant but whatever the economic ideology the reality especially in African countries was governance based on patronage. When superpower control switched, as it did in Somalia for example, patronage systems were thrown into chaos. Somalia remains one of the most unstable countries in Africa to this day.

Many of the earliest critiques of Western aid came from a leftist or Marxist perspective, arguing that aid was a tool of capitalist interests. Such critiques focused particularly on the World Bank as an instrument of US policy.[21] Indebtedness to the World Bank was seen as a means by which countries were tied into Western interests and into a Western capitalist approach to development. This criticism of aid has continued into recent times. In *'What's the matter with foreign aid?'* published in 2002, David Sogge argued that- *'Posing as a solution, foreign aid has become a problem as it is harnessed to market rules...'*[22] A review of aid published by the New Internationalist magazine in 2007[23] criticises aid as a tool of free-market institutions and a means of domination by Western capitalism, contrary to the interests of workers internationally. But the real problem was not the imposition of a particular economic ideology but the failure to adapt to the political realities facing the new post-colonial governments and especially the role of patronage.

After a period of lavish support for huge infrastructure projects as rewards for political allies in the earlier phases of the Cold War (although much of it as loans) Western aid coalesced around the 'Washington Consensus', a conflation of neo-liberal economics and conservative preferences for non-intrusive government. Acceptance of the Washington Consensus became a condition and primary objective for aid. Initially this reflected the clash of Cold War ideologies but later it came to reflect the growing influence of Western business over aid and their desire to gain easy access to markets in poorer countries, especially for the extraction of raw materials.

Because huge loans had been incurred during the earlier period of infrastructural development, states had no option but to comply. This enabled the World Bank, acting on behalf of the USA, to impose Structural Adjustment Policies (SAPs) -drastic cuts in the state and its services on the basis that free trade would bring about prosperity and this in turn would lead towards human development. The earlier phase of aid had resulted in massive patronage systems that had to be supported with large amounts of easy cash. The new policies not only reduced the amounts of cash available but required the deliberate dismantling of state services and widespread loss of jobs. The dictators of the Cold War era could no longer maintain stability through payouts and the inevitable result was a wave of violent conflict across Africa.

---

[21] Lappe, Collins and Kinley (1975)

[22] Sogge (2002) p21

[23] Black (2007)

In Zaire, for example, President Mobutu had received massive support as an ally against his communist-leaning rivals. He deployed patronage on such a scale that he had become a symbol of corruption.[24] Jobs in the military, police, health and education were allocated on the basis of patronage rather than merit or qualification. Despite the distortions caused by patronage, government services were quite extensive and effective, especially in relation to education. Mobutu bought political support and paid off potential enemies and by avoiding violent conflict, Mobutu had been able to facilitate a reasonable degree of development. But with the introduction of SAPs the big payments stopped and the conditions for aid were tightened. Mobutu could no longer pay for peace. He could no longer hand out ministerial positions to keep enemies quiet or if he did, the appointment was no longer valuable enough to prevent a challenge.

Disgruntled police and soldiers took to the streets and the country was thrown into a political crisis. Other countries saw a chance to loot Zaire's massive mineral wealth. An invasion led to the overthrow of Mobutu and instability throughout the 1990s. His successors could do no better. Extensive violence together with the failure of the health system were the main reasons for the disastrous famine of 2004-6 in which four million people are thought to have died.

The outbreak of wars in many countries, especially in Africa, from the 1980s onwards can be attributed to the direct assault on patronage systems caused by the sudden imposition of Structural Adjustment Policies. The importance of patronage as a feature of governance in poorer countries has been hugely underestimated and generally ignored by the aid system.

Even today patronage systems are generally disregarded by aid agencies and equated with 'corruption'. This leads agencies to minimise support for state services and instead set up rival private (charitable) services that take staff away from the public sector. Vigorous efforts to stamp out 'corruption' can lead to unintended destabilisation.

The Washington Consensus is still the orthodoxy underlying Western aid, but the failure of SAPs did not go unnoticed at the World Bank. It rebranded itself as the leading researcher and thinker on poverty and continues to produce some of the most authoritative

---

[24]   This section is based on a study for DFID: Vaux, T et al (2007)

studies available to the aid community. Aware that SAPs had done little to help poor people, it linked its future lending to Poverty Reduction Strategy Papers (PRSPs). The intention was that national governments would take the lead in developing their own approach to reducing poverty, working with a wide range of actors including civil society. International charities including Oxfam generally welcomed the idea and worked to increase the level of engagement of civil society. But the results were disappointing. Production of PRSPs was made a condition for further international aid and governments began to treat the whole exercise as an imposition by the West. The representation of government at discussions about PRSPs slid down to junior levels and the work of drafting a PRSP was often delegated to a foreign consultant.

The PRSP process exposed the mismatch between Western assumptions and the political reality in poorer countries. While civil society was perceived in the West as a positive influence allowing the views of poor people to be heard, it was often perceived by national governments as a front for political opposition and this was indeed the case in many countries. Unable to access aid money channelled through government, opposition parties set up NGOs to attract aid that could then be used to support their own patronage networks. International charities hoping to bring about changes in government policy easily fell into the habit of funding such organisations, and their efforts to influence government reinforced the suspicion that the real motive was political. What international charities hoped were democratic campaigns for change were often treated as an assault on the ruling party. This eventually led to the discrediting and abandonment of PRSPs.

Foreign funding could make matters very tricky for local NGOs. Governments introduced limitations and legal restrictions on NGOs and subjected them to close scrutiny. The more the Western aid system identified 'good governance' as the key to development and focused on issues of democratic governance, encouraging participation and accountability, the more governments became suspicious of civil society and of aid in general. By ignoring the role of patronage, or directly trying to stamp it out, aid agencies further alienated national governments. When Western states needed the support of national governments in the Global War on Terror, leaders realised that they could safely ignore all such demands and continue to receive aid because they were too important to fail. Uganda, Ethiopia, Kenya and Rwanda, for example, pursued policies that were very different from classical notions of 'good government' (human rights violations, manipulation of elections, extensions of Presidential tenure, brazen corruption etc) but continued to receive substantial amounts of aid and accolades for their achievements.

The World Bank responded to these trends by becoming more like a conventional bank, with national governments as clients. It stopped dictating the terms of development and instead responded to requests for finance coming from governments. Proposals were assessed mainly against commercial rather than ideological criteria. In effect, if a government wanted to borrow, the Bank would lend money but like a good bank manager, the Bank investigated the issues relating to the loan. This provided the impetus for further development of the Bank's research and analysis. It could draw attention to relevant research but, especially after the Paris Agreement in 2005, the national government would be free to decide whether to take any notice.

Global economic development had begun to lift many countries such as Vietnam and Bangladesh out of the category receiving extremely easy terms for Bank loans and this meant that governments had greater reason to scrutinise projects. In the past and in the case of the poorest countries, repayments might begin after ten or twenty years and interest rates hovered a little above zero and so national governments knew that repayment would not be their responsibility. This encouraged them to take loans irresponsibly and this had led to the huge mountain of debt that became the subject of much concern in the early years of the twenty- first century. Realising that they had made the loans in an irresponsible manner, donor governments agreed to write off most of the debts. Since then, with tighter terms, national governments have begun to take more responsibility. This is a reflection of a wider process by which the terms of engagement between Western aid and national governments are becoming more equal.

In 2007, Riddell noted that- *'Bank and Fund (International Monetary Fund) staff continue to 'encourage' aid recipients to adopt and implement a number of macro-economic policies strikingly similar to, and as restrictive as, many of those advocated and promoted in the past.'* [25] But in the last

---

[25]    Riddell (2007) p365

decade, the Bank has become less evangelical about the 'free market' or 'Washington Consensus approach', more pragmatic and much more responsive to the needs of client governments rather than donor governments.[26]

The Bank now focuses less on downsizing the state and even encourages states to extend their role. As an example, the Bank has encouraged states to invest more heavily in the prevention or mitigation of disasters and runs a separate fund, the Global Facility for Disaster Risk Reduction (GFDRR), for this purpose. The Bank's rationale is that disasters should be considered as a major risk to public finances and economic prosperity. The Bank acknowledges that disasters have particularly dire consequences for the poorest people and at the same time notes that the Treasury loses income from taxes and may have to pay out huge sums for reconstruction. The approach combines poverty reduction with fiscal prudence.

The Bank has calculated that an investment in Disaster Risk Reduction (DRR) will produce a very good economic return, much higher than investment in the form of project aid. As a result, DRR has become an increasing focus for international aid. This has been given further impetus by global concerns about climate change and the pledge of huge sums to prevent or alleviate the disasters likely to arise from rising sea levels, increasing volatility in weather, floods etc. Climate change is now a major 'growth point' in the aid system. The challenge, however, is to ensure that DRR does not simply benefit the national finances and the general population but explicitly helps those who are most at risk –very poor people.[27]

The failure of SAPs and PRSPs, together with growing impatience with 'good governance' opened the way for national governments to turn the tables on donor governments especially after the Global War on Terror made many of them actual or potential allies. At the same time, Western donors had become painfully aware that the widespread failure of aid projects could be attributed mainly to lack of 'ownership'

---

[26] This is based on an unpublished study I conducted for the World Bank in 2015

[27] I return to this theme and updated work of the World Bank in Chapter Ten

by national governments.[28] They were ready to negotiate the control of aid inputs. New principles for the conduct of aid were set out in the Paris Declaration of 2005. Most crucially they committed donors to the principle of 'Alignment' —meaning the alignment of aid with the policy of the national government. Wherever possible, aid would be channelled through the state in the form of General Budget Support (GBS). Another crucial principle was Harmonisation. Donors would coordinate their actions around support for the government and ensure that programmes and approaches were consistent. Instead of donors taking up many different projects they agreed, as a general principle, to pursue Sector Wide Approaches (SWAps) in which donors worked together, using pooled funds, to support government policy in a specific sector.

Alignment created a bureaucratic difficulty for some Western aid departments because civil servants are accountable to their Parliaments (and people) rather than to recipient governments. There was unease about processes such as GBS which made it impossible to pinpoint the use of aid funds. Theoretically aid given in this form could be attached to any government expenditure. This created a crisis in Uganda when President Museveni appointed more than a hundred 'special advisers' paid by the public purse but regarded by donors as purely political supporters. President Museveni also used public money to buy himself an expensive aeroplane. Donors protested but Museveni's record on poverty reduction was good and his support for the African Union military force in Somalia was an overwhelming priority for Western governments and so aid to Uganda resumed on the same terms. In general the new Paris Declaration arrangements appear to work rather better than those that preceded it.

But the 2005 Paris Declaration did not work so well in relation to 'fragile states' (those suffering serious political difficulties and in some cases violent conflict). The difficulties of using aid in such countries had led the OECD/DAC to develop guiding principles[29] which emphasized that each context should be examined separately and donors should use great caution in order to 'do no harm'. These cautious principles contrasted with the blind trust implied by the Paris

---

28  Easterly (2006)
29  OECD/DAC (2007)

principle of Alignment. In many fragile states, the national government was itself a cause of instability. However, before donors could find a way of resolving this apparent contradiction, the 'securitization' of aid following the Global War on Terror made it impossible to conduct the analysis simply on the basis of government capacities. Many of the world's poorest people live in 'fragile states' but they are also extremely prone to violence, or to harbour violence. Countries such as Somalia are increasingly viewed as security threats rather than as opportunities to reduce extreme poverty.

Effective work in fragile states requires extensive analysis on a case by case basis but this is pointless if the analysis is ignored. Fragile states might also benefit from having long-term dedicated aid staff based in those countries who could learn about the complexities and find ways to use aid effectively and not do harm. But relentless pressure to reduce the overhead costs of donor agencies and at the same time spend ever-increasing budgets means aid in these countries is now positively dangerous.

As well as the pressure to spend more funds than they can handle aid managers in donor organisations also face pressure to meet internal targets and to reach global aid targets, notably the Millennium Development Goals (MDGs). Launched in 2000 the MDGs were developed mainly by the UN with interventions from Western states. They did not necessarily reflect what individual national governments wanted to do and became one of the issues leading towards the Paris Declaration. They also constrained the freedom of aid managers to find the best response to a specific situation. In effect they consolidated a top-down approach to aid that had developed over the previous decades.

As with any other form of targeted development, the danger with the MDGs was that issues not covered would be neglected and that statistics would be manipulated to give a misleading impression of success. This led, for example, to campaigns to register girls for education but then ignore them when they dropped out of schooling later. There was also a tendency to present progress towards MDGs as if it was a result of aid and nothing else. This has enabled the aid system to take credit for China's extraordinary achievement in reducing extreme poverty.

When the MDGs were reviewed and renegotiated in 2015, national governments pressed for a much more flexible set of objectives. The new Sustainable Development Goals include practically any sort of development activity and have little use in focusing aid. But then, focusing aid around Western priorities and ways of thinking was always a mistake.

In relation to disasters there has been a similar trend towards national governments taking back control. In 2003 Western donors set up a Good Humanitarian Donorship Initiative which developed twenty three 'Principles and Good Practice of Humanitarian Donorship'. Principle Five reaffirms the *'primary responsibility of states for the victims of humanitarian emergencies within their own borders'* and gives a commitment under Principle Seven to *'Strengthen the capacity of affected countries and local communities to prevent, prepare for, mitigate and respond to humanitarian crises with the goal of ensuring that governments and local communities are better able to meet their responsibilities and coordinate effectively with humanitarian partners.'*

As nation states began to assert greater control over the aid system, international charities took the logical step of seeking to make those governments more accountable to the people through the work of civil society and by making aid directly accountable to poor people. Agencies created a Humanitarian Accountability Project which aimed to strengthen rights of consultation and participation for the beneficiaries of aid. But this set the international charities at odds with national NGOs and with national governments which perceived this as an attempt to bypass them as representative voices of the people. There was no way in which the international charities could be held accountable to the people because each one would claim that the responsibility lay with another charity. Only national government could be held truly accountable.

This has led to tensions between national NGOs and international charities, parallel to those between national governments and Western donors. It is the culmination of a long process of re-balancing power between the aid system, NGOs and national governments. Aid resources flow from donors to charities (or UN agencies) to NGOs or governments. The dominant form of accountability is upwards towards the donor and cannot be reversed unless the resources are in the control of the people, the NGOs or the government.

By insisting that NGOs become more accountable to the people, the aid system weakens their position. Although international charities like to use the term 'partners', such NGOs might more accurately be described as 'contractors'. Aid funding has a particular danger of discouraging voluntarism. If a local organisation undertakes work for an aid agency it will normally be paid but when the aid stops the staff cannot be paid. Staff working on one activity may be paid and others are not. The infusion of aid money creates considerable tensions within NGOs as well as between different NGOs. In addition, the most competent staff of NGOs often leave their jobs in order to work directly for the international charities at much higher rates of pay. The result is that NGOs come and go rapidly. The aid system has created many 'briefcase' NGOs –small businesses working openly as contractors for aid agencies and without principle or grassroots support.

Another negative effect of the aid system is that it lures competent staff away from government service. As Ghani and Lockhart observe- *'The aid system as currently configured tends to undermine rather than support state institutions. The thousands of small projects designed to aid a particular school, village or district end up recruiting the very teachers, administrators, and doctors they are designed to support, to work instead as secretaries and drivers for international staff.'* [30]

Aid has a strong tendency to undermine and extract capacity for use abroad rather than build it in country. These problems have become particularly apparent in Afghanistan and Iraq where 'mission creep' led to the destruction of existing capacity (the Taliban in Afghanistan and the Baath party in Iraq) and the obligation to build states from scratch. Fifteen years later these Western creations still appear to be dependent on Western support , highly unstable and liable to revert to major conflict at any time. Western states hugely underestimated the costs of state-building and ended up with cost-cutting that led directly to failure. [31]

These vast undertakings of state-building have accelerated the expansion of aid budgets spectacularly- *'Between 1990 and 2000 aid levels rose nearly threefold from $2.1billion to $5.9billion -and in 2005/6 amounted to over $10billion. In the last year for which data are available, 2008, the best 'guesstimate' was a total of some $18billion up about $3billion from the previous year.'* [32]

---

[30] Ghani and Lockhart (2008) p98

[31] Stewart and Knaus (2011)

[32] Barnett ad Weiss (2013) p29

But as shown earlier, aid has not made much contribution to the eradication of extreme poverty. This is largely attributable to economic growth coupled with pro-poor social policies, especially in China. Globalisation has led to a period of rapid economic growth globally and even the countries of Sub-Saharan Africa have been buoyed up by the opportunities to engage in global trade at reasonable cost. The gradual erosion of tariffs had begun to benefit poorer countries or at least give them the means to tackle poverty even if they lacked the will.

The recent moves against globalisation, especially in the USA but reflected also in the UK's withdrawal from the EU, threaten to reintroduce protectionism and reverse the generally benign global conditions that have prevailed in the last two decades. Following this argument, the best hope for poor people may lie in continued economic growth allowing them scope to put pressure on national governments that will have little excuse not to address poverty.

The notion that huge increases in aid will help poor people nevertheless persists and the logic of the Marshall Plan approach to poorer countries still finds proponents especially within the aid system which of course stands to gain considerably from such a process. They have found a voice in prominent economist Jeffrey Sachs who claims that more aid money will bring about 'the end of poverty'.[33] His arguments have been endorsed by Bono, Bob Geldof and other celebrities. But this simply opens the door for governments to waste more money on extravagant ventures such as state-building in Afghanistan and Iraq or on promoting trade agreements along protectionist lines. Aid as currently configured does not do much to help very poor people and certainly does not bring about permanent change as China and India have done through a combination of growth and policy. As Angus Deaton has shown in his book 'The Great Escape', these two countries are responsible for most of the reduction in extreme poverty but between them received only 2.6% of total aid.[34] Deaton goes on to directly dismiss what he describes as the 'hydraulic' theory that money pumped into the aid system at one end results in proportionate poverty reduction at the other.

---

[33] Sachs (2005)
[34] The figure is from 2010. Deaton (2013) p277

Up to now aid and the relief of poverty has followed a top-down trajectory, assuming that benefits would trickle down through the system and eventually bring benefits for the poorest people but it is now time to move beyond that. Processes of economic growth and democratisation must ultimately drive the process but the world is sufficiently wealthy (and unacceptably unequal) to open up the possibility for a global agreement to end extreme poverty by ensuring that poor people get cash directly into their hands. This will enable them to reach out to the lowest rungs of the economic ladder and then pull themselves out of poverty on a permanent basis.

# CHAPTER THREE

# THE ATROPHY OF CHARITY

A id workers start out idealistic and fearless and become cynical and cautious. The same is true of aid institutions, especially charities. An 'established' aid agency is almost inevitably part of the 'establishment'. It becomes too big to take risks or to challenge prevalent power. This is sad but worth taking into account when we consider the evolution of the aid system after World War II.

The danger for charities is that they start by trying to help or augment the state. The state may be glad to receive this help and then hands over the responsibility to the charity. The charity is glad to receive funding from the state but the people who are to be helped now have no way of holding the state to account. One charity can pass the buck to another. Systems for addressing social problems become haphazard and unaccountable.

This is what has happened with aid and it has taken place both in relation to donor governments and in relation to national governments. It applies in development work as well as so-called 'humanitarian' work. The aid system takes over responsibility for poor people and the victims of disasters and is paid to do so. But no poor person has any claim over the system. Failure to provide aid can always be attributed to lack of funds or arbitrary decisions in a distant donor capital.

Meanwhile the charity has become bigger and bigger. Many people appear to be dependent on it. If the charity notices that the things it is paid to do are not the right ones, it cannot afford to challenge the donor. Other charities are waiting to snap up contracts. It must continue and generally keep quiet about what it knows or only select those bits of information that will not harm its position. The charity atrophies away from its idealistic intentions and becomes very like a commercial contractor.

The temptation to take over the roles and responsibilities of the state presents a particularly persistent dilemma and goes back way beyond World War II. The history of modern humanitarianism is often traced back to Henri Dunant's outrage that soldiers were left dying on the battlefield at Solferino in Italy in 1859.[35] He was angry because the military authorities had huge capacities for waging war but took no care of soldiers once they were wounded. He established the International Committee of the Red Cross (ICRC) in order to ensure that 'non-combatants' (initially soldiers who were no longer fighting and later the civilian victims of war) should be regarded as neutral and given rights of protection and care. These principles were internationally accepted and expanded through a series of Geneva Conventions. The latest (focused on civil wars) were endorsed by most nations in 1989.

Dunant's work focused on the role of the state. He was outraged because prisoners of war were treated badly, sometimes as if they were still an active enemy. He developed a role for the ICRC in upholding minimum standards for the care of prisoners of war, exchanging information and facilitating return to their own country. The idea was that the ICRC would monitor and encourage compliance with these standards by working behind the scenes rather than taking on the role itself. The unique advantage for the ICRC is that it has secured a firm legal basis for its work through international treaties. States in conflict saw an advantage for themselves in the protection of prisoners –their own soldiers would also be protected from abuse if they became prisoners.

In so far as the ICRC holds states accountable for non-combatants and assists them in a protection role its work is uncontroversial and widely applauded. Problems arise because the ICRC has gradually extended its role to include provision of humanitarian aid to populations affected by wars. This is where difficulties begin to arise. It seems likely that the attacks on the ICRC in Iraq and Afghanistan happened because the ICRC was seen as a humanitarian aid agency like any other and part of the general Western intervention rather than as a unique neutral body concerned with the conduct of war. The ICRC is also open to the

---

[35]  Bugnion (2003)

criticism that it is taking on responsibilities that properly lie with the parties in conflict.

Florence Nightingale, had struggled with the same issues in relation to the British military authorities during the 1856 Crimean War and she criticised the ICRC for going beyond the role of holding states to account.[36] Nightingale became famous in the UK because she was portrayed in the British media as 'The Lady with a Lamp' who passed through the wards in the military hospital at Scutari, caring for soldiers during the Crimean War. In fact she was not acting primarily as a nurse (she was not qualified) but gathering information. She would sit with dying men, listening to their stories and sympathising with their suffering but also taking notes and analysing what was happening.

She listened carefully to the way patients described their experiences and noted down their comments on the care they received. She used these records to build up statistics on the causes of death at the Scutari hospital in the Crimea. From conversations with soldiers in the wards she realised that more soldiers were dying from ill-health than from battle wounds. Her work took place before scientific discoveries about the transmission of infectious diseases. At that time the application of leeches was still common, based on ancient Greek theories about the role of 'the four elements', but Nightingale opposed this practice on the basis of empirical observation. She had noticed that it just did not work. Instead she argued for much higher levels of hygiene and cleanliness. She had enough influence with the military authorities (she came from a well-known family) to make them change the practices in the hospital and this resulted in higher survival rates for the soldiers in the Scutari wards. Nurses were regarded as little more than servants but Nightingale demonstrated the importance of high quality nursing and the need for training.

Despite public adulation for the few cases where she was directly able to help individual soldiers, Nightingale kept her focus on the role of the authorities. She used statistics as the main basis for her arguments. She found that out of 20,400 British soldiers killed in the Crimean War, only 2,600 had died in battle. These figures were obtained from an internal military report but the report had been suppressed in order to avoid public criticism of the army. Nightingale saw that change

---

[36]   The following is based mainly on Mulley (2009)

would only happen if the public became aware of what was going on. She was outraged that despite the internal report, no changes had been made and the same would happen again in the next war. She contacted the report's authors and enlisted the support of a pioneer in the new discipline of statistics, William Farr, to produce a new starker version of the report based not only on military evidence but also her own direct experience. From her own observation backed by statistics, Nightingale pointed out that the site of the Scutari hospital had been badly chosen and it had been badly run by the military authorities. She calculated the number of unnecessary deaths and laid the responsibility squarely on specific military and political figures.

She delivered the report in person to the military authorities but they barred publication on the grounds that the report contained confidential information. When they continued to prevaricate, Nightingale passed the report to the famous author Harriet Martineau who published a condensed version as a small book 'England and her Soldiers'. This became immensely popular and caused an outcry against the military authorities. The arguments reached a wider audience by the clever use, almost for the first time, of graphics that made it easy for the general reader to understand the evidence. Nightingale and Martineau followed up with a public campaign to make the authorities take action.

The results were dramatic. Belatedly the military authorities rushed to take action to improve their care for soldiers. An Army Medical School and an Army Statistics Department were established as a direct result of Nightingale's work. Thanks to the resulting improvements in hygiene and health care, the mortality of soldiers based in the UK fell by 50% over the following decade.

Nightingale continued her work of encouraging a listening-based, empirical approach to health. She founded a nursing school but insisted that it should be integrated into a hospital, St Thomas's in London, so that the nurses would have practical experience. She used her gift for communication in 'Notes on Nursing', a handbook for nurses that has been influential ever since it was published in 1859. In spite of advances in science its emphasis on listening to the patient has remained relevant and the book was reprinted as late as 1974.

Nightingale resisted the temptation to live up to her popular 'Lady with a Lamp' persona. She avoided getting deeply involved in the nursing institute that she had established and instead spread her scope of concern to soldiers stationed in India. She found out that there was a very high rate of mortality. Because of a serious illness (which eventually killed her), she could not travel to India but she studied documents and interviewed many people with direct experience of India. She identified problems in basic hygiene and public health. Her work not only led to a huge improvement in the health of soldiers in India but may have had wider effects. She published a guide on village sanitation in India that was taken up by the colonial authorities.

Nightingale's focus never shifted from the role of the state. While researching issues relating to sanitation in India she became convinced that British rule did not improve the lives of the Indian people and she became an active supporter of the British Committee of the Indian National Congress which was founded in 1889 and played a key role in India's path to independence in 1947.

Nightingale is an example of a philanthropist who refused to comply with a misguided public stereotype (The Lady with a Lamp) that would have enabled her to receive public adulation and no doubt found a sizeable charity. She continued challenging authority and, as in the case of Henri Dunant and the ICRC, criticising those who veered towards the institutionalisation of charity. But public opinion is stubborn and she remains best known as The Lady with a Lamp and for founding the UK's first professional nursing school (now based at Guy's Hospital in London). Her subversive challenge to the military authorities, leaking of classified documents and espousal of India's independence remain much less well known.

The central role for the nation state was a relatively new concept in Nightingale's time. There were still sprawling empires instead of states and in the UK many responsibilities had only recently transferred from the level of communities and counties towards central government. But the spread of transport and communications made this an inevitable and necessary process. Nevertheless, communities and individuals are naturally inclined to take on (or take back) those responsibilities. Theoretically anything that local charity does raises a question about the failure of the state to do something that local people consider to be necessary.

But public opinion (in the UK at least) remains in a different mode, tending to regard charitable activity very highly and, as in Nightingale's case, rating it higher than more fundamental efforts to change national policies even though these may have far greater results than individual acts of charity. In this climate of public opinion it is very hard for those who start out as reforming idealists not to end up supporting institutions that cause further confusion about the role of the state. Having founded a charitable institution they have to promote its survival by singing its praises, regardless of the truth. The atrophy does not come from within but because of pressures from outside.

These processes may be observed in the case of the UK's best known charities, Save the Children Fund and Oxfam. At the end of World War I, Eglantyne Webb and her sister Dorothy were outraged by the continuation of a British embargo on food supplies to Germany long after the Armistice had been signed.[37] Tens of thousands of children in Germany were dying of starvation but when Webb tried to raise funds to help them she was confronted with the argument that *today's German children could be tomorrow's enemy*. Eglantyne Webb argued that children, as non-combatants, should have absolute rights to protection and care but this brought her into direct confrontation with the government.

The sisters launched a 'Fight the Famine' Council in 1919 with the primary objective of lifting the embargo but the mood in parliament and among the public remained negative. Most people, Eglantyne reported, *'considered it unpatriotic to feed the children of enemies'*. Eglantyne was arrested while demonstrating in Trafalgar Square in London and put on trial for handing out posters on which was written- *'What does Britain stand for? Starving babies, torturing women, killing the old.'* She was sentenced to eleven days in prison or a fine of £5 (which was paid on her behalf). The Jebbs continued their campaigning and criticism of the government. The embargo was finally lifted but only after many thousands of further deaths. The Jebbs turned their attention to new and equally dire situations in Ukraine and Russia, trying to draw the attention of the public and the government to the terrible famine which eventually killed millions of people.

The fund established in 1919 to provide help for German children was never a primary focus for the Jebbs —in fact its income decreased over the following decade and no institution was created until much

---

[37]    The account of the Jebb sisters in this section is based on Mulley (2009)

later. The sisters were much more concerned with the need to lift the embargo and then to draw attention to a series of disasters during the 1920s. Eglantyne confessed that she was not particularly fond of children but recognised that a focus on children was a way to draw attention. She recognised that helping individual children or raising funds for specific problems was not enough and that the best way forward was to make governments recognise their responsibilities towards children. She worked tirelessly on this and was instrumental in bringing about The Declaration of the Rights of the Child in 1924, one of the earliest such international treaties. The Declaration was expanded in 1959 and formed the basis for the 1989 UN Convention on the Rights of the Child.

But for many people in the UK it is the fund established in 1919 that is best known because this developed into the Save the Children Fund, which is now the world's largest children's charity. Eglantyne Jebb's view of what Britain stood for in 1919 might not go down well with today's more establishment-minded supporters.

But like Florence Nightingale, the Jebb sisters were absorbed into the public consciousness or prejudice and it is the notion of raising funds to help individual children that is now their most prominent legacy. As the Save the Children Fund grew in size, it moved closer to the government, initially proposing projects for government funding, then taking on projects designed by government and finally becoming a 'contractor of choice' working on the UK government's behalf.[38] The possibility that a Save the Children poster today would accuse the government of 'starving babies, torturing women, killing the old' is remote. If the UK government chose to cut off funding, Save the Children would face financial ruin.[39]

Save the Children has continued to make use of the public preference for helping children rather than any other category of person even though this does not work well in many situations and in many societies. Children are supposedly 'innocent' but this implies that in some way their parents and other relatives are guilty. Especially in poorer societies, children are, in any case, totally dependent on

---

[38]  See Gill (2016) p250

[39]  Income from the British Government was about a third of total income in 2014 – Gill (2016) p250

their parents and cannot survive in isolation without them and so a comprehensive view of the family as a whole is a much better approach for an aid agency and one that many aid workers in Save the Children recognise. But public prejudice has its uses. The myth of innocent children enables Save the Children to raise funds even from those who are sceptical about aid in general.

The danger arises if the agency that raises funds for children tries to use those funds exclusively. This happened quite widely during the Ethiopia Famine of 1984.[40] Children were separated out into segregated 'child feeding centres' and only the most severely malnourished were given food. Mothers had to abandon their other children at home and attend while a single child was fed. On those days mothers were unable to work. They would return home to find the other children hungry and might reasonably ask what right a foreign aid agency has to decide how food is used within the family. It might be the case that feeding another child or a parent might give the family unit a better chance of survival. These are sensitive issues that only poor people themselves are in a position to address.

In the case of Ethiopia it was found that the overall nutritional status of the family was likely to decline when a child was taken into selective feeding. After much debate among aid workers, agencies turned to providing general rations for the whole family. But lorries delivering bags of food are not as photogenic as foreign nurses holding starving children and so 'selective feeding' has never entirely vanished from the charitable repertoire.

Some charities have found it productive (of funds) to go a step further and establish a link between a specific donor and a specific child. 'Child sponsorship' is a hugely damaging form of aid that is perpetuated simply because of self-indulgence by those members of the public who insist on using it. Firstly it is extremely wasteful of resources because of all the letter- writing and exchange of presents that has to be organised. Secondly for every child selected there are many who are excluded and this is fundamentally unfair as well as creating divisions and tensions in the societies and communities affected.

In practice the aid agencies that raise their funds through a focus on children generally broaden the scope of their activities. Both

---

[40] See Vaux (2001) Chapter Two

UNICEF and Save the Children are very well aware that the mother may be a much more appropriate focus for concern and assistance than the children because it is the mother who, in many societies, has the main responsibility for their well-being and if the mother fails, the children fail. Even if they run child sponsorship programmes, reputable agencies shift their focus to an even broader concern for children with a community or even within a nation and they use child sponsorship money to bring about changes in government practice that may benefit children.

All this involves aid agencies in contortions. Some organisations including Oxfam, have taken the decision not to use child sponsorship. Instead they make use of donors' desire for a direct link by showing a particular child and naming a sum that will give that child, for example, an education suggesting an appropriate monthly sum that might allow the donor to imagine that they were funding that particular child. Because of intense competition between the charities, none of them is willing to confront public prejudice openly.

Aid workers are left to manipulate around the possible negative effects of donor prejudice and in many cases they can do so successfully. They can even make use of prejudices, such as the concept of children as 'innocent', in order to secure support from those who might otherwise be hostile to aid. An agency claiming to work for children is likely to be given a freer hand by any government than one declaring that its objective is human rights or government accountability. The argument for a special status for children has been used to gain access to war areas. At the height of Sudan's civil war in the 1980s, UNICEF successfully negotiated an access agreement, known as Operation Lifeline Sudan (OLS), to allow aid to be delivered to famine areas. UN organisations can only act with the permission of the UN member state in which they operate but Sudan chose to allow deliveries even into areas held by their enemy, the Sudan People's Liberation Army (SPLA). On the basis that aid was being delivered for the general benefit of children, UNICEF was able to deliver a wide range of relief goods and opened the way for many other agencies to use the same 'lifeline', ostensibly in the name of children. Of course, when the food arrived it was distributed within families and communities according to their own preferences. In a war context it was impossible to insist that food went only to children.

Similarly, during the 1996-2006 war in Nepal, Save the Children and UNICEF promoted the notion that schools should be treated as 'Zones of Peace' in which military action was prohibited. This notion received formal support from both sides but the practice on the ground was variable and uncertain. Some commanders of the Royal Nepal Army refused to vacate schools because they wanted to use them as military bases. The Royal Nepal Police posted contingents in schools without giving any warning. This led the Maoist rebels to attack schools. The Maoists continued to recruit young people from the schools. Ultimately the claim of schools as 'Zones of Peace' did not make much difference. With regard to both the Sudan and Nepal cases it was the interests of the warring parties that really dictated the action rather than their expressions of goodwill. In Sudan both sides used the 'lifeline' to deliver food to their military forces and it is arguable that Operation Lifeline Sudan fuelled and perpetuated the war. In Nepal commanders on the ground did whatever they liked in the schools knowing that there could be no sanction against them. The intervention of aid agencies had no significant effect.

Part of the argument behind the Schools as Zones of Peace concept was that children should not be subjected to political pressures. Some Nepali commentators questioned whether it was right to regard schoolchildren, who might be up to eighteen years old, as non-political beings. Arguably the children had every right to engage in debates about the issues underlying the war (poverty and the rights of women were the main ones) and even to take sides if they wished. Aid agencies might reply that they were simply using the supposed innocence of children as a ploy to increase their safety.

The story of Save the Children and the use of the supposed 'innocence' of children show the two sides to the atrophy of charity. Firstly the determination to put responsibilities squarely on governments becomes gradually transposed into a tendency to grow a large institution capable of doing government's work for it. Secondly, the use of child innocence as an instrument for aid comes up against the interests and customs of families and potentially the right of children to be treated as responsible beings. For one or other reason it simply does not work.

These problems only arise because the donor public misunderstand the issues and think that a simple focus on children avoids all the dilemmas and difficulties of aid. It does not. It simply passes on the problems to aid workers, with the added difficulty of an arbitrary preference for children.

Although Oxfam is, in my opinion, the most honest aid agency, its trajectory is essentially the same as for other aid institutions and it is likely that all charities that grow to become 'too big to fail' suffer an erosion of principle and honesty. Arguably, this is simply a factor in the growth of organisations and as each charity becomes too big, new ones or different types of organisation may step forward to fill the gaps. This is what I believe is happening now.

Oxfam began during World War II. Nazi forces occupying Greece had requisitioned all available food and other supplies, causing widespread starvation. As a proportion of lives lost against the total population, the famine in Greece was one of the worst in history. According to some estimates up to five hundred thousand people died between 1941 and 1944 out of a population of just seven million.[41] Food was offered by Greek people living abroad and by other sympathisers but the Allies imposed a blockade in order to weaken the Nazi forces.

They refused to allow any exceptions to the blockade, arguing that aid would be looted and used by the Nazis. British Prime Minister Churchill used the Nazi blockade of the UK as a defence for his 'total war' policy.

Committees were formed in London and elsewhere in the UK to oppose this policy on the grounds that the Greek citizens had shown no inclination to support the Nazis and should not be punished. They felt that the extent of suffering in Greece could not be justified and requested that the blockade be lifted to allow supplies to reach the civilian population. The ICRC offered to ensure safe delivery of the food and to minimise seizures by the Nazis. The case was raised in the House of Lords and Parliament but Minister of Economic Warfare Hugh Dalton, strongly backed by Winston Churchill, refused to make any concessions. Although the famine relief committees were successful in raising funds, food was delivered to Greece only after the war was over.

The Oxford Committee would have disbanded at the end of the war if it had not been for the efforts of Edith Pye. She had been deputed from the central committee in London to support what was

---

[41] Ref

known as the Oxford Committee for Famine Relief, founded in 1942.[42] Unlike other members of the committee, Pye had long been involved in helping refugees and war victims in Europe during the period after World War I. She had visited the Balkans and documented the ongoing effects of war. Aware of wider problems of famine and distress, she urged the Oxford committee to continue its work.

As 'chief strategist and organiser', Pye now called for a response to starvation in post-war Germany. Just as had happened after World War I, the Allies still maintained an embargo on sending food to Germany but a visit to Berlin in October 1946 by the publisher Victor Gollancz, acting for the Oxford Committee, provided clear evidence that starvation was now developing into famine. Faced with eyewitness reports, the government finally gave way, lifted the blockade and even provided an airlift for food parcels donated by the public.

The Oxford Committee was given the use of a shop in the centre of Oxford for collecting these food parcels and began to sell second-hand goods donated by the public. This initial fundraising venture developed into a chain of shops giving the Committee the means to continue its work and offer assistance abroad. As the work progressed beyond famine relief the Committee adopted its cable address 'Oxfam' as a title that better reflected the widening scope of its activities.

The Jebb sisters and Edith Pye were influenced by the Quaker principle of 'speaking truth to power'. Especially in their early work they acted directly on the moral imperative of challenging injustice, regardless whether there was a chance of success or the consequences for those making the demand. Fundraising and direct relief operations were less important than bringing about changes in government action. Charities were thought to be too small to make more than a token gesture in order to show that giving aid was possible.

Influencing government becomes more difficult when charities start to take money from government and especially when they build up responsibilities that only continue if they receive government support. This is what has happened to most charities in the field of international aid. When I joined Oxfam in the 1970s government funding was limited to 10% of total income and this was increased to 20% in the 1980s. After that the idea of a limit was dropped and the focus was on maximizing

---

[42]  The following is based on Oxfam's official history- Black (1992)

income from whatever source. By the time I conducted an evaluation of Oxfam for DFID in 2010[43] this had become a serious problem because Oxfam's survival had come to depend on government funding. A proportion of this funding was 'unrestricted' in the form of a block grant payment under a Programme Partnership Agreement (PPA) but the majority was 'restricted' –tied to specific projects. The proportion of 'unrestricted' funds (i.e. available for Oxfam to use independently was falling rapidly. My report noted that '*Although exact figures are not available, the percentage of unrestricted funds is estimated to have fallen from over 70% to below 40% in the last decade.*' I found that there was widespread concern about this within Oxfam- '*Many Oxfam staff expressed concern that it will become increasingly difficult to maintain characteristics of flexibility, innovation etc that are facilitated by unrestricted funding.*'

The trend towards dependence on government was long-term and had begun in the 1970s but it was unfortunate that this sudden increase in dependency coincided with the rising agenda of the Global War on Terror. This was not entirely coincidental because aid budgets had been hugely increased following the 9/11 event but they were much more tightly controlled around Western security interests, as explained earlier. A further factor was donors, especially the EU and DFID had begun to demand much higher levels of contribution from the implementing agency. This put enormous strain on 'unrestricted' funds. Oxfam faced the additional difficulty that it maintained perhaps the largest 'public policy' department of any of the international charities and played an active role in analysing and reporting on the issues underlying its work. Ironically, the cost of doing this increasingly added to Oxfam's difficulty in speaking out against government. It simply could not afford to cause offence.

Having reached such a high level of dependency it might have been better for Oxfam to scale back its public policy work or to acknowledge explicitly in each report what the financial interests of the agency are in each case. Very often Oxfam is commenting on situations in which it stands to secure contract funding depending whether donors choose one path or another. Calling for more aid begins to look like a call for more aid for Oxfam.

---

43    Vaux (2010)

On the crisis in Yemen, for example, Oxfam has published a paper drawing attention to the fact that continuing UK arms sales to Saudi Arabia add to the suffering of the people of Yemen and the humanitarian disaster that Oxfam is responding to. But its criticism is qualified by the observation that *'Britain should be proud of the £55m it has already given to Yemen to meet its growing humanitarian needs.'*[44] Oxfam does not mention that it is a recipient of DFID funding and therefore has a certain interest in making this statement but in fact Oxfam is a major recipient of DFID funding in Yemen.[45] By contrast The Guardian newspaper puts the issue squarely on its editorial page noting that- *'The UK, which has licensed £3.3bn worth of arms sales since the Yemen conflict began, boasts of increasing aid by £37m. The pledge would be laughable if it were not so shameful.'*[46]

Oxfam can no longer afford to be so blunt nor could Save the Children today accuse the UK government of starving babies, as Eglantyne Webb did in 1919.

The work of DFID is surely a matter for critical analysis by charities such as Oxfam and Save the Children. Reputable critics have raised many concerns about aid and even suggested that it does more harm than good. Surely this issue deserves careful attention but the charities avoid enquiring too closely into the hand that feeds them. Instead their stock comment on aid issues is to call for more.

This is a pity because although DFID commissions evaluations and is examined by government bodies such as the National Audit Office, charities such as Oxfam and Save the Children have direct experience of DFID in the field and could provide a useful analysis if they chose to be honest about it. But the close financial linkages between the charities and DFID probably make this impossible today.

The comments on arms sales to Saudi Arabia and their role in the Yemen conflict may also be modified because charities have been

---

[44]   Oxfam: *British Aid and British Arms —a coherent approach to Yemen?,* Oxfam Briefing Note 11 September 2015

[45]   According to DFID's Operational Plan for Yemen, Oxfam is one of its four main INGO partners. DFID website accessed via https://www.gov.uk/government/world/organisations/dfid-yemen

[46]   The Guardian: *Arms sales to Saudi Arabia: we must stop enabling the killing,* 7th November 2016

steered away from comment on such issues in the past. Oxfam's support for the Campaign Against the Arms Trade in 1985 led to a full enquiry into Oxfam's campaigning by the Charity Commissioners. Oxfam was ordered to stop its involvement in the campaign and to avoid other 'political' forms of campaigning.[47] Recent tightening of controls on lobbying groups may have made the charities even more nervous.

The problem from the point of view of the public is that these influences are not made explicit. It would surely be better if Oxfam came clean on these restrictions but this might seem to undermine its credibility as a commentator on global poverty issues.

In 2014 total government and institutional funding accounted for 60% of Save the Children's annual income.[48] Perhaps the most pernicious effect of this increasing dependence is that it makes the flow of aid decidedly top-down rather than bottom-up. In the 1970s my task as an Oxfam Field Director was to gather up requests from local organisations and then fund as many as possible within a limited budget but today's aid managers are tied much more tightly to running large donor-funded projects for which they need NGOs simply as contractors.

This has put strain into the relationship between international charities and local NGOs. Added to this the international charities have become more prescriptive especially in relation to disaster relief. They have turned disaster relief from something that everyone can help with into something that only 'professional' aid workers can provide and it has to meet with standards that have been set by the Western charities. The Sphere Standards, first introduced in 1998, were put forward as a way to avoid situations in which smaller, less experienced charities took on major responsibilities in relief camps and then failed to carry them out, as had happened with disastrous effect in the Goma camps after the Rwanda Genocide in 1994. Agencies also hoped that by setting standards at a very high level they would ensure adequate financing from donors and would not be forced to run services in which, for example, the amounts of food or water being delivered were less than was needed.

---

[47]  Black (1992) pp278-283
[48]  Gill (2016) p250

But the effects have not been as was apparently expected. Local organisations have been discouraged from responding to disasters because they lack 'professional competence' (i.e. knowledge of the standards) and donors have not necessarily provided enough funding to reach the standards and so the same compromises still have to be made. Local NGOs find themselves caught in an impossible situation in which they are doomed to fail.

Another problem for local NGOs is that humanitarian standards have driven up the demand for technicians and specialists but generally only the biggest international charities can afford to maintain the 'surge capacity' of trained staff and specialist equipment. In effect, the standards have simply consolidated the power of a small group of international charities, who happened to be the ones who promoted them in the first place.

International charities express willingness to mobilise local populations in order to press for their 'rights' in relation to national government. The paradigm of 'from poverty to power'[49] is a dominant part of today's charitable thinking. But the increasing dependence of the charities on donor governments makes the issue of 'foreign funding' all the more sensitive. Unsurprisingly, national governments are not keen on being influenced by foreign organisations using local NGOs as a front, especially when the real source of funds turns out to be a foreign, and potentially hostile, government.

It is impossible for the big international charities to turn back. They cannot recreate themselves to represent the disinterested fury of their founders. If truth is to be told to power, it will be by organisations with less self-interest. The atrophy of many Western charities has reached a point at which they are part of the problem rather than part of the solution.

---

[49]   This is the title of a book published by Oxfam about such processes of change: Green (2008)

# CHAPTER FOUR

# DOES AID WORK?

This apparently simple question is difficult to answer because there is little agreement about what aid is for. The question will have different answers depending on the assumed purpose for aid and this in itself is a telling argument that the issue of international aid needs some serious rethinking.

Aid is variously used to support international trade, gain trade access for Western countries, promote good governance, democracy, human rights and global security, and to reduce international migration. Indeed, the reduction of poverty and distress do not always get a mention when politicians justify or criticise aid budgets and it has become increasingly common to justify aid on the basis of the national interest of donor countries. Even if poverty reduction is cited as a purpose, it may be simply an instrument for achieving other objectives, such as reducing terrorism.

A fundamental problem for those who seek to justify aid as a path towards poverty reduction is that, as noted earlier, the main changes have not come from aid but from social policy in China and the general process of economic development in India and East Asia. Progress in Africa, where a great deal of aid has been focused, is meagre. There is substantial evidence that aid has serious negative effects on poor people, especially by causing instability as in the case of the World Bank's Structural Adjustment Policies referred to earlier.

The measurement of changes in extreme poverty is problematic. The 'dollar a day' (or similar levels) of income is the one most widely accepted but income is only a proxy for the actual level of deprivation and suffering. It simply has to be assumed that at an extraordinarily low level of income, deprivation and suffering is likely to be high. It may also be assumed that such a low level of income makes a person vulnerable to risk, especially of violence. Extreme poverty and distress go together and in the absence of a means of measuring distress, income poverty is the best marker available.

The World Bank has put considerable effort into making the statistics relating to extreme poverty as accurate as possible. It has moved away from figures based on overall national income and explored census and other data. Statistics available from poorer countries are not very reliable and there are inconsistencies in the start dates and coverage of the World Bank analysis. The Bank began to collect figures for incomes of less than $1 per day from 1979 but variants between ways of measuring income, exchange rates and other factors led the Bank to revise its definition to $1.25 in 2008 and $1.90 in 2015. There is considerable debate about these levels and about the compatibility of figures collected using different levels but the time series from 1979 now seems to be reliable.[50] The World Bank found that the number of extremely poor people for all developing countries excluding China was 1.1 billion in 1981 and 1.12 billion in 2008, falling to around 800 million more recently.[51] The reduction in extreme poverty has come almost entirely from China with progress in India also during the recent years of its economic uplift.

The figure of a billion extremely poor people is used widely by commentators but comes from two different methods of calculation. The World Bank figures are based on numbers of very poor people within countries whereas another approach, used by Paul Collier in his book *The Bottom Billion*[52] results from adding up the populations of countries deemed to be extremely poor. As it happens the results are

50    Blog by Joliffe and Prydz (2015) http://blogs.worldbank.org/developmenttalk/print/
      international-poverty- line-has-just-been-raised-190-day-global-poverty-basically-
      unchanged-how-even The World Bank 2105 Global Monitoring Report re-calcu-
      lates figures based on $1.90 per day see http://www.worldbank.org/en/publication/
      global-monitoring-report On this basis the World Bank projects a total of only
      700 million in extreme poverty in 2015
51    Ruth Alexander, BBC News 9/3/2012 http://www.bbc.co.uk/news/maga-
      zine-17312819
52    Collier (2007)

similar but the latter method is not so useful in demonstrating global trends and the critical importance of China and India.

Collier's approach points instead to the important problem of fragile and failing states –those that are caught in 'poverty traps' and make relatively little progress in relation to poverty, as has been the case in many countries of Sub-Saharan Africa. Collier's analysis is useful because aid has been focused on conflict affected countries in Africa (see Chapter Five) but this should not detract from the big lesson that the greatest single reduction in poverty have come from national governments receiving very little aid. We must begin to answer the question whether aid works by noting that it has not contributed much to the elimination of extreme poverty in the last thirty years.

These different approaches raise the important issue of inequality. Most aid statistics (such as for progress in health and education) focus on whole countries but these often reflect increasing inequalities within those countries rather than the advances of poor people.[53] The World Bank has found that global inequality is increasing rapidly[54] and this has made the task of charting extreme poverty more difficult because there are now large numbers of people who are very poor even within relatively rich countries. Although the most extreme cases may now be concentrated in India and Sub-Saharan Africa there are very large numbers of people elsewhere who are so poor that they are a concern of global humanity. This suggests that the challenge of global poverty in the years ahead is to devise the means to ensure that there is a 'bottom line' below which people in any country do not fall.

There is a valid argument that inequality in wealth creates inequalities in power and this puts the rich in a position to exploit very poor people. Oxfam has raised concerns about the extraordinary wealth of a very small number of people.[55] This leads to proposals for heavier taxation of rich people and corporations in poorer countries. This is laudable but it may be somewhat unrealistic to expect the people and corporations enjoying huge wealth and huge power to vote for their own demise. The process of change by tackling wealth will be a very

---

53   Deaton (2016)

54   World Bank (2016)

55   Oxfam (2015) *Inequality and the end of extreme poverty,* Oxfam media Briefing 21 September 2015

long and probably painful one. There is no guarantee that loss of wealth in the higher echelons will ever make much difference to the poorest people. Indeed, a counter-argument might be that the economic growth fostered by the rich is the best chance of progress for the poor. My aim in this book is to envisage a system that, regardless of the role of the richest people, ensures that extreme poverty has limits –a global welfare state.

What is the role of the aid system? Having failed to make much discernible impact on extreme poverty so far, the aid system may nevertheless wish to cast itself in a leading role in the next phases of poverty eradication. We should be cautious about this because the aid system has shown itself weak at analysing and responding to its deficiencies. The aid system has yet to acknowledge that its role in eradicating extreme poverty has been so limited and instead likes to claim China's success as its own.

Looking at the system in greater detail reveals that it has very little capacity for learning. Evidence for the achievements and failures of aid might be expected to come from evaluation processes but this source provides very little of significant value. In particular, very few evaluations by aid agencies have been made available publicly until quite recently. When I conducted a review of humanitarian evaluations for ALNAP in 2005,[56] only 43 evaluations had been deposited for public reference (out of thousands of projects conducted every year) and only eight of these were general evaluations focused on a disaster or a sector rather than on individual projects. UNHCR and the EU were honourable exceptions with policies of publishing evaluation of all programmes. In other cases evaluations were generally conducted when there was a specific problem and were often treated as 'internal'. Because they were not published, the evaluators were free to be critical if they wished but there was no guarantee that the agency would take any notice. This began to change about a decade ago when aid budgets increased dramatically, agencies became more dependent on donors and the donors began to demand evaluation reports.

By 2015 there were 1,100 evaluations available on the ALNAP database and most international charities now post large numbers

---

[56]   ALNAP (2005) *ALNAP Review of Humanitarian Action –evaluation utilisation,* ODI London, p37

of documents called evaluations on their websites. But the pressure for publication has had a negative effect. Because they are likely to be published and scrutinised by a donor government, evaluations are much more tightly managed by the organisations being evaluated and focus on projecting the reputation of the agency rather than finding out what is going on. Although DFID calls for evaluations of work done by agencies using its funds, it does not have sufficient staff to manage the process itself and even if an 'independent' consultant is given the task of evaluation, the process is tightly managed by the organisation being evaluated. In my experience of dozens of evaluations, criticism of the agency is scrutinised with particular care (in some cases this is the only part of a draft report to be taken seriously) and the consultant will be asked to remove such negative comment. The reason given is often 'lack of evidence' or 'the issue is beyond the Terms of Reference' but such limitations rarely apply in the case of positive comments. If the consultant is reluctant to comply the agency may require the consultant to extend the process through countless drafts and withhold payments until the agency is satisfied.

Although evaluations may be commissioned from 'independent' consultants, most consultants develop close links with a particular client or group of clients. By working regularly for the same agency they develop expertise about that agency and this may qualify them for the next job but this also makes them beholden to the agency and dependent on it. Although still described as 'independent' the consultant (or more likely consulting company) has an interest in providing satisfaction for the client rather than critical scrutiny. The process is driven by two main factors –the need to tick the box marked 'evaluation' and competition between agencies. The box must be ticked in such a way that no advantage is given to competitors.

Some agencies have dropped the pretence of 'independent' evaluation and instead allow reports by in-house staff to be presented as if they were evaluations. These often turn out to be little more than progress reports with a bias towards success and achievement. There is a strong tendency in such reports to equate outputs (lists of what the agency has delivered) with impact (the effect on people in need). This means that even if inappropriate assistance is delivered, the agency can present its work as a success.

With donors such as DFID giving control of evaluation to implementing agencies, it is not surprising that the Terms of Reference are drawn up in such a way as to ensure a positive report. Typically this reduces the focus of the evaluation to an assessment whether the stated outputs have been achieved (what was formerly known as an 'output to purpose review') and the question whether the project achieved relevant and sustainable results is bypassed, often on the grounds that evidence is lacking. Although the OECD/DAC introduced wide-ranging evaluation criteria (and these may still be referred to in the Terms of Reference), the way in which evaluations are managed brings the focus back to what was delivered on the grounds that the evidence for wider results is less 'robust'.

This trend applies in all forms of evaluation including humanitarian aid. Indeed, because humanitarian aid often has a very high profile and may seriously affect the agency's reputation, the trend to manipulate is stronger. Up to around 2006, the UK fundraising consortium the Disaster Emergency Committee (DEC) published a series of influential evaluations that helped to advise international charities on the wider aspects of their disaster response and to review the sector as a whole. An evaluation of the response in Kosovo after the 1999 exodus, for example, led to extensive debate about the difficulties of working alongside NATO and other military forces. An evaluation (in which I was Team Leader) after the Gujarat earthquake in 2001 raised questions about the slow transition to recovery and the limited application of Red Cross principles, notably building on local capacities and reducing future vulnerabilities. But this changed when parts of a DEC evaluation in Southern Africa were picked up in the media as indications of failure. An early version of the evaluation of aid responses to the Indian Ocean Tsunami (in which I was again Team Leader) was leaked to the press and formed the basis for criticism on the BBC Newsnight programme.

The international charities forming the DEC were afraid that such criticism could reduce public support and so they decided to limit the scope of evaluations to an audit process – simply ensuring that funds were used for their stated purpose. Issues such as the validity of the purpose or adjustments made during the course of the response were excluded. Instead, the DEC urged individual members of the consortium to conduct their own evaluations but this put evaluation back into the hands of those who were being evaluated, with all the limitations and opportunities for 'spin' described above. Because the members of the DEC were competing for public approval, they also competed to put forward positive results in these evaluations.

Project evaluations, especially if doctored in the interests of the agency, are in any case very little help in putting together a comprehensive picture of aid or answering the question whether aid works. There is much greater potential in large-scale evaluations conducted, commissioned and directly managed by donors such as the series of studies published by the Tsunami Evaluation Coalition (TEC). These helped to stimulate critical thinking about humanitarian aid and resulted in important reviews by donors. The Coalition drew attention to the lack of continuity between different 'phases' of disaster response, arising because of the different mandates of the main actors. They pointed towards a lack of overall leadership in humanitarian crises and the need for greater coordination of the sectors. The TEC studies helped to bring about the UN Cluster system of coordination in place today.

For a few years after 2006 donors took the trouble to manage comprehensive evaluations and they yielded important results. But this was an extremely demanding process and donors are extremely short of time. The pressure to reduce the 'overhead costs' of aid departments increased as budgets rose and the 'head count' was held back. This led donors to give a greater role to the UN (and particularly the Office for Coordination of Humanitarian Assistance –OCHA) to conduct large-scale evaluations of humanitarian operations. But through the Cluster System' of aid coordination the UN had become the main player in humanitarian responses and it was in effect evaluating itself. The UN developed a process called Inter Agency Humanitarian Evaluation (IAHE) intended to provide independent assessment of the overall aid response. In the process in South Sudan, which I led in 2015, the UN tried to limit the evaluation to a simple process of assessing whether outputs matched the stated purpose and strongly discouraged my efforts to examine whether the overall aid operation was appropriate. Unable to accept these pressures, I resigned from the evaluation team.[57]

In conclusion, there is too much 'spin' in current evaluation processes to provide a reliable pointer towards the effectiveness of aid. Other approaches have been tried but none of them is satisfactory.

---

[57] Vaux (2015) My report written in mid-2015 was never accepted by the UN or published. A new version put together by OCHA and other team members was published in March 2016, a year after the field work. See Inter Agency Standing Committee (2016)

The EU AidWatch programme simply measures whether EU member states are making progress towards achieving the aid target of 0.7% of GDP.[58] Not all states have even agreed to this target. The whole exercise relies on what Deaton (2013) calls the 'hydraulic' assumption that the results of aid are directly proportional to the scale of the inputs. More aid means more result. This is similar to the evaluation process of listing outputs delivered and just as meaningless. Similarly, the OECD has published surveys of aid effectiveness but these are simply assessments of compliance with the Paris Declaration. The World Bank Global Monitoring Report focuses on changes in global poverty but not on the specific contribution of aid.[59]

A more comprehensive approach is taken in the 'Quality of Overseas Development Assistance' Index developed by the Brookings Institution and Center for Global Development in the USA. This uses four dimensions to measure aid effectiveness – 'maximising efficiency', 'fostering institutions', 'reducing administrative burden on recipients' and 'transparency and learning'. The Brookings Index is the most sophisticated attempt yet but it still measures proxies rather than results and the proxies are simply aid processes rather than aid results.

A similar approach is used in the Real Aid survey that has been published annually by ActionAid.[60] It measures donor performance against specific criteria selected by ActionAid including whether aid is targeted towards the poorest people. This is certainly a step further than simply looking at outputs and processes but it still falls short of measuring results. Moreover, ActionAid's sample is too small for the sweeping conclusions drawn from it. The survey covers just seven countries without distinguishing between different donors and the responses are based on small-scale selective opinion surveys. The results for the different criteria are then aggregated into a single Index. ActionAid finds that Real Aid (aid compliant with the criteria) increased from 51% in 2005 to 55% in 2009.[61] This is heartening but it is not a reliable basis for conclusions about aid.

---

[58]  This target dates back may years but was reaffirmed by EU states in 2005. See AidWatch website

[59]  http://www.worldbank.org/en/publication/global-monitoring-report

[60]  ActionAid (2011) Real Aid –ending aid dependency, ActionAid London

[61]  ActionAid

Faced with increasing public criticism, mainly from right-wing media, DFID has introduced a 'results agenda' intended to focus attention on the ultimate goal of bringing about results for poor people. The UK government has set up an Independent Commission on Aid Impact (ICAI) to review the work of DFID and report to the Parliamentary International Development Committee. This confirms that methods of assessment used so far have not only focused on the 'quantity' rather than 'quality' of aid but actually distorted aid planning in favour of activity that is more susceptible to that type of measure-

'We found that the results agenda has helped to bring greater discipline in the measurement of results and greater accountability for the delivery of UK aid. These achievements have, however, involved some important trade-offs. Some of DFID's tools and processes for measuring results have had the unintended effect of focussing attention on quantity of results over their quality.'

The ICAI then puts its finger on the nub of the problem. The most important results of aid can only be measured by applying timescales much greater than DFID management systems can cope with-

'DFID's programmes have an average programme length of just three years. Transformational impact will, however, often be possible only over several programme cycles and this should be recognised explicitly in programme design. This is particularly the case in conflict-affected and fragile states.'[62]

In a recent review of DFID's support to Fragile States (those that are deeply affected by political instability and conflict), the ICAI noted that the UK nearly doubled its allocation of aid for fragile states between 2011 and 2014[63] but- 'At the time that the scale up decision was made, DFID was unprepared to manage the scale of additional funds allocated to fragile states. The processes that were used to develop plans and allocate funds were not fit for purpose and led to over-ambitious goal-setting and accelerated programming ahead of management and delivery capacity.'

This finding points towards the root of the problem. Aid planning perspectives are far too short and this is exacerbated because the

---

[62]    ICAI (2015) DFID's Approach to Delivering Impact, Summary at http://icai. independent.gov.uk/report/dfids- approach-to-delivering-impact/

[63]    ICAI (2015) The Scale-up of DFID's Support to Fragile States, Summary at http://icai.independent.gov.uk/report/assessing-impact-scale-dfids-support-fragile-states/

politicians in charge of aid change rapidly. Even time scales of two to three years are beyond the concern of many Secretaries of State. Managers do not gain credit by painstakingly following up on the programmes devised by their predecessors. They prefer to sweep the past away and introduce a new 'magic bullet' but then move on before the deficiencies of the magic bullet become too evident. DFID's leaders tend to underestimate the difficulty of working in situations such as fragile states in which guides and policies can easily be harmful and aid solutions must be tailored to specific circumstances, as the OECD/ DAC Principles demand.

Nevertheless senior managers like to change the priorities rapidly. In the last decade it has shifted around from governance to services to livelihoods to economic growth. All this time the attempt to concentrate attention is thwarted by pressures coming from outside the department to take account of the Western security agenda, trade interests and other concerns.

Effective aid management in fragile states is extremely challenging and basically the systems and political pressures make it impossible for DFID to be successful, especially if it cannot be entirely clear whether the objective is to address poverty or support Western security. The nearest DFID is likely to come to success is explored in the case study of Nepal presented in Chapter Six. If DFID took on the full staff and overhead costs necessary for such a task and allowed the flexibility necessary to respond to unique challenges, it would face sharp criticism for being wasteful and inefficient. It is a no win situation leading to the conclusion that aid may not be the best way to approach the challenge of global poverty.

Academics provide increasing analysis of aid but their work is limited by two main factors. Firstly, many academics depend on DFID for the finance of their research programmes and this creates 'spin' in the results. Secondly the nature of academic enquiry usually entails either micro-studies that cannot be generalised or macro studies that lack empirical evidence. Moreover, academics are generally wary of answering the big question whether aid works or do so in a way that adds to the uncertainty and confusion about the issue. Roger Riddell presented his answer to the question 'Does Foreign Aid Really Work?' in an encyclopaedic 500-page collection of examples published in 2007.

[64] He finds that aid works in some cases but not in others and, in a final chapter titled 'Why Aid Isn't Working' identifies many problems without giving a clear answer to the initial question. In general commentators tend to assume that the answer lies in making various adjustments to aid practice rather than wondering whether it is the right tool.

Riddell divides the problems with aid into two types: those created by the donors and those that come about because of the circumstances faced by recipients of aid and recipient countries. Among those created by the donors he notes that a great deal of aid, perhaps 60%, is still tied back to products and services originating in the donor country. This includes not only materials but also consultancy fees, expatriate salaries and commercial profits for companies managing aid programmes. This problem appears to be insoluble because DFID lacks the staff t manage programmes or to even to work directly with the national government. Therefore it tends to employ a commercial company, or sometimes and international charity, to take on the management of a very large programme. As shown in the Nepal case in Chapter Six, DFID does not even have the staff to detect when things are going seriously wrong and the companies have little interest in disclosing problems so long as they are paid.

On the recipient side Riddell draws attention to the problem of 'patrimonialism'. He finds a fundamental contradiction between what aid seeks to do and where it seeks to do it. Many of the poorest people in the world (setting aside China and India for the moment) live in the states with the least capacity to deliver poverty reduction programmes and in some cases there is only a limited commitment to the issue. Riddell points out the implication that donors should either shift their focus towards less poor people in countries where aid is most likely to be effective or they must grapple with the difficulties of working in situations that are least conducive to aid. Neither appears to be a realistic course. DFID is tied by public opinion, concerns about fragile states as sources of terrorism and its public service agreement to focus on poverty. If aid is to be 'successful' it cannot be focused on poverty.

This fundamental dilemma has been taken up by other authors. Giles Bolton who worked for DFID in Africa gives his gloomy conclusion in the title of his book -'Aid and other dirty business —an insider reveals how

---

[64]    Riddell, R (2007)

*good intentions have failed the world's poor'*. He argues that the West should be much more serious about the difficulties of aid. Greater resources should be provided but only if the 'quality' improves. This leads back to the problem that Western governments will not permit aid departments to take on the huge numbers of staff that would be necessary to significantly improve the quality of aid.

Matthew Lockwood, an experienced aid manager as well as an academic[65], observes that for most of Africa aid simply adds to the problem of bad government. In his view, aid channelled through bad governments makes them worse and aid cannot do much unless there is already good leadership- *'to achieve rapid and sustained development, the nature of politics and the state in African countries will have to be transformed by leaders who have a combination of both the commitment and political power to overcome clientelism...'* (p132).

Since DFID does not have the power to transform the political landscape of Africa the implication might again be that aid, at least in the form generally understood, is the wrong tool. African economist Dambiso Moyo, in her book *'Dead Aid'*, also focuses on the fact that aid boosts patronage networks and these in turn foster corruption and undermine good governance. Former World Bank spokesman Robert Calderisi provides a similar analysis of the problems but, like Lockwood, reaches conclusions that imply a return to colonial controls. He considers that the West should- *'Require all heads of state and senior officials to open their bank accounts to public scrutiny'.*[66]

For much of the last two decades the magic bullet has been 'good governance' but far from promoting good governance, aid undermines it. Angus Deaton puts the issue particularly clearly- *When the "conditions for development" are present, aid is not required. When local conditions are hostile to development, aid is not useful, and it will do harm if it perpetuates those conditions."*[67] Nevertheless aid agencies keep trying to achieve the impossible and keep coming to the same conclusion – that aid cannot change a situation that is not already conducive to aid. Trends in Western countries towards greater 'austerity' are likely to reduce aid management still further while the growing assertiveness of

---

[65] Lockwood (2005)

[66] Calderisi (2006) p208

[67] Deaton (2013) p273

national governments will ensure that aid managers cannot do much to influence states that are not already committed to poverty reduction.

In my experience the issue that causes most trouble to DFID managers is the huge increase in budgets. In 2005, having just delivered a report to DFID Mozambique on the danger that aid could exacerbate political turbulence, I crossed over at the airport with Gordon Brown, the UK Chancellor at that time, who had come to announce an immediate 30% increase in the DFID budget for Mozambique. DFID managers had to switch their attention to spending more and the risk of doing harm had to be set aside.

An imbalance between aid objectives and management capacity together with rapid acceleration in aid spending inevitably lead to dangerous and harmful situations. CDA's Listening Project in Afghanistan summarizes the issue from the perspective of government officials-

*'Many people were perplexed about the process by which aid flows into Afghanistan and into their communities, and why donors push to disburse funds quickly to meet external deadlines. In Kabul, people knowledgeable about the aid system expressed frustration with donors who often change funding structures and rules to spend money more quickly. People insisted that when the process is speeded up, it creates opportunities for the money to be stolen.*

*'Officials in one ministry provided an example of just how donor pressure to spend quickly undermines policies meant to reduce corruption and to build community capacity and ownership. Normally funds go to the community in three instalments, and each disbursement has to be spent before the next one arrives. The first portion comes from the communities and they have to raise the funds, put them into an account and only then is the funding from the donors added. However, one bilateral donor insisted that the full amount be provided to the villages at one time. The program staff expressed concern that the money could be stolen if given in this way. However, the donor insisted that their fiscal year was ending and that the partners had to spend the money quickly. They did as the donors demanded, and the money was gone.'* [68]

Aid managers get caught up in these pressures. As Michela Wrong observes (in an analysis of the problems faced by a Kenyan whistleblower)- *'In any development organisation whether USAID or Oxfam, the World Bank or World Vision, career progress is measured in how*

---

[68]   Anderson et al (2012) p110 based on Listening Project Report, Afghanistan

*much money an official succeeds in 'pushing out of the door'. No one gets Brownie points back at head office for closing down a programme or putting a relationship with a client government on ice, even if this was, in fact, the most constructive course of action. Humanitarian organisations may talk about making themselves redundant, but their annual reports rarely boast about offices closed or staff laid off. Organisations' internalised incentives all work in the opposite direction....'* [69]

Wrong notes how this tendency is compounded by the short-term deployments of field staff- *'At precisely the moment when he has reached a mature understanding of just how formidable the system he hopes to reform really is, the director is pulled out.'* [70] Muhammad Yunus, founder of the Grameen Bank in Bangladesh, noted the same characteristic of aid agencies- *'If you are a young ambitious officer of a donor agency hoping to move up quickly, you choose the project which carries the biggest price tag. In one go, you move a lot of money, and your name moves up the promotion ladder.'* [71]

Pressure to spend aid money fast leads to waste and corruption but the much greater danger is that it will destabilise the patronage systems that underpin governance in many parts of the world, especially in Africa (see Chapter Five). As Angus Deaton concludes- *'giving more aid than we currently give, at least if it were given as it is given now, would make things worse, not better.'* [72] To be effective in fragile states using a conventional aid approach (projects and programmes), DFID would need to increase its staff hugely or else focus on a very small number of projects that were very closely researched and monitored. Neither is possible in the current climate and the trends may make the situation worse so we have to think outside the box. Deaton challenges the underlying assumption that aid is the proper tool to address problems of development and argues instead that *'What surely ought to happen is what happened in the now-rich world, where countries developed in their own way, in their own time, under their own political and economic structures.'* [73]

This might be better than a continuation of the status quo but it

[69]   Wrong (2009) p189
[70]   Ibid
[71]   Yunus (1998) p16
[72]   Deaton (2016) p272
[73]   Deaton (2016) p312

is not the only answer. Aid can be used not only to empower poor people directly but also to help generate the conditions in which the governments of poorer countries take responsibility for eliminating extreme poverty –in other words take over the management of what has hitherto been the prerogative of aid agencies. It may be unrealistic to expect the impetus for such a change to come from the aid system. The problem for many of us who work within the system is to recognise that our time has passed. The lead must come from poor people and their governments, or not at all.

Jonathan Glennie, in his book 'The Trouble with Aid –why less could mean more in Africa' [74] argues for a reduction in the volume of aid to African countries so that tighter control can be kept on corruption and better choices made between aid options. He considers that the expansion of aid has been far too rapid and has far outstripped the capacity of institutions to absorb it. This is true but the ability of poor people to absorb money is practically endless and perhaps a way can be found to bypass the process of state-building and simply ensure that the poorest people get help. If aid money could be transferred directly to poor people they could devise their own priorities and programmes, and be in a better position to hold their governments to account.

---

[74]   Glennie (2008)

# CHAPTER FIVE

# PATRONAGE, POVERTY AND VIOLENCE

The World Bank in its 2011 World Development Report[75] finds that insecurity '*has become a primary development challenge of our time. One-and-a-half billion people live in areas affected by fragility, conflict, or large-scale, organized criminal violence, and no low-income fragile or conflict-affected country has yet to achieve a single United Nations Millennium Development Goal.*'[76]

The security services in poorer countries tend to serve their political masters rather than the people and have the least interest in serving the poorest people who have neither money nor political influence. Police, judiciary and military forces are likely to exploit rather than protect the poorest people. Therefore the security of very poor people depends on their ability to serve a patron and receive protection in return. Poverty and insecurity sustain the patronage systems that are a notable feature of the poorest countries. In a vicious circle, patronage systems make countries poorer because they undermine democratic governance.

In the absence of an effective state, patronage systems can be a source of security for poor people and they may also be a source

---

75  World Bank (2011) *Conflict, Security and Development,* World Bank, Washington DC http://siteresources.worldbank.org/INTWDRS/Resources/WDR2011_Full_Text.pdf

76  Op cit p1

of violence because patrons fight among themselves, demand support from their clients and attack those from rival patronage networks. Patronage systems can be organised along 'tribal' lines but it might be equally true to say that tribal identities are formed on the basis of patronage. Attempts to challenge patronage systems strike at the heart of social systems and may seriously affect the security of poor people. The aid system tends to ignore or overlook patronage systems and in the process may do a great deal of harm by causing conflict and reducing the meagre base of protection that patronage provides.

In a lecture delivered in 2009, Alex de Waal observed that- *'International policy tends to be guided by models that are framed by certain norms of what a state 'ought' to look like and how it 'ought' to run.... Patronage is the basic principle for how those countries actually function... Patronage can be inefficient and corrupt, and can be a factor that contributes to political and economic crisis and even war. But patronage systems can also function as a repository of trust and security. In these countries they are recognised as a fact of social life, and consequently are seen as legitimate. It is expected that political leaders will use them to secure their power and reward their followers.'* [77]

A synthesis of studies of patronage systems concluded that- *'These (patronage) systems have evolved to protect the interests of a restricted elite, who will in turn seek to preserve the system from potentially disruptive attempts at reform. It could even be argued that such dysfunctional systems achieve, at times, a considerable degree of resilience, particularly when this term is applied to the successful pursuit of regime survival and conflict containment.'* [78]

The dominant patronage arrangements are those run by the government in power and aid has a strong tendency to reinforce them and by implication marginalise other patronage networks, creating

---

[77] Alex de Waal: *Fixing the Political Marketplace: How we can make peace without functioning state institutions?* Fifteenth Christian Michelsen Lecture, Bergen 15 October 2009. Writing some years later Alex de Waal takes a less sanguine view of patronage as the basis for an exploitative business model in De Waal (2015a). See Chapter Seven of this book on South Sudan

[78] Africa Power and Politics Programme et al (2012) *The Political Economy of Development in Africa: A Joint Statement from five research programmes, April 2012,* Africa Power and Politics p10

tensions that in some situations lead to violent conflict. In countries with limited ability to raise funds through taxation, aid can become a major attraction to patrons competing for political power because it will provide the means with which to rewards clients. The promise of access to aid coffers can be an incentive for the attempt to overthrow the government in power.

Equally, the government in power can reward clients with aid money and projects or punish opponents by denying them access to aid money. For example, northern Uganda which challenged President Museveni long ago is still an area of the country deprived of aid investment and this continues to exacerbate tensions that could lead to violence along tribal lines. Stability can come from the overwhelming dominance of a single patronage system, as in Uganda, or from a balance of power between such groups as in Nigeria.

The Nigeria example is particularly interesting because the basis of power sharing is mysterious, at least to outsiders. At the time of Nigeria's independence, political power was contested between three main ethnic (or patronage) groups. One of these groups, the Igbo people of the south-east, staked a claim to the country's biggest source of revenue- oil. Colonel Ojukwu declared independence for 'Biafra' and promised the Igbo people that they would no longer need to share their oil wealth with the rest of Nigeria. The Hausa-dominated north and Yoruba people in the south-west determined to put down the rebellion. The war was bitter and caused immense suffering for poorer people in Biafra who were unable to obtain food because of a Nigerian blockade.

Eventually Nigerian military forces succeeded in defeating Ojukwu and he fled the country. Reflecting on these events Nigerian leaders concluded that there had to be a balance of power in which each of the main ethnic groups would have a share, or more cynically, 'a time to eat'. The balance of power necessary to preserve peace was institutionalised as a rotating Presidency. The disadvantage was that Presidents were chosen because of their ethnic background and their acceptability to their supporters. Good governance was not the top consideration and over the following decades, Nigeria suffered a series of corrupt and ineffective Presidents interspersed with military rule which was just as corrupt and ineffective.[79] Nigeria became infamous for the vast sums of

---

[79]    Maier, K *This House has Fallen –Nigeria in Crisis,* Penguin Books (2000)

money expropriated by venous leaders but there was a considerable degree of uncertainty about being President and most of them decided not only to exploit their advantage as much as possible but also to salt the profits abroad rather than invest it in Nigeria. Hence, despite the massive revenues from oil, Nigerian development stalled.

But the big achievement was that this system of rotating patronage kept the peace. After the attempted secession of Biafra, Nigeria did not return to civil war and the three parts of the country held together. Although peace was maintained at the national level, conflicts broke out in many parts of the country, reflecting local struggles for control over resources and rivalries of smaller patronage systems. Tribal identity was not the only basis for conflict. Religion also became an issue that could be used to divide people and force them to support one patron or another for their own defence. Aspiring patrons exploited tensions between the native population in some areas and those who had migrated from outside. But so long as the centre remained strong, based on the three-way balance of power, a local challenge could either be absorbed into the oil-based national patronage arrangements or crushed by the military.

In 2002 the Nigerian Presidency decided to study the nature of these ongoing conflicts and (with DFID support) I joined up with a team of Nigerian academics.[80] The central issue was quickly identified as patronage or, as the Nigerian academics preferred to call it 'prebendal politics'. Although Nigerians instantly recognise the crucial importance of patronage and the process has received considerable attention from African academics[81], the issue is generally airbrushed out of aid planning.

Individual aid managers may be well aware of the importance of patronage systems but they are often cautious about making explicit reference to it, perhaps because it has been identified with 'corruption'. But patronage is a great deal more than 'corruption' and this term is not really useful at all in describing the actual system of governance rather than the one that is assumed to be in existence for the purposes of aid. This is a fundamental reason why so much aid is misguided and has negative consequences, especially in Africa.

---

[80] DFID (2002)
[81] See Adebayo Adedeji Ed (1999)

From a Western perspective patronage may appear to be unfair because it is exclusive and has little to do with abilities, but it includes obligations of caring for poor people, from the same family or tribe, that even the most corrupt and vicious leaders cannot ignore. At best, patronage systems can provide security, and do so at many levels. For example, a patron must allow poor relatives to come and live in his house. This provides a social support system that aid has yet to equal and there is a danger that aid efforts to introduce 'pro-poor development', 'good governance' and 'rights-based approaches' will undermine it. Much of aid has been directly or indirectly concerned with overthrowing patronage systems but this can lead, at least in the short term, to instability, insecurity and conflict.

Democracy makes patronage systems more competitive and favours confrontation ('winner takes all') rather than compromise. If rival patrons cannot find a way to share benefits peacefully then violent conflict is a likely result. The cost of manipulating democratic systems and bureaucracies increases the demands on patrons and makes them resort to extreme measures in order to extract benefits from power.

Conflicts in Africa can be modelled as an interaction of Greed and Grievance. If a leader oversteps the mark (Greed) there is likely to be Grievance among followers who are not sufficiently rewarded and among opposing groups that have lost out. These contests are often fought out over access to government finance (aid) and natural resources such as oil and other minerals. A series of studies which I conducted for DFID from 2002 onwards indicated that poor people certainly had Grievances about unemployment and political exclusion but these were not driving forces in the conflicts that have plagued the continent. After the colonial period, Africa's wars have not been revolutionary in the sense that poor people join in the struggle to overthrow elite leaders but struggles between elite groups. Very often an apparent rebellion is simply a political demand to be recognised and bought off. As soon as money or jobs are offered to the leaders of the rebellion it collapses and (at best) poor people return to their homes no better off. This is the logic of insurrections such as Joseph Kony's in Uganda and neighbouring countries. The aim is to be bought off. Aid fails to address such problems – it is unlikely to be used directly to buy off villains such as Kony. Aid also exacerbates such rivalries because aid makes political power more worth fighting for.

Aid does most damage when it applies global panjandrums in inappropriate situations, such as the application of Structural Adjustment Policies in Mobutu's Zaire as described earlier. But there have been many other panjandrums including 'good governance' that have had perverse effects. The fundamental problem with aid is that it comes with ideological baggage. This is especially dangerous in Africa because aid represents such a large proportion of national finances and because rivalries can so readily take on tribal, religious and personal dimensions.

At the root of the problem, aid represents an attempt to alter another society and it generally does so without sufficient knowledge or apprehension that the effects may be far different from those intended. In northern Nigeria DFID found that the rate of enrolment of girls into school was very low and, because this was a DFID priority and Millennium Development Goal, launched an aid programme to enrol more girls and generally improve girls' education. This worthy objective was applied in an extremely sensitive area and without sufficient caution and consultation. There had been extensive violence in the past over religious matters in the north. Islamic conservatives were locked into a struggle with moderates and the issue of Sharia Law had become a focus of political and tribal contention. But DFID was determined to go ahead with its girls' education programme. This could be regarded as a brave move but it was foolhardy in the context. A movement was formed in the north to oppose Western education and took on the name 'Western education is forbidden' or Boko Haram.

It might be an exaggeration to say that DFID created Boko Haram but DFID certainly made matters worse. The programme had to be suspended and today Boko Haram is a major threat to global security. Not only has it abducted Nigerian girls in order to prevent them from receiving a Western education, it has also extended its scope far north into the Saharan region and linked up with sinister terrorist organisations including Al Qaeda.

From a Western perspective the aim of encouraging girls' education cannot be questioned but in northern Nigeria it is highly controversial and even the national government would have to tread carefully in order to promote it. Arguably, a way could have been found through intensive negotiation with political and religious leaders. DFID did not have the capacity or processes to handle such a difficult issue with adequate care.

Fatima Adamu, a Muslim academic from the north who worked with me on an unpublished review of DFID's programme in 2004 (when DFID was just starting to support girls' education) felt that DFID should have built up its work more slowly focusing on the negotiating skills of local women and approaching the issue of girls' education much more obliquely. She was confident that this could have been done in a small low-key experiment- *'Women's gender roles in society have given them skills that are relevant in conflict management and prevention. The role of women as agents of peace was reiterated by almost every group we met in Jigawa State. A representative of the Herdsmen Association pinpointed not only the negotiating skills of women, but also the influence they have over their children who are sent to graze livestock, which may then enter a farm and cause damage to crops. This is one of the most common causes of disputes and conflict between farmers and pastoralists. The special position of women in society that enables them to play crucial roles in the peace of a community should be sourced, tapped and utilized by development projects for conflict prevention and resolution as well as conflict management.'*

DFID was already supporting an organisation in the north called Women's Rights Advancement and Protection Alternative (WRAPA) and received clear warning how difficult and dangerous these issues were. This organisation was denounced for un-Islamic behaviour by an influential community leader after the Friday prayer. The audience in the mosque was ready to take to the streets in protest and there was a serious risk of violence against WRAPA but the group had made good links with the Imam and other community leaders who intervened to stop the situation escalating. The group offered to defend their actions under Islamic law and *'after a lengthy debate using Islamic literature the community members were convinced about the sincerity of WRAPA officials and the program'*.

But in a large-scale programme with targets and timelines there was little room for such cautious and tentative exploration. The attempt to promote girls' education was not totally misguided but it was misguided to proceed without extensive capacity and an open timescale. The work should have proceeded at a pace dictated by local women and it should have recognised that there would be opponents and that their potential for disruption would have to be taken into account and limited. As the IPCR conflict study for DFID in Nigeria warned- *'Those who feel excluded are likely to take action to assert their interests. Therefore any strategy for change must fully recognise the negative as well as the positive.'* But instead the programme became caught up in DFID and UN targets timescales; it was rushed along too fast. DFID managers in Nigeria had no choice but to frame their programmes around the MDGs: these were strongly supported by the Prime Minister, Tony Blair and Chancellor Gordon Brown. The OECD/DAC Principles for Engagement in Fragile States advise that above all aid should 'Do No Harm'. This is practically impossible when the aid budget is being constantly increased, staff cut, and the targets and timescales are imposed from outside.

It is not impossible to help poor people but it cannot be done by the aid system. Money could have been made available to girls from poorer backgrounds in northern Nigeria and their families could have taken the lead in deciding whether to use the money to acquire education and, if so, whether to seek a Western education in government schools or attend the Islamic schools. In that case the decision would have been made by those who knew most about the risks and would be most affected by the consequences. But the aid system ultimately likes to behave as 'nanny' and decide what is best, where and when. Ultimately this comes about because those who support aid and provide the money want to take the credit for what has been done. They cannot let go.

The overall problem is not that the overall objectives of aid are wrong but that its timescales and methods are wrong. This happens because the aid system decides too much and gives too little room for people to decide for themselves. My Nigerian academic colleagues found that poor people interviewed during these studies- *'take a long view of conflict as a sign that democracy is maturing and opening up previously closed space.'*[82] They regarded conflict as necessary in order to overcome their own powerlessness and were not satisfied with patronage systems that so often led to violent conflict and provided them with very little support. In one of the local studies poor people spoke about the need for 'direct action' but of course this posed problems for DFID. In Jigawa State-*'Because of bureaucratic inefficiencies and fierce political competition the people of the wetlands suffer unnecessarily from flood and drought. Sometimes the channels silt up blocking the flow of water and causing loss of crops. But the people are not supposed to open*

---

82    Vaux, T with F Adamu, A Akintaye, K Fayamu and L Obafemi (2004)
      *Mainstreaming Conflict - report for DFID Nigeria*, unpublished report

*them without the permission of the authorities.'* Some of the villagers were considering direct action but recognised that this could lead to conflict, and possibly violent conflict. They contacted the managers of a DFID project who advised them to take up the issue with traditional leaders and by that means secure support from the river basin authorities. At the time of the conflict study the situation had become very tense and the report raises a question about DFID's role- *'At what point is direct action justified and what is the position of DFID if people feel that they must go outside the strict parameters of the law?'* If DFID was simply giving money to poor people it could have avoided responsibility for what they chose to do, but then it would also have to give up any control over the 'programme' or better still give up the idea of programmes entirely.

Patronage is a striking example of the more general observation that the social and political systems with which aid interacts are too complex and too delicate to be addressed by an aid donor; they can only be addressed by the people themselves and this can only be done by reversing the lines of control so that poor people are in charge of resources.

Rigid notions such as 'good governance' cause serious trouble when applied to systems of governance that do not conform to Western expectations. Giles Bolton, who worked for DFID in Rwanda, asks his readers to imagine what it would be like to be 'President for a Day' in a typical but imaginary African country.[83] To get to where he is, the President has had to promise favours to various groups and interests and they keep reminding him that these promises have to be fulfilled, debts repaid and their support assured for the future. Otherwise they will cause mayhem of one kind or another. Although he sets out to serve the poor, the President finds himself a hostage to the competing interests of the rich and powerful. To outsiders he might be 'corrupt' but to himself and his associates he is fulfilling his moral duty. In the African expression he is being a 'Big Man'.

Paul Collier extends consideration of the dilemmas of African rule by pointing out that the President not only faces the possibility of being deposed by political rivals but also by his own military forces

---

[83]   Bolton (2008)

unless he keeps them fully satisfied.[84] He has no choice but to pay off the military and even maintain bloated security forces even though aid organisations are likely to object and demand 'security sector reform' as a condition or priority for aid. Collecting taxes is extremely difficult because there are few people able to pay and little capacity for tax collection. So Presidents have to use aid money to fill holes in their budgets. Employment in government posts is one of the greatest sources of patronage and government policy can come to revolve, in practice at least, around patronage rather than around development.[85]

One of the most damaging aspects of the patronage system is the tendency to rotate Ministers and officials very fast (for patronage reasons) and then for each Minister to change his staff (patronage again). Donors may invest heavily in equipping and training a government department and express satisfaction with the apparent 'commitment' of the Minister. But then a new Minister comes in who is likely to change everything. His focus is on providing jobs for associates rather than on making the health or education system work.

Describing the political process in Kenya, Michela Wrong reports (on the basis of other studies) that when Kenyatta was President, his Kikuyu tribe accounting for just 20.8% of the population, claimed between 28.6% and 31.6% of cabinet seats while the Kelanjin tribe, accounting for 11.5% of the population, held only between 4.8% and 9.6% of the seats. When a Kalenjin, President Moi, took over, the Kikuyu share of cabinet seats fell to just 4% while the Kalenjin's share soared to 22%. It was the same story with permanent secretaries. The representation of Kikuyus went down from 37.5% under Kenyatta to 8.7% under Moi, while the Kalenjin went up from 4.3% to 34.8%.[86]

Aid managers generally know about such issues but cannot do much about them because of pressures from higher up the aid system. So they continue to pour money into aid projects through government and simply repeat assurances that, despite evidence from the past, this

---

[84]  Collier (2009)
[85]  De Waal (2015a) describes conflict in the Horn of Africa in terms of rival-
     ries between business-patronage networks, making development generally
     irrelevant to their aims
[86]  Wrong (2012) p52

time the President or Minister really is 'committed' to development and the project is 'owned' by the government.

In Africa, tribal identities form the basis for political cronyism but essentially it is not so very different from the political shenanigans of Western countries (appeasing back-benchers, lobbying, hiring ex-Ministers as consultants, pork-barrelling etc) except that the African version is labelled as corruption. The problem is that the aid system behaves as if they did not exist either in the West or in the countries where they operate.

The issue is most obvious in Africa but it is also important in every other country. In 2006, Jamaica recorded the highest level of homicides per capita in the world and DFID, which had retained a presence in Jamaica largely because of Commonwealth connections, commissioned a study of violence extending across the Caribbean region.[87] One of DFID's main interests was in the police forces. DFID had provided substantial amounts of equipment and training for the police but had not succeeded in 'reform'. Police services had continued in the same mode as in colonial times, supporting the interests and plans of elite groups and political leaders. This included an ambiguous relationship with gangs that smuggled drugs and weapons across the region. These gangs were a ready source of income for high level police officers and politicians. Because police appointments could be lucrative, promotions and appointments were highly politicised and even Jamaica's most progressive governments were afraid to act against the police.

One of the proposed ways forward was to appoint an independent Commissioner who could receive direct input from the public (i.e. complaints) at different levels. But the police were ready to portray this modest step as an attack on the police as an institution and they were ready to launch a campaign portraying politicians as being 'soft on crime'.

With DFID funding, retired police officers from the UK had been posted to the Caribbean and put into senior posts in an effort to demonstrate British approaches to policing. They were supposed to train Jamaican counterparts. But these officers were not used to the

---

[87]  Extending across the Caribbean although rather unevenly. The unpublished report is Vaux, T and A Harriott (2008) *Small States Big Problems: Strategic Conflict and Security Assessment –Caribbean*. This section draws on Harriott, A (2000) –see bibliography.

subtle webs of political protection that enabled Jamaican police officers to maintain links with the gangs and ignore calls for reform. In practice the British officers were sidelined. Their Jamaican deputies remained in control and they retreated into a pleasant but unproductive Caribbean inaction.

Aid systems tend to avoid politics and therefore act as if politics do not matter. The attempt to make services more useful for poor people inevitably involves a challenge to established power but the aid system focuses instead on technological change, training and capacity building when the problem is not skill but power. This weakness is recognised by managers in DFID, who have made serious efforts to study 'drivers of change' and conduct political economy studies, but at the end of the day they simply have to spend the budget. They are not in a position to bargain aid against reforms. Instead they have to beg to be allowed to spend more. With no possibility of aid altering political realities, we come back to the observation that aid may work where the political circumstances are conducive (and where there is probably no significant problem of poverty) but not in circumstances that are difficult (but where there are likely to be huge problems of poverty and distress).

The ability of aid agencies to influence politics in favour of poor people has been further undermined by the dominance of the global security agenda after 9/11. In 2011, I had the opportunity to work on a political economy study with local academics based in Bishkek in Kyrgyzstan.[88] The focus was on the national education system. Donors in the education sector had been disappointed to find that, following many years of aid support, educational standards as measured by the Program for International Student Assessment (PISA), had plummeted from among of the highest during the Soviet period to last position (65th) in 2009. A high proportion of children continued to enrol in school but more than 80% of Kyrgyzstan's 15-year olds had only achieved reading skills below Level 2, which is the baseline level of proficiency. In other words school leavers could not read. This was embarrassing to the government and they agreed to work with the donors to find out what was happening –hence the political economy study.

---

[88]   Vaux, T and M Ryabkov (2011) *Political Economy Analysis of the Education Sector in Kyrgyzstan,* unpublished report for the European Commission

After the collapse of the Soviet Union, Kyrgyzstan experienced a sharp economic decline accompanied by rampant inflation. The level of funding for school upkeep and teacher salaries remained fixed in money terms but its value declined because of inflation. At the same time, the share of the national budget allocated for education significantly decreased. In some cases, local government had felt obliged to step in and pay for heating and school upkeep but there was a serious nationwide problem with teacher salaries.

Research showed that Kyrgyzstan still had just about enough good teachers (despite an exodus of Russian-speakers) but teachers felt obliged to find other part-time work and very often they would pay classroom assistants and senior pupils to do the teaching for them. A UNICEF report found that- *'In many cases schools continue to claim salaries for teachers who are no longer there or remain absent for long periods. This leads to under-reporting of teacher shortages...'* [89] Official figures for Jalal-Abad, for example, showed a shortfall of 3.8% in teacher numbers but the actual shortage, as revealed in UNICEF research, was 28.4%. Similarly, official figures showed a student-teacher ratio of 15:1 but the real ratio was up to 45:1. Official figures showed that students were still doing well in examinations but the external PISA tests showed that they were not even learning basic skills. The reality was that it had become possible to buy educational certificates.

Education was said to be free and this was a condition of donor support; it was illegal to charge for state education. But parents were under strong pressure to meet the deficit in school running costs and to pay top-ups for teacher salaries as an incentive for them to work. Where parents could afford to do this, schools could maintain a high standard but elsewhere the quality declined drastically, especially in rural areas, where poverty was mainly concentrated. In effect this meant that some schools became privatised in the sense that they catered to fee-paying parents. Children whose parents were unable to pay were not allowed to continue at the school. Selection by payment was illegal in government schools but the practice was not reported to the higher authorities. It emerged from our political economy study that inspectors were being paid off and there were indications that

---

[89]  UNICEF (2009) *Survival Strategies of Schools in the Kyrgyz Republic: a school-level analysis of teacher shortages,* UNICEF Bishkek

the inspectors passed on part of the proceeds to officials higher up in the Ministry. In fact the staffing in the Ministry was a huge patronage network centred around the Minister.

Donors had initially been alerted to the scale of problems because of the results of the PISA tests. They recognised that there might be a confrontation with the government and joined together in a Sector-Wide Approach (SWAp). They commissioned the political economy study which provided evidence of even deeper problems. The Ministry was no longer staffed by education professionals but by unqualified persons who happened to be favoured by the Minister. The new staff were not properly qualified to oversee educational policy and had strong incentives (because of their loyalty to the Minister) not to raise difficulties and problems.

Wealthy urban people, enjoying significant political influence, were perfectly satisfied with this arrangement because they could send their children to what were in effect elite private schools subsidized by the state. They could obtain a top class education much more cheaply in these schools than in purely 'private' schools such as the international schools. But the overall effect of these failures of the education system was to exacerbate inequalities across the country and especially between urban and rural areas. According to data obtained from the World Bank, the cost of education had become a major expenditure for all families, accounting for over 20% on average but very much higher among the poorest families.

The Kyrgyzstan political economy study concluded with an assessment of a strategy to achieve change. The central government was likely to respond to pressure from powerful urban elites rather than the rural poor but some local parliamentarians had protested against what was happening and for them rural votes were important. Also, most of the head teachers had a strong professional interest in the quality of education and would make efforts to challenge abuses and improve the system. Donors had some leverage because they could threaten to withdraw aid. But in the last resort it proved impossible to move along this path. Firstly donor representatives were under intense pressure to achieve the Millennium Development Goals and, depending what statistics were used, it was still possible to argue that there was progress. School enrolments, a particular focus of the MDGs, were very high, including among girls. But secondly, donors were impotent because the driving force behind aid programmes in Kyrgyzstan was to reward the country for its support for NATO's actions in Afghanistan. The main airbase for military forces entering and leaving Afghanistan was located in Kyrgyzstan. It was under threat because Russia wanted to close it. Aid was a bargaining chip in this high level political tussle. In effect the aid programme had nothing to do with poverty reduction but represented 'soft diplomacy'. This was well understood by the authorities in Bishkek and they rightly anticipated that the donors would do little more than issue a mild protest and the education system could be left as it was. So in the end nothing changed, inequalities increased and poor people lost out on education. It is by no means impossible that the grievances of poor people in Kyrgyzstan will be mobilised by politicians seeking to challenge the existing political clique and plunge the country into violence, as has happened in the past.

The dangers of aid are nowhere more starkly demonstrated than in the case of Rwanda around the time of the 1994 genocide. A study by Peter Uvin, who lived and worked in Rwanda for several years, concludes that- *'The process of development and the international aid given to promote it interacted with the forces of exclusion, inequality, pauperization, racism, and oppression that laid the foundation for the 1994 genocide.'* [90] In other words, aid may not have directly caused the genocide but it exacerbated some of the factors that did.

Colonial history had exaggerated the differences between Hutus and Tutsis and there had been serious outbreaks of violence after independence as democracy gradually took power away from the minority Tutsis, favoured by the Belgians, and transferred it to the majority Hutus. Leading Tutsis fled to Uganda where they were given support and military roles by President Museveni. In the eyes of the Hutu majority this represented a serious threat which was compounded by an incursion of Ugandan Tutsis into northern Rwanda in 1992.

Rwanda attracted a high level of aid because it had a strong government capable of managing projects effectively. Donors took the opportunity to deliver large amounts of aid, and much of it passed through central government to the local government structure, the communes. The communes were regarded by aid agencies as an unusually efficient form of local government allowing aid to be

---

[90]    Uvin (1998) p3

delivered right down to local level. But according to Uvin's study local participation was an illusion-'*Commune personnel are not even remotely accountable to the population but solely to the vertical structure from which they receive detailed marching orders.*' [91]

The flow of money to the communes was tightly controlled by the centre and came under the control of a hard-line Hutu faction in Kigali. The heads of the communes, the burgomasters, owed their allegiance to this clique and need not be accountable to the people. They used aid to consolidate control over the people and to marginalise the Tutsis. The President came under pressure internationally to make concessions to the Tutsis in order to achieve peace after the 1992 incursion but the clique in Kigali opposed this and hatched a plot to eliminate the threat permanently. Instructions for the genocide were sent out early in 1994 and when the call came the burgomasters and local Hutu leadership were ready to play their part. The trigger was the shooting down of the airplane bringing the President back from peace talks in Tanzania. The Hutu clique spread the rumour that this had been the work of the Tutsis and the massacres, which had been planned beforehand, started immediately and simultaneously across all parts of the country. Inevitably there was resistance by Tutsis, giving rise to further rumours that this was a Tutsi insurrection. An increasing number of Hutu people took part in the violence, now regarding it perhaps as a matter of self defence.

Aid caused the concentration of political power that made the genocide possible but the aid system remained unaware of this process or unable to do anything about it-'*High paid consultants trained burgomasters and their personnel in methods of programming, monitoring, evaluation, and beneficiary participation; technical consultants wrote down detailed communal development plans; foreign experts wrote lengthy reports on local development –but the gap between rhetoric and reality never closed. As the technical assistants attached to communal support projects observed bitterly after years of work- "communal development projects served to allow the burgomasters to better control their population."*' [92]

By controlling aid flows, burgomasters became very powerful but their power depended on their relations with the central government. The aid system ignored what was in effect a patronage

---

[91]    Ibid p25

[92]    Ibid –referring to a report from for the Swiss Development Corporation

system running on aid money. Uvin found that the World Bank and aid agencies working in Rwanda *adopted a myth of apolitical development*.[93]

There was a history of tribal massacres in Rwanda (and also among ethnic Hutus and Tutsis in Burundi) and this made it plausible that at some point the Tutsis would strike back, especially as they enjoyed Ugandan support. In seeking to consolidate its power the Hutu clique spread these fears and encouraged Hutus to make plans in case the Tutsis rebelled. Whether they really believed in the Tutsi threat is uncertain –they may simply have used it as a way to seize power from the President.

No aid worker predicted the disaster. Uvin himself had lived in Rwanda for years but admits that matters were not nearly so clear before the genocide as afterwards with the benefit of hindsight. I visited Rwanda myself in the early 1980s and recorded an impression of a haven of tranquillity among nations in chaos. Rwanda was often described by aid workers as Switzerland in Africa –a country in which a pattern of decentralized communes guaranteed a lasting peace.

Uvin's book was published in 1999 but the lessons have not been learnt. The scale of aid for Africa increased steadily and the level of management ('overhead costs') declined making it even less likely that the aid system would recognise such dangers. Aid agencies do not demonstrate their effectiveness by analysing their impact on power structures but by giving out the numbers of schools and hospitals, attendances, enrolments and examination results.

The main problems arise from the flow of resources through power structures that can use aid for their own purposes but there are also negative side effects from specific aid activity. The provision of services can be deeply divisive. Aid money provided with the intention of helping all areas and groups can be manipulated to favour specific areas and peoples, excluding others. It is impossible and possibly undesirable for aid managers to micro-manage such a process. In Rwanda's neighbour Burundi aid channelled through the Tutsi-dominated government had been used to improve schools in Tutsi areas and Hutu areas were excluded. This added to ongoing tensions and has been cited as a

---

[93]    Ibid p45

cause of later violence.[94] Education can also have an impact on conflict because of the way that histories are taught in the syllabus. Even the style of teaching can predispose children towards authoritarian forms of behaviour that may facilitate the concentration of power (as in Rwanda) and lead to conflict. In 2000, UNICEF published a paper on *'The Two Faces of Education'* which noted that-

*Prejudiced children are more likely to be moralistic, to dichotomize the world, to externalise conflict, and to have higher need of definiteness... Under classroom conditions of inter-ethnic tension and conflict, such characteristics unavoidably find their way into the classroom and must be taken into account if the peace-destroying impact of education is to be minimized.*[95]

Decentralisation is often viewed as a way of balancing central against local power but it can also strengthen local power bases. During the war from 1993 to 1996, Bosnia was divided into Bosniak-majority and Croat-majority. Schools in each area taught their own aggressive view of history. In this way the education system prepared children to accept the process of 'ethnic cleansing'.[96] On a larger scale the break-up of Yugoslavia led to sharp divisions between ways of teaching history in the different elements remaining. The Serbian claim to Kosovo, based on a history of conflict with Turkey in the Middle Ages, was taught as fact to both Serbian and Kosovar children. Having to accept Serbian propaganda in schools became one of the grievances of the Kosovar population. In all these cases the use of language in the schools was also a crucial issue, often leading to discrimination against ethnic opponents and minorities.[97]

But generally in the aid system, education is measured in quantity rather than quality. Donors assume that the more services (such as education) being provided, the greater the chance of peace. But a multi-donor evaluation of aid to South Sudan after the 2005 Peace Agreement showed an inverse relationship between the spread of services and the level of peace. The reasons for this are not entirely clear. A possible explanation may be that women and children, who were most closely

---

94  Smith and Vaux (2003) p10
95  Bush, K and D Saltarelli (2000) *The Two Faces of Education in Ethnic Conflict*, UNICEF Innocenti Research Centre, Florence
96  Smith and Vaux (2003) p24
97  Smith and Vaux (2003) passim

associated with the provision of education and other services, had no influence over decisions relating to violent conflict which were taken by men. The provision of services had no bearing on what were in effect tribal wars. But the theory that services bring peace had been the foundation for international aid strategy in South Sudan after the Peace Agreement. The spread of services was expected to provide a 'peace dividend' which would reward peacefulness and reduce conflict.[98]

In a review of *'Service Delivery in Countries Emerging from Conflict'* fellow-consultant Emma Visman and I examined four different countries and found no evidence that provision of services contributes to peace.[99] A similar conclusion was reached in a literature review (in which I participated) in 2011- *'Service delivery, depending on how it is undertaken (exclusively versus inclusively, by which type of provider, and to which groups of people) can contribute either positively, negatively or neutrally to wider state-building and peace- building processes. The exact conditions under which its positive contributions can be assured are not clearly outlined in the literature...'*[100]

The aid system works on the basis of general assumptions that may not be true in relation to each situation but they do not take the trouble to analyse each case separately or explore the political economy implications of what they are doing. Similarly they do not undertake sufficient consultation with the affected people. But even if they did the overwhelming pressure on the aid system to spend money, comply with higher donor policy and reduce overhead costs would render such exercises futile.

Another area in which false assumptions can be made relates to the role of natural resources in violent conflict. Paul Collier has found that the presence of rich natural resources correlates with conflict and this has led some organisations to conclude that a ban on the trade of certain natural resources would lead to an end to conflict.[101] But natural

---

[98] Bennett et al (2010)

[99] Vaux and Visman (2005)

[100] Practical Action, Save the Children, CfBT (2011) p44

[101] Collier, P et al (2003) *Breaking the Conflict Trap —civil war and development policy*, World Bank Policy Research Report. This has been questioned in Suhrka, A and I Samset (2007) *What's in a figure? Estimating recurrence of civil war*, International Peacekeeping vol 14 no 2 pp195-203 and questioned in

resources do not necessarily cause conflict. Take Nigeria's three way balance, for example, and consider that diamond-rich Botswana has been one of Africa's most stable countries.

A new type of campaigning organisation has emerged, especially in the USA, focused on this issue of the linkage between natural resources, poverty and violence. The 'blood diamonds' campaign is perhaps the best known example and typically draws on support from celebrities in order to gain publicity and widen public support. A similar campaign has focused on the rare earths and other valuable minerals mined in the eastern parts of the DRC. The Kivu Provinces became a focus for intense international attention because of widely-reported sexual violence against women. Some of the world's rarest and most valuable minerals were being mined in this area and some of these are used in mobile phones, providing a direct link to people, especially young people, in the West. It was readily assumed that wealth from mining was a major factor driving the violence. Mining paid for guns and this was the basis for violent conflict. On this assumption, The Enough Project launched its *'Can You Hear Congo Now?'* campaign in 2009.[102]

Although the campaign achieved widespread endorsement and celebrity support in the USA it was ultimately harmful because of a misunderstanding about the nature of the problem. Weapons were not being purchased from the proceeds of mining. They were already widely available in Kivu and cheap. Long periods of war had flooded the area with arms. The problem was not the weaponry or the local warlords but the inability of the state to control the violence. Ultimately it was a matter of competing patronage networks —the state's against those of local warlords and their patrons in other African countries.

For poor people in the region, mining was one of the few activities available other than fighting. It was the only source of livelihood for many families because there was not enough stability or security for farming. Most of the mining was not conducted by big companies but by hundreds of thousands of 'artisanal' miners who dug pits and extracted minerals by hand. The products of this 'artisanal' mining were sold at

Keen, D (2000) *'Incentives and Disincentives for Violence'* and other articles in Berdal, M and D Malone (eds) (2000) *Greed and Grievance —economic agendas in civil wars, Lynne Rienner*

[102]  Seay in de Waal (2015)

very low prices to merchants. The miners remained poor but if mining ceased, they would be desperate.

The campaign by *The Enough Project* succeeded in bringing about an international trading ban on the four principal minerals extracted in eastern DRC. Merchants dealing in these minerals faced heavy fines and possible imprisonment. The effect of the ban went far wider than the four minerals because it was impossible for merchants to be sure that other consignments of minerals were not tainted. Faced with the threat of severe punishments by the USA, and risking criticism by consumers fired up by celebrities, traders withdrew from the mining business completely. Mineral trade in the DRC collapsed and this caused a serious loss of state revenues derived from taxes on exports, making it even more difficult for the state to constrain the violence.

The most direct and serious effect, however, was loss of the livelihoods of artisanal miners not only in the Kivu Provinces but all over the country. Mining activists in DRC have estimated that two million miners were put out of work.[103] Far from reducing conflict the campaign left miners with little alternative but to join the armed groups.[104]

The crucial failure of the campaign had been lack of analysis and lack of dialogue with local organisations, notably the miners' unions. It is not only campaigning groups in the USA that suffer from this deficiency. In a study conducted in DRC a few years earlier I had found that DFID's focus was on helping large mining companies in Katanga to run welfare projects in the communities around their mines. This arose because of pressures on DFID to promote the activities of British companies. At first this appeared to be a wasteful but probably harmless activity but my discussions with miners' unions revealed that the companies in Katanga were putting large numbers of 'artisanal' miners out of work. They had reduced the labour force by introducing mechanization and they had used their political influence in DRC (and especially in Katanga) to secure special deals that enabled them to produce materials more cheaply than the local 'artisanal' mines.

Drawing on a report by a local organisation and discussions with labour unions, the study pointed out to DFID that '*the sale and gift of mining concessions during the war now threatens to end this livelihood (artisanal mining)as large companies come into DRC using capital*

---

[103] Seay (2015) p128
[104] Seay (2015) p129

intensive methods that require very few workers. Hundreds of thousands of 'artisanal' miners, many of them with experience of fighting, may now lose their livelihood.'[105] Instead of DFID supporting welfare activities by the companies the study advised that- 'A better response would be to require companies to use middle technology methods that required a labour force rather than the current high technology approaches that bring no employment opportunities.'[106]

The study pointed out that the mining issue was embroiled in DRC politics at all different levels- 'As the temperature increases, aid will be more politicised and the political implications of aid will need to be considered very carefully. Aid for the state must not lead to exclusion of the opposition. Aid for the centre must not undermine the decentralization process. Support for the government must not be seen as condoning kleptocracy and violation of human rights. Aid agencies will need to be a little more detached and a little tougher in their demands... Withdrawal of support from the state will also have direct political implications. There is no doubt that DRC is one of the world's neediest countries. But these factors must not lead to an assumption that the more aid is given the more stable the country will be. The reverse could equally be true. Aid can add to tensions as well as reduce them.' (Op cit p35)

There was no disagreement from aid managers working for DFID in DRC but the messages were not acceptable higher up. DFID in the DRC was obliged to spend more and more money with lower overhead costs. The notion of persuading companies to focus on employing poor people rather than making profits got nowhere, of course.

The fundamental reason for the mistaken assumptions of The Enough Project was lack of consultation with the people affected and with those who might represent them, especially the miners' unions. It is the same problem with DFID. But the minerals campaign was driven by a desire to equal the spectacular 'blood diamonds campaign' and it was very difficult for the organisers to go back and admit that they had been badly wrong. Consultation, as in most cases, would raise so many difficulties that inaction would seem better than action, and inaction is death to the aid system.

---

[105]  Based on Pact (2007) Researching Natural resources and trade flows in the Great Lakes Region, Pact report for DFID, USAID and COMESA p6 which warns that the numbers affected could be more than a million.

[106]  Vaux, T et al (2007)

# CHAPTER SIX

# CAN AID WORK? A CASE STUDY FROM NEPAL

In Nepal over the decade from 2000, the conditions for using aid as a means of poverty reduction were optimal. The purpose of aid was not greatly distorted by the Global War on Terror because Nepal has no significant Muslim population and although the US Ambassador styled the Maoist insurgents as 'terrorists' this was really another label for 'communists' and harkened back to an earlier era. Trade promotion was not a serious objective for aid because Nepal's trade is almost exclusively with India. The UK's recruitment of Gurkha mercenaries to serve in the British army, gave a reason for friendly relations and reasonably high levels of aid but it did introduce an element of additional support for the Nepal government and the royal family in the war against the Maoists. But perhaps the most significant point is that aid workers found Nepal an extraordinarily pleasant place to live and tended to stay for long periods of time, getting to know the country better than aid staff usually do. Some had lived in Nepal for decades and were deeply committed to poverty reduction.

The war had begun in 1996 when one of several 'communist' parties in Nepal left mainstream politics and launched a rebellion in the style of Chairman Mao, retreating to remote rural areas and seeking support from among the oppressed peasantry. In labelling the Maoists as terrorists the US Ambassador did not receive the wholehearted support of other embassies and aid departments. There was a degree of sympathy for the Maoists especially when aid managers began to realise that the Maoist agenda for poverty reduction was rather similar to their own. Nevertheless the official position of Western countries remained strongly opposed to the Maoists and aligned with a government that, they had to admit, was not only corrupt but the real cause of poverty.

Nepal's inability to address poverty issues was deep rooted. The monarchy wielded considerable powers and could overthrow politicians at whim. Political parties acted as patronage systems that exploited brief periods in power in order to reward themselves and their followers. Governments came and went with bewildering speed leaving a trail of corruption and unfulfilled promises. Because today's opposition was likely to be tomorrow's government, a culture of impunity developed. Despite the disappearance of huge sums from the national finances, much of it derived from aid, politicians were never held to account. Politicians spoke out against each other but behind the scenes made deals that allowed them all to participate in impoverishing the nation, and rural people in particular.

Western observers suspected that the Maoist leadership, which came from the high caste Hindu elite, was simply using the rebellion to get into power, and indeed this is what actually happened, at least to a very considerable extent. When the war ended in 2005 the Maoists formed a government that was not much less corrupt than its predecessors and almost as ineffective. But in the process the Maoists unleashed the anger and determination of poor people and exposed the problems of development and the deficiencies of aid.

The fruitless politics of Nepal did not come about by accident but because it suited its superpower neighbours, China and India. Neither wanted the other to achieve dominance over Nepal and so they favoured a situation of instability in which Nepal was weak and dependent. At various times India favoured and provided refuge to leading politicians including the Maoists. India provided massive aid for roads but these were designed to allow Indian troops to move along the border in case of an incursion from China. China was irritated by the Maoists' use of their former leader's name and showed little sympathy for the rebellion. They focused on maintaining the power balance with India to ensure that Nepal did not become a base for Tibetan or other forms of resistance within China itself. China provided Nepal with assurances against annexation by India, as had happened in the case of another Himalayan kingdom, Sikkim. In this context of superpower rivalry, the

Maoist rebellion was useful as a means of keeping Nepal weak and malleable, but it is unlikely that either of the great regional powers wanted it to succeed.

The history of Nepal is one of extraction of wealth from rural areas and concentration of wealth in the capital, Kathmandu. The ownership of land was closely controlled by the monarchy and its associates and the country was run on a feudal basis. Peasant farmers generally did not own land and women had no rights to property. Debts to landlords had resulted in the widespread practice of bonded labour, a form of slavery.

The monarchy styled Nepal as a Hindu Kingdom[107] and claimed a position at the top of a Hindu hierarchy but in reality at least half the population were not Hindus but Buddhists, animists and followers of other localised religions. Hinduism was prominent in the Kathmandu Valley but not so much elsewhere especially in the hills and mountains. Lower caste (or outcaste) Hindus and adherents of all other religions were treated as inferiors. Their well-being was disregarded by the ruling Hindu elite. The isolation of elite Hindus in the Kathmandu valley made them unaware or uncaring towards the deep poverty and suffering of the rural areas.

Taxation was mostly directed towards the upkeep of the monarchy, the police and the military forces. Poverty reduction became an issue for government only so far as aid agencies made it so and paid for it. Practically the entire 'development' budget was funded by aid agencies. Although some aid managers had stayed in Nepal for long periods the aid system as a whole had fallen into the control of the Kathmandu-based Hindu elite of Brahmins and Kshatriyas (*Bahuns* and *Chettris* in Nepal). The Nepali language itself was a source of discrimination. It was required as a qualification for government jobs and this put minorities at a disadvantage. English was the preserve of a highly educated elite, mostly Brahmin, and by giving preference to English-speakers the aid system allowed elite groups to take almost complete control of local staffing, using each further recruitment to favour relatives so that the

---

[107]   The monarchy came very close to an abrupt end in 2001 when the Crown Prince murdered most of his relatives but his unpopular uncle managed to salvage the monarchy for a few more years until it was finally swept away when the Maoists came to power in 2005.

staff of each aid agency came to resemble an extended family. Because foreign managers gain much of their knowledge from their local staff this meant that their understanding of Nepal became biased. Local staff in Kathmandu had little interest in leaving the capital and arranged matters so that huge amounts of time were taken up in workshops, trainings and other 'capacity' building, often entailing long periods of time in luxury hotels.

Another effect was that rural programmes mainly benefitted the elite classes rather than poor people. When projects were selected and implemented Brahmin field workers decided who should benefit and who should be excluded. Old patterns of discrimination were reinforced through aid. Whether corruption played a significant role in these arrangements is difficult to know but there were many allegations.

DFID recognised that the war had altered the entire context for aid and in 2002 decided to undertake a conflict analysis and use this as the basis for a review of ongoing programmes. The resulting Strategic Conflict Assessment (SCA) found that aid tended to help the elite rather than poor people and also that poor people were unable to interact with the aid system- *'If the villager comes to Kathmandu he may be unable to meet with aid staff because they are involved in a constant round of 'workshops' at luxury hotels. By allowing extravagance in its own processes, and spending disproportionate amounts on its own machinery rather than on the poor, aid has become part of the problem —a cause of conflict.'* The report noted that one of DFID's partner NGOs with 81 staff spent over 3,800 person-days (47 days per person in a year) in workshops and trainings, nearly all in the Kathmandu valley.

The staffing of aid agencies was a particularly sensitive issue identified in the DFID conflict analysis- *'Aid agencies are staffed almost entirely by non-poor groups, and there is a very high concentration of Brahmins. The reason is not necessarily that caste considerations have been used overtly in recruitment —although this does seem to happen. But suitability for jobs is often based on behaviours associated with elite social groups. Education is given immense importance, and acts as a barrier to prevent low caste and poorer groups from finding jobs.'*

Aid agencies generally made English a requirement even in jobs where it was not necessary. If poor Nepalese people go to school at all they attend state schools in which the language of instruction is Nepali. Anyone proficient in English is likely to have gone to a private school in which instruction is through English medium (this is still the case today). This means that only better-off people could get jobs with aid agencies. The report also pointed out that the representation of women in aid agencies was very low and the lack of women's voice was one of the reasons for the failure of so many aid programmes. Aid staff complained about low participation of women in meetings about development projects, and used this as an argument that they were not much interested, but this happened largely because aid agencies were not sensitive to the heavy workload of women and their inability to attend meetings called at unsuitable times or involving long periods of time- *'Studies suggest that women in rural areas work for 18 hours a day. For women, time is scarce and therefore an aid culture that demands attendance in many meetings is a form of discrimination.'*

Many aid agency staff were surprised to find that the Maoists blamed international aid for the country's underdevelopment and developed proposals for reforming the aid system.[108] They criticised the huge amounts of aid spent in Kathmandu. They argued that aid money should not be spent on workshops but on 'direct delivery' of benefits to the people. The Maoists actively took up agendas that the aid agencies had barely touched on, such as bonded labour and the status of women. Much of their support came from very poor people in rural areas and rural women played a particularly active role in the armed struggle. Many Maoist followers viewed their purpose as the eradication of poverty and rights for women.

DFID's conflict study in 2002 noted that- *'The Maoists have been able to exploit a genuine sense of grievance caused by the failure of governance and focused attention on the exclusion of poor people from political power. They have been able to link their political cause to discrimination based on caste, ethnicity, religion and gender. In effect they have seized the development agenda from both the government and the international agencies. This is not because the Maoists have found development solutions but because government and international aid have failed.'*[109]

---

[108]  Best known through their '40-point Programme' but reflecting massive research by one of the Maoist leaders, Baburam Bhattarai —see Bhattarai (2003)

[109]  Vaux, T (2002) *Nepal Strategic Conflict Assessment*, unpublished paper for DFID

Surrounded by elite local staff many aid workers found reasons to dismiss these claims and pour scorn on the rebellion but by 2002 the Maoists had taken control of most rural areas and aid agencies now lacked access to the areas where they were supposed to work. Government officials retreated to fortified district towns and to Kathmandu. This may have suited many of them very well because services were much better than in the rural areas and they could gain access to the English-speaking schools that were the passport into elite jobs.

The Maoists took a strong stance against American organisations and any organisation receiving US funding. Otherwise they did not prevent agencies from reaching rural areas but watched them in case they were spying for the government. Their main demand was that agencies should deliver direct benefits to the people. They also insisted that aid agencies should have the agreement of the people and they favoured open public meetings for dialogue between the agency and the people.

The Maoist rebellion forced aid agencies to rethink their strategies and ways of working. Some managers looked for ways of co-existing or even collaborating with the Maoists. Some local NGOs opened up secret back-channels of communication which could be used even by donor governments such as DFID which began to move steadily towards a more neutral position in the war.

DFID began to pass more funding through NGOs including those that were known to have Maoist sympathies and connections. Although the overall aid system had been criticised as elitist and Kathmandu-centric, there had been examples of aid delivering results directly to very poor people. For example, the Swiss Development Cooperation (SDC) had introduced and promoted community forestry. All forests had been declared the property of the crown and people had been debarred from entering the forests. Lack of firewood had become a serious problem for poor people. Corruption in the government's forestry department had led to massive destruction of forests. SDC did not succeed in opening up the biggest forests, as they initially hoped, but they did persuade the government to allow small wood-plots to be allocated to villagers and run by them. These 'Forest Users Groups' proved to be extremely successful and showed that village people were capable of overcoming their internal problems if given the chance to tackle an issue that deeply concerned them.

The reason why so much aid failed or made inequalities worse was that it was not simply influenced by people from elite backgrounds in the government and aid agencies but channelled through elite groups at village level. In particular, aid had been delivered through Village Development Committees (VDCs) that reflected the stranglehold of rich people over the poor. VDCs were dominated by high caste landowners with only a token presence of poorer people and women. The Brahmin staff of aid agencies generally ignored or denied these problems. A UNDP project which I reviewed in 2004 was intended to raise incomes in poor communities. It collected requests from everyone but poor families typically put forward very modest proposals, perhaps for an animal or some tools, while the wealthier families, with the benefit of education and wider contacts (and acting as hosts for UNDP's visiting Brahmin staff), put forward much more ambitious schemes, such as a shop or an agricultural development project. The poor family got a goat worth five dollars while the high caste family got a shop worth thousands of dollars. Reports might show that the project enjoyed full participation of the people including the poorest groups but in reality it exacerbated inequalities and this was the kind of activity that had driven poor people towards rebellion.[110]

The Maoists began to question these processes in the areas they controlled. They organised discussions in villages about aid programmes and insisted that aid agencies must openly explain their intentions to a full assembly of local people. But the most important changes came about because the elite groups fled from the villages when the Maoists took charge. Development and poverty reduction were now much more straightforward. But a majority of aid agencies failed to recognise this. They avoided areas of Maoist control and allowed themselves to be predisposed against the Maoists by propaganda put out by elite groups including their own staff. Some agencies devoted even more of their time and resources to conferences in the Kathmandu Valley.

For those that turned their attention to poverty reduction in rural areas the problem was that the Maoists were in favour of 'direct delivery' but not much else. They did not want aid agencies to try

---

[110] The above case study derives from an unpublished UNDP Programme Review from a Conflict Perspective conducted by myself and Nepalese consultants

to organise the people because this could compete with their own work. For aid agencies this might be frustrating but it was not a major obstacle in so far as the Maoists shared the same objective of poverty reduction. Agencies had to leave the Maoists to organise discussions on issues such as bonded labour and women's rights.

The Royal Nepal Army (RNA) became increasingly concerned about aid activity in Maoist areas and frequently prevented aid agencies from travel, ostensibly for their own safety. In order to minimise obstruction both by the Maoists and by the army, DFID took the lead in developing a set of 'Principles of Engagement' and these were developed into the more practical Basic Operating Guidelines (BOGs) which specified how agencies would operate in the war context. The BOGs provided assurance to the parties in conflict, for example, that aid agencies would not carry arms or allow armed personnel to use their vehicles.[111] Printed on a single laminated sheet, the BOGs were used as a laissez-passer by aid workers travelling in contested areas. The system was backed up by specialist staff who investigated any problems arising. When a violation occurred, a group of the aid agencies would find ways to convey their concerns the government or Maoists as necessary. In general this worked very well: the number of attacks and disruptions was reduced considerably and aid workers were able to travel more widely.

Some military commanders refused to acknowledge the BOGs and continued to obstruct aid but the official position was to facilitate the delivery of aid on the basis that this would help to win 'hearts and minds'. An army General and member of the National Security Committee gave me an assurance that- *'there are strong instructions from senior command to the security forces to respect your neutrality'* but the reason he gave was that- *'development will help prevent people from joining the Maoists'*. Development aid, in this view, was to be portrayed as the gift of a beneficent government. The General was concerned that *'the rebels have been taking advantage of these (aid) resources to use them against the government'*. The only issue on which the army refused to compromise with the aid agencies was a prohibition against water pipes and other such equipment which, in the army's opinion, might be

---

[111]   Vaux, T (2003) *The Basic Operating Guidelines in Practice –Report for DFID Nepal,* unpublished

used to make bombs.

The official position of the Maoists, as stated to me through intermediaries, was that they would support the delivery of aid provided firstly that US organisations were not involved and secondly that aid programmes complied with the Maoist 40-point programme and in particular the preference for 'direct delivery'.

The government made no attempt to negotiate but tried to crush the rebellion by force. A State of Emergency was declared in November 2001 and this continued until the end of the war in 2005. The security forces were given license to arrest and detain people without question. There were gross human rights violations by the security forces and these turned some sections of civil society, including some of the media, into critics of government. But they could do little against the strong grip of the regional superpowers which dictated the realities of political life in Nepal.

DFID in Nepal took the lead in developing the BOGs and was able to deliver aid widely because of the apparent position of neutrality. Without warning the UK Ministry of Defence (MoD) in London decided to provide helicopters for the Royal Nepal Army (RNA). This resulted from the UK's ongoing military connection with Nepal focused around Gurkha recruitment but it threatened to overthrow DFID's aid arrangements and put DFID staff and partners at risk. The MoD gave assurances that the helicopters would be used only for transport and not for attack but few people believed this. No-one knew how the Maoists would react but fortunately they chose to ignore the helicopters and continued to support the BOGs access agreement. The significance of this episode is to show that DFID Nepal had been pursuing a course approaching neutrality but this was not the formal UK position and had not been communicated, it seems, to the MoD. It was fortunate that the results were not more serious.

In the course of the war, DFID managers in Nepal had substantially rethought their relations with the Maoists but the US Ambassador, unable to travel safely out of Kathmandu, remained fixed in the view that the Maoists were 'terrorists' and this made it difficult for Western allies to take a different view. The label 'Maoist' meant that Western capitals could not envisage any kind of dialogue. The fact that this was a rebellion of and for poor people never became established and so what DFID did in Nepal can be regarded as an outlier, a sign of disinterest from the centre rather than interest. The helicopter incident seems to be evidence of this. The UK and US focus was on Afghanistan and Iraq; Nepal had no significance. Aid managers on the ground were able to improve the effectiveness of aid only because they were left alone. The trend since then has been to reinforce the importance of geo-strategic interests. In my later work for DFID around 2008, I was repeatedly asked to focus on the tiny Muslim communities on the Indian border to see if they might be at risk of 'radicalisation'.

In the policy paper 'Preventing Violent Conflict' DFID drew the following conclusions from Nepal- *'DFID's conflict analysis revealed that very little of DFID's development assistance reached the excluded rural poor, and that DFID's approach failed to change the dynamics that generated and sustained the conflict. As a result of the assessment, DFID fundamentally re-orientated its development programme, as well as staffing and management systems, in order to tackle the political, economic and social exclusion underlying Nepal's civil war.'*[112]

In detail-

*'Before the conflict analysis was undertaken in 2002, DFID Nepal along with the majority of other donors, saw conflict as a risk to be avoided rather than as the operating reality. The Nepal Government referred to a 'law and order problem' and actively discouraged donors from using the word 'conflict'. Development assistance consequently tended to avoid areas where there were security risks, and all too often reached only as far as District Headquarters, rather than the people in the more remote conflict-affected areas.'*[113]

One of the most successful measures adopted by DFID was the introduction of 'public audit'. Under this process, all the people affected by a programme are invited at regular intervals to hear a presentation of the facts about the programme including financial details, and then have the opportunity to question the aid workers and managers, as well as anyone else involved in running it such as a local committee. The process has been used and promoted by other organisations but was new to DFID in Nepal. Part of the rationale was that these meetings enabled the Maoists and their representatives to decide for themselves whether to cooperate with the aid programme and they could ask

---

[112]  DFID (2006) p29
[113]  DFID (2006) p29

questions about it. But there was no need for aid agencies to negotiate directly with the Maoists.

I am not sure whether DFID ever considered switching from a project approach to cash-based distributions, which would have gone much further to reflect the Maoists' 'direct delivery' principle and empower the people. Probably the objection would be that the Maoists would take advantage and seize the cash. Against this it could be argued that the Maoists could not afford to offend the people so directly and would fall victim to their own preference for open discussions and public audit. The real problem probably lies in the pre-conceptions of senior managers and politicians in the aid system who basically do not trust poor people.

Another piece of good fortune is that during this period DFID was not under pressure from London to spend more funds. The assumption was that spending would be difficult during the war but DFID budgets increased hugely after the end of the war —when the old distortions of aid programmes resumed and it became difficult to deliver aid to poor people.

Otherwise the main problem that DFID managers in Nepal had to contend with was that most of their programmes were too rigid to adapt to changing circumstances. Typically they were designed to run for five years, had been designed before the changes caused by war and were set in stone in the form of contracts with large commercial companies whose task was simply to implement what had been agreed.

DFID's Rural Access Project (RAP) had been planned in the late 1990s when the war had already begun but it was not taken into account in the planning except as a possible operational hazard. Roads in different parts of Nepal had been identified for upgrade or construction. The planning of the project reflected progressive thinking about road construction derived from a 'green roads' approach already developed by SDC and others in Nepal. Instead of using heavy machinery the roads were to be built using manual labour drawn from local communities. The roads were relatively simple un-tarred structures intended to facilitate trade between villages and towns. It was anticipated that maintenance would be undertaken voluntarily by local people because they would see the benefits of the road. The project sought to strengthen the livelihoods of the road-builders by introducing savings and credit schemes.

When the project started in August 2001 the war was at its height. During the first year progress on some roads was halted by high levels of insecurity and managers began to prioritise peaceful sections of road. Road-building was slower than projected but the main problem was that the sections of road were disjointed. The project worked on stretches of road they could reach and ignored others. The result was a patchwork of short pieces of road with no linkages between towns and villages. People saw no benefit in maintaining the roads and allowed them to deteriorate and Nepal's terrain makes this a very rapid process. Roads were being destroyed as fast as they were being made. By 2005 DFID became aware that the project had gone seriously wrong. I was given the task, with an experienced international engineer, of reviewing the project taking into account the war context.[114] We found that after four years of the five-year project, no road had been completed and most of the work that had been done had been wasted. Local people were alienated and disinterested. The project was due to close the following year with practically nothing achieved but it was extended to continue until February 2007 at a total cost of £32million. At the time of the review, road sections were scattered all over the country, the project was 77% through its timetable and 79% of the budget had been spent.

The contracting company pointed out that they had kept within the terms of the contract and that the failure of the project was because of the war. The reviewers wondered why the company had done so little to alert DFID to the crisis or to suggest ways of working that would minimise the effects of the war. We found that by the time of the review 41% of the funds had been spent on overhead costs. The contractors had done very well and clearly had not regarded it as their task to ensure that the project made sense in the new context. DFID was equally at fault for allowing this to happen.

The review maintained that the problems caused by the war could have been overcome by adjusting the project design. Agreements could have been made to complete high profile sections that would benefit rural communities and create indirect pressure on the Maoists not to disrupt the project. It was possible to negotiate with the Maoists through back-channels, as DFID had done in other cases. Unfortunately these theories could not be tested because the war ended in 2005 and

---

[114]    Vaux, T, J Howe and B Basayat (2005) *Rural Access Programme (RAP) –Fundamental Review*, unpublished paper for DFID

circumstances changed. Overall the expenditure during the war years, around £20million, was almost entirely wasted except for the wages provided to labourers on the pointless exercises in road-building.

The use of large commercial companies, five-year designs, minimal supervision and failure to adapt to a changing situation is typical of aid programmes and the problems have been exacerbated by the relentless pressure to spend more and faster. DFID in Nepal managed to avoid geo-political problems and did well to adapt its largely humanitarian aid in war areas but the system would not allow the renegotiation and reformulation of most of the long-term development programmes. With extreme poverty now concentrating more in fragile states, such as Nepal, where circumstances change fast and instability causes fundamental shifts, this inability to be flexible and responsive practically debars DFID and similar organisations from significant achievement.

Such problems are not confined to periods of outright war. Fragile states shift from war into periods of uneasy peace in which the centrifugal forces that cause war remain dormant. In the case of Nepal problems of inequality and injustice that had underpinned the Maoist rebellion re-emerged as soon as the war ended in 2005. The Maoists decided to re-enter the political arena as a political party. Despite disgruntlement among hard-line cadres, who believed nothing had been achieved by the war, the Maoist leadership stood for election and became the largest political party. Although they initially achieved some minor successes on behalf of poor people, the Maoists were drawn into the same patronage problems that had beset previous governments. In order to secure popular support they built up patronage networks, using their position in government. They paid off their supporters and focused on keeping power. Corruption and nepotism were unavoidable.

The war had given very poor people a glimpse of a different sort of future and the aid agencies had, for a short while, given serious attention to their problems. But at the end of the war this momentum was quickly lost. Power and wealth returned to Kathmandu and the interests of poor people were undermined by patronage networks that favoured wealthier classes. The education sector, which I had the opportunity to review in 2008 and again in 2010, provides a good example. During the war, the Maoists had made teachers in rural areas work hard because they were held accountable to the people. A teacher who did not work or who discriminated against poorer children or dalits (outcastes) would be made to face a people's court or simply punished by Maoist cadres. But the resumption of normality removed this pressure and teachers reverted to former practices of absenteeism. Many of them delegated their work to unqualified substitutes. They enjoyed impunity because they were protected by powerful unions linked to even more powerful political parties.

The education sector was heavily funded by donors and during the war they had insisted that the government should allow independent monitoring. This process revealed that class sizes had become extremely unequal because teachers who could escape from Maoist areas had taken refuge in district towns and in Kathmandu. Many were reluctant to return to the rural areas and this resulted in a huge imbalance in the distribution of teachers. A break in the recruitment of teachers during the war years then led to a dearth of teachers especially in the highly-populated plains areas where classes of over 150 children were now reported. Attempts to rationalise the spread of teachers was opposed by the teacher unions which simply blocked any transfers. They calculated that they would attract teachers from other unions if they resisted postings and, if challenged, they mobilised support from Kathmandu politicians. The political parties competed to secure teachers as members by granting greater and greater license for misbehaviour. The situation degenerated to the point that teachers were invulnerable to direction from the Ministry of Education.

The quality of education for poorer people declined drastically. It was impossible to mobilise political pressure, partly because of the politicised unions but also because the country's wealthy elite had no use for state schools. During the war years they had developed the habit of sending their children to private schools, in district towns and Kathmandu, where they would learn English. This would qualify them for high-paid jobs or at the very least enable them to seek work abroad, notably in the Gulf states. Even teachers in the state system commonly sent their children to private schools.

Instead of challenging this system, the Maoists joined in, creating their own teacher union and competing with the other parties. Head teachers and School Management Committees (SMCs) could not impose discipline. The 2006 monitoring report noted a high dropout rate especially among children in over-sized classes. Nearly half of children who enrolled in Grade 1 either dropped out or had to repeat the class because they failed the end-of-year examination. Only 16% of children completed primary education and only 5% achieved the basic School Leaving Certificate (SLC) at the end of secondary school. Only 20% of children from state schools obtained the SLC compared with 80% from private schools.

Donors expressed concern about these findings but realised that the Ministry lacked the power or motive to tackle the politicised unions. Subsidies from donors continued but the quality of education declined still more. By 2010 the problems had been further institutionalised-[115] *'Teachers who are centrally employed enjoy security of employment and pension rights that create a sense of impunity for their actions in terms of accountability to local populations. This is reflected in high levels of teacher absenteeism, poor timekeeping and the common practice of teachers having second jobs.'*

In 2008 the main concern had been the rate of failure in the final examination that might open the way to further education or employment. But in 2010 the reviewers found that the examination pass rates had suddenly improved. Perhaps the quality of education had improved dramatically? But the explanation was that, faced with the displeasure of donors, the education system had facilitated cheating as a way to improve the results. With or without a bribe, teachers ensured that children passed their examinations. No other significant changes had taken place.

In an education system that was becoming increasingly demoralised, teachers now extended their opportunities for making money by charging students for advance copies of model answers to exam questions or for exam passes outright. This further increased inequalities because only those children with money could afford to pass exams –precisely the opposite of what the donors intended.

While the state education system suffered from these problems, private education flourished. Owners of private schools prevented the involvement of teacher unions. Although teachers in private schools were less well paid they had to work much harder –otherwise they could be sacked. The private system delivered much better results

---

[115]  Pherali, T, A Smith and T Vaux (2011) *A Political Economy Analysis of the Education Sector in Nepal,* paper for the EU http://uir.ulster.ac.uk/30667/1/ Pherali_Smith_Vaux_%282011%29AugFull FINAL-FINAL.pdf

even without the need for cheating and so employers came to prefer pupils from the private sector. Above all, private education was valued because it was almost always in English medium compared with state education which was almost always in Nepali. Language increased the sharp divide between the poor and the rich and became an insurmountable obstacle for poor people, however clever.

Donors began to wonder whether they should be supporting Nepal's education system at all. The problems seemed to be deeply political and intractable. Nepal was beginning to flex its muscles following the Paris Declaration of 2005, which committed donors to Alignment with the wishes of the host government. But the biggest factor was that donors were under increasing pressure from their head offices to deliver on the Millennium Development Goals (MDGs). The enrolment of girls into schools was a top priority. Thanks to a programme run by UNICEF, offering incentives to girls enrolling for school, the enrolment figures for Nepal were still impressive and so managers in Nepal could justify further expenditure on the basis of demonstrable progress towards the MDG. The fact that girls dropped out after enrolling and failed to complete their education was not covered by the MDG and could be ignored – and it was.

This case study shows the importance of aid managers living in a country for long enough to see beyond the appearances presented by those with vested interests in aid. It shows that they can respond imaginatively to war and find ways to deliver aid to poor people if left free from pressures such as those arising from the Global War on Terror. Nevertheless they remain constrained by institutional realities notably the fixed contracts with companies which have come to be the dominant form of aid delivery. All these problems are exacerbated because the aid programme is mainly shaped by the pressure to spend funds. These factors together indicate that the current aid system is not a good way of helping poor people and might be replaced by something better.

# CHAPTER SEVEN

# HUMANITY AT WAR – CASE STUDIES FROM SOMALIA AND SOUTH SUDAN

In March 2017 the UN described the situation as in Somalia, South Sudan, Yemen and Northern Somalia as the greatest humanitarian crisis since 1945 and said that over twenty million people were at risk of starvation and that over $4.4billion was needed.[116] Although aid agencies generally like to avoid identifying war as the cause of the disaster and instead present it as crop failure or simply 'starvation' there was no getting away from the fact that the principal reason for the humanitarian crisis in each of the four countries was war and it was the failure of global security arrangements that had brought about the crisis.

Nevertheless the focus of the UN was on raising funds for humanitarian aid rather than focusing on the possibilities for preventing or limiting the violence. This comes about essentially because the UN consists of a cluster of aid agencies that have evolved, as described in Chapter One, to handle aid rather than tackle root causes. Instead of applying pressure around the UN Security Council, they give the impression that the crisis can be satisfactorily addressed if enough funds

---

[116]  *The third horseman returns,* The Economist April 1st 2017

are provided. The pressure to tackle the roots of the problem eases off and people in Western countries take some satisfaction that they have, at least, sent some money directly to an aid agency or indirectly through their government. International charities become enthusiastic followers and raise very large amounts of money.

In this Chapter, I examine two of these cases, showing two sides to the problem. In Somalia, an obsessive US focus on the Global War on Terror was the main cause of suffering while in South Sudan the 'international community' was too disinterested to intervene to stop a pointless war. The underlying problem issue is the decline in global security from the high and objective standards set in the UN Charter and the selective and self-interested security agenda that we see today, especially since the launch of the Global war on Terror.

Somalia has been a victim of the Western security agenda for a very long time. During the Cold War its opportunistic leader President Mohammed Siyad Barre changed from a pro- USSR to a pro-USA position, leading to civil war in Somalia, the division of the country and persistent military interference from Ethiopia. Consensus among the Somali clans broke down and the northern part of the country, formerly British Somaliland, broke away after a bitter and destructive war. In the rest of Somalia, rebellion against Siyad Barre eventually ousted him but while departing from the country he ravaged the riverine areas, seized all the food and caused a terrible famine in 1990-1991. This was one of very few occasions when I have actually seen adults die in front of me.[117]

Such was the horror of te images coming from Somalia that US President Bush ordered a humanitarian intervention which, as described in Chapter One, degenerated into the fiasco of a Hollywood film, the alienation of Somalis and subsequent aversion of the USA to intervene for humanitarian reasons anywhere else.

Somalia's history of war throws into doubt the theory that conflicts in Africa are largely driven by contests over resources or by ancient hatreds between tribes. Somalis follow a single religion and belong to a single ethnic group with a common heritage of pastoralism (with some exceptions to be described later). Somalia has no significant natural resources except cattle and cattle-raiding has never taken place on a huge scale as it has in Sudan. The Somali clans have generally managed to

---

[117] Vaux (2001) See Chapter Six

moderate competition for grazing lands effectively whereas disputes can more easily split along tribal lines in South Sudan. The main explanation for Somalia's instability lies in international and regional interference. This raises questions whether Western aid is an appropriate response.

Although Somalis form a single major ethnic group they are divided into clans and these sub- divisions have been exploited by political leaders who, when faced with difficulties, call on support from regional neighbours and manipulate international intervention for their own purposes. Ethiopia, Kenya, Uganda and the USA have been particularly intrusive. Traditional cross-border grazing by pastoralists provides an easy excuse for neighbours, especially Ethiopia, to launch military action into Somalia and interfere in its politics. Historically pastoralists were able to ignore the colonial 'lines on the map' and move across the region as if there were no borders. They could take their animals where there was fodder and water. But political and military entanglements in the post-colonial period have strengthened the borders, limited the movement of pastoralists and caused a poverty crisis. Ethiopia, in particular, has been concerned about political movements based in the arid region known as the Ogaden. Kenya has been concerned about 'shiftas' —gangs that attack trade routes and engage in looting, venturing far into the north of Kenya.

Very little food-grain is produced in Somalia and pastoralists rely on selling animals and buying food-grain from others both within and outside Somalia. This has encouraged the development of an extensive and effective commercial sector, which now also handles substantial flows of money from Somalis who have migrated or fled abroad. With its long coastline and fishing industry, Somalia has been a source of seamen many of whom have settled abroad. There is a sizeable Somali community that has lived for many years in the UK.

One of the only areas where food is produced is along the Juba and Shebelle rivers but Somalis prefer not to engage in agriculture and this work is dominated by Bantu tribes. They are particularly vulnerable because they are not part of the Somali clan system that dominates national politics.

The US intervention was officially justified purely on the basis of humanitarian needs but there has been much suspicion, especially among Somalis, about the real motivation and considerable speculation that it was more to do with re-asserting American control, attacking Islam and exploiting oil resources that had recently been discovered in the Ogaden region. Whatever the truth about that (the oil never materialized in significant amounts) the result of the intervention was a disaster in itself. The American invasion force became embroiled in conflict with Somali clans and the conflict began to take on the appearance of an American attack on Islam. This strengthened Islamists in Somalia, previously a tiny minority without much influence, and led to the formation of an Islamist movement, Al Shabaab which, after the 9/11 event, made links with Al Qaeda and other extremists.[118] Their credibility as a Somali protection force was strengthened when the US encouraged incursions by the regional neighbours. With US backing, the African Union deployed a military force consisting mainly of Ethiopian, Kenyan and Ugandan troops but this simply added to Somali suspicions and resistance. The Islamists continued to gain support and eventually established a government in Somalia.

The overwhelming priority of the USA then became the defeat and destruction of the Al Shabaab 'terrorists'.[119] In effect, starvation became a tool in the Global War on Terror. The US set up a puppet government in opposition to Al Shabaab. From 2006 onwards power was contested between this Western-backed Transitional Federal Government (TFG) and the Islamists. Humanitarian aid continued but the situation became very dangerous for aid workers because Somalis made no distinction between the military, political and humanitarian interventions that, as they well knew, were being orchestrated by the USA. Aid workers retreated first to armed compounds in Mogadiscio and then to Nairobi in Kenya. This undermined the remaining credibility of aid operations- *'the fundraising, the decision- making and most of the program design was conducted hundreds of miles away from the location of the crisis —and in many cases by individuals who had never been to the scene of the crisis, or at least not for some time.'[120]* Aid managers were not directly present to negotiate and explain. They could not even assess the problems and needs. The risks and difficulties were passed on to local NGOs and Somali companies.

---

[118]  Al Shabaab was preceded by the Islamic Union of Courts but for the sake of simplicity, the term Al Shabaab is used throughout this Chapter.

[119]  Al Shabaab had been added to a list of terrorist organisations by the Office of Foreign Asset Control in 2008. See Maxwell and Fitzpatrick (2012) p9

[120]  Maxwell et al (2012) p2

Western aid, along with Western military and diplomatic efforts, was focused on dislodging the Islamists. There was no effort to engage in dialogue. With exclusive access to Western support, including humanitarian aid, President Sharif of the TFG, waged war and dispensed patronage to his close associates, exacerbating tensions among the clans. The President made little effort to spread out the resources that he received from outside. As a Saferworld report describes, 'the elders say the President's sub-clan dominates senior level government posts which were supposed to be apportioned based on the clan rule in which all government posts are divided between the four major clans and a group of smaller clans.'[121] Conflict between the clans, also involving Al-Shabaab, created widespread insecurity. Pastoralists were unable to move freely, rains failed and famine conditions began to develop in 2010.

Although conditions were serious across the whole of Somalia the most serious effects (as had been the case in 1990-1) were felt by the Bantu minorities who depended on agriculture. The drought affected the whole region including large areas of Ethiopia and Kenya but by far the worst rain failure was in Somalia and the famine, when it was eventually declared by the UN, was concentrated in a very limited area of Somalia.

International charities, notably Save the Children and Oxfam, called attention to the drought and warned of famine but (following the general custom of attributing disasters to 'Acts of God' in order to maximize the public response) downplayed the significance of the war.[122] Even so, lack of sympathetic press coverage (the situation was too dangerous for most reporters and most of the news was focused on the war against Al Shabaab) led to only a limited public response.

Nevertheless the humanitarian response would have been much larger if the USA, as might be expected, poured funds into Somalia as a way of gaining support. But instead the USA adopted a deliberate policy of starvation. American food aid was withdrawn in 2009, just as the famine was beginning to develop. The reason given was the risk that it would directly or indirectly benefit Al-Shabaab. The USA also imposed a restriction on other forms of aid, requiring agencies

---

[121] Saferworld (2012) *Mogadiscio rising? Conflict and governance dynamics in the Somali capital,* Saferworld London
[122] Save the Children and Oxfam (2012)

to prove that nothing received from the USA could possibly reach Al Shabaab. Agencies were threatened with a complete ban from receiving US government aid anywhere in the world. This was an impossible condition and severely curtailed aid efforts at the most crucial time.

The Bantu peoples in the areas suffering extremes of famine had come under the control of Al Shabaab. They may not have had much choice about this (they were animists rather than Muslims) but it is possible that they saw Al Shabaab as a source of protection. One study of the famine found that Al Shabaab- *'represents to some extent a political voice of the minority populations (the Reewin clan and Bantu tribes) and draws its rank and file from those peoples.'*[123]

The US embargo not only deterred agencies from providing aid but also led them to reduce their estimates of need to what they thought could be delivered, rather than what was really needed.[124] This undermined international calls for emergency action. Nevertheless, many Somalis, especially those with money or with relatives abroad, could still arrange imports through traders. The Somali commercial sector was extraordinarily robust and could deliver food almost anywhere even at the height of the war and famine.

As in 1990, it was the Bantu minority that suffered most. They lacked the money and relatives abroad to help them. A global spike in food prices in 2011 made the situation suddenly much worse. The price of food rose to the point that poor people all over the country were unable to buy it. The famine spread far beyond the Bantu peoples in the riverine areas and although traders could still bring in food, people were unable to pay for it.

With few direct reports from aid workers and unable to visit Somalia themselves, journalists relied on interviews with people fleeing out of Somalia especially those who went to the huge relief camp at Dadaab in Kenya, which became the biggest in the world. But the reports of deaths were still second-hand and failed to elicit an overwhelming global demand for action. The fact that the famine had been caused by the USA made aid agencies and other Western governments cagey about their descriptions of the problem and this perhaps weakened their arguments.

---

[123] Majid and McDowell (2012)
[124] Save the Children and Oxfam (2012)

In these circumstances the decision of the UN to declare a 'famine' (in the UN's technical definition of the most extreme form of starvation) was a bold move. The USA was still using famine to undermine Al Shabaab and this was an act of defiance even though the USA was not explicitly blamed for the situation.

Western donors could now respond without having to go against the US position —they could simply refer to the fact of a famine as declared by the UN. In 2012- *'funding from donors nearly doubled overnight and a major humanitarian effort quickly ramped up. But for many affected groups —already displaced, malnourished, and tragically in many cases already suffering high levels of human mortality- the response was too late.'* [125] Even so, when the UN called for aid to be delivered on an emergency basis, it was criticised in the USA, notably in the New York Times, for 'politicising' the famine.

The next problem was how to deliver aid quickly. New supplies of food aid from the USA would take months to arrive and aid agencies doubted whether large volumes could be handled without interference not only from Al-Shabaab but from government (TFG) supporters. The answer was to use 'the Somali method'. Somalis living abroad had developed ways to send money to their relatives through Somali companies and traders. Mobile phone companies had found ways to transfer cash from abroad by phone and even the warring clans respected the importance of signal relay stations. Finally freed from fear of repercussions from the USA if they could not trace every single donation to its final user, the aid agencies moved into action and did what they should have been doing much earlier.

In a review of Oxfam's operations conducted in 2010[126] I found that- *'Oxfam has used remittance companies not only to transfer funds but also to deliver or oversee programmes through local organisations in insecure areas. This has enabled Oxfam not only to provide humanitarian support but also to attempt development work to provide a measure of local stability. Although Oxfam is not the only agency to do this it appears to have taken the lead.'*[127]

---

[125]  Maxwell et al (2012) p1
[126]  Vaux (2010) This was part of a wider evaluation of Oxfam's work for DFID. The report was not published.
[127]  Vaux (2010) Notes on Somalia and Somaliland

The difficulties of these cash distributions have been critically examined in academic studies and the general conclusion is that they were very successful.[128] Staff in some agencies feared that the widespread use of commercial companies might undermine respect for humanitarianism but in reality the companies were much more respected than the agencies. Others feared that money would be useless if there was no food available but as Amartya Sen had shown as far back as 1981, famines are not caused by lack of food availability but by lack of entitlement to food.[129] Money creates an entitlement —or in other words, Somali merchants could be relied upon to bring in food from across the region if the price was right.

An interesting aspect of the Somalia crisis was that, other than the Somali companies, Turkey emerged as the most effective aid actor. Its Islamic background and abstention from a direct role in the Global War on Terror made it widely acceptable in Somalia. People were willing to believe that Turkish aid was based on Islamic solidarity and there was no need for other explanations. Turkish aid workers, many of them volunteers, were able to travel much more freely and widely than other nationalities- '*Somali people welcomed the Turkish preference for direct contact with local people and the prominent involvement of its private sector. Up to 500 Turkish aid workers, teachers and engineers are currently in Mogadiscio.*'[130]

By contrast the established Western aid system had done badly. Aid workers had retreated into their compounds and to distant cities where they lived in luxury and drew handsome allowances for the 'hardship' they suffered. The American focus on terrorism had seriously distorted the humanitarian response while international charities had been held back by fear of punishment by the USA and lack of public interest. The UN's decision to shame the international community and the use of cash distributions finally brought the situation under control but only after thousands of people had died in the famine.

---

128  Bradbury, M (2010) *State-building, counter-terrorism and licensing humanitarianism in Somalia,* Tufts University. See Chapter Eleven of the present book for further evidence and wider consideration of this issue.

129  Sen (1981)

130  Bradbury (2010) p20

Somalia was a victim of US interests, and specifically the Global War on Terror. The case also demonstrates how tightly unified the aid system has become. The USA was able to browbeat practically all the agencies into following its punitive approach and using starvation as a political tool. With the possible exceptions of the ICRC and MSF France, aid agencies were too dependent on US funding and US influence on its allies, to pursue an independent course.

The issue of independence is now critical for aid agencies because the funding they receive from government donors has become so distorted by political objectives. The aid system as a whole has become more dependent on donors and, as the system expands, it has developed its own rigidities arising from competition among agencies and an increasing tendency to generate policies and priorities from central concerns rather than respond to situations on the ground. Donors have come under increasing pressure from sceptical parliamentarians to justify what they are doing and this has tended to harden policies and priorities. Donors have to show that their aid is coherently planned and directed. International charities and others then compete for the funding that arises from this planning. They respond to what is on offer and they are more likely to win the contract if they comply closely with the donor's preconceptions rather than put forward arguments for a different approach.

This can be illustrated from another part of my mission to Somalia in 2010 focused on Oxfam's work with pastoralists in the northern unrecognised state of Somaliland, adjacent to Ethiopia. The last time I had been in this area was in 2000 when I conducted a study for Oxfam comparing food aid and cash aid as a response to recurrent periods of starvation and suffering.[131] Rainfall in the Ogaden semi-desert extending across the boundaries of Ethiopia, Somalia and Kenya had always been patchy and sporadic. Pastoralists move their herds to whatever areas had received rain and where grass can be found. Conflict between the states of the Horn of Africa had led to strict controls on their movements. Some pastoralists have responded by travelling to distant areas in order to get sway away from the military forces harassing them. This caused them to stay away from their home areas for very long periods and some had practically abandoned their wives and children

---

[131]  Vaux (2000) unpublished

in relief camps. Others were facing up to the possibility of ending the pastoralist way of life by raising cattle in one place, bringing fodder to cattle rather than taking cattle to grass.The European Commission Humanitarian Office (ECHO) had spent huge sums on these relief camps and decided in 2010 to launch a regional programme to try to limit the effects of drought by supporting pastoralists to work with governments to secure free migration across the region. ECHO designed a programme to be focused on Somaliland and Ethiopia, avoiding the difficulties of work in Somalia. ECHO laid down clear guidelines as to what was required and called for agencies to put forward bids to undertake the work. Oxfam had undertaken a quick Participatory Capacity and Vulnerability Analysis (PCVA) in Somaliland but in order to persuade ECHO that it was expert on issues of pastoralism in the Horn of Africa decided to follow a model already developed, and apparently successful, in northern Kenya. Oxfam won the contract but the plan reflected a combination of ECHO requirements and Oxfam's regional model rather than the local assessment.

Unfortunately the circumstances in Somaliland proved to be completely different from those in Kenya. In Kenya, Oxfam's aim had been to change the policies of a government that was powerful and well-resourced but showed little concern for pastoralists. Therefore Oxfam had created new organisations representing pastoralists to challenge and influence the government. It was the kind of 'from poverty to power' approach that Oxfam was promoting globally at that time.[132] By contrast, the government of Somaliland was highly focused on pastoralism and sympathetic to it. Ministers kept animals either directly or through family connections. There was no need to campaign for changes in policy. Government-backed pastoralist associations already existed and were doing a good job representing pastoralist interests when needed. The problem in Somaliland was that some forms of migration had become impossible and pastoralists were having to adapt their way of life.

The creation of new pastoralist associations by Oxfam caused confusion and a degree of resentment from the authorities. The programme was set on a regional basis and did well in Ethiopia where new pastoralist associations were useful in pressurizing a government

---

[132] Represented by the Oxfam publication Green (2008)

that, as in Kenya, was sceptical or even hostile towards pastoralists. The problem faced by pastoralists in Somaliland was not government recognition but the increasing practice of keeping animals in one place rather than moving across the grasslands. Pastoralists knew that keeping animals in one place put great pressure on water sources and created veterinary risks but they were finding that rains were less reliable and the obstacles to migration had become overwhelming, especially in the form of insecurity across the region following continuous war. Farmers had begun to enclose land with thorn hedges and there were disputes over land ownership and access. Some of the enclosed areas were sited across routes normally used for animal movements. There were increasing numbers of clashes between herders.

These problems were discussed with me openly by Oxfam's highly motivated local staff and by government officials. They pointed out that ECHO's desire for a regional programme together with Oxfam's learning from Kenya had created a 'one-size-fits-all' solution that was irrelevant and possibly harmful in Somaliland. It divided pastoralists from each other and divided pastoralists from the government. Government officials and local staff lamented that Oxfam had not followed the findings of its initial assessment and built on institutions that were already there, helping them to adapt to new situations. Needless to say the programme had little useful effect in Somaliland and the trend towards keeping animals in the same location rather than migrating has become more serious.[133]

The Somalia case study has shown the damage that can be caused by the 'securitization' of aid and the dependence of the aid system on Western donors especially the USA. The Somaliland case shows how this dependence extends to a more bureaucratic level because aid planning flows top down and commercial rivalry between aid agencies leads to further distortion. A third major failing of the aid system is its tendency to apply humanitarian solutions when security solutions would be better. This also is a reflection of its dependence on donors. Whatever approach donors take to a political problem, the aid system follows. Questioning and campaigning is muted because the aid system's default position is to run humanitarian relief programmes. This is their lifeblood and so they do not stand out against it even if it is the wrong path to take.

---

[133]  Shepherds Staying Put, The Economist June 10th 2017 p50

This has been the case in South Sudan where the aid system has been drawn into hugely expensive and ineffective relief operations when a political or security solution is needed. Instead of stopping to consider the wider question whether humanitarian relief is the right tool, aid agencies get drawn into a maelstrom of competition with each other both in relation to funds and public profile. Once drawn into the system they cannot step back and argue that humanitarian aid is not the answer. They praise donors for their generosity and fail to hold them to account for doing so little about the causes of the problem.

The peace agreement that separated South Sudan from the north in 2006 and later led to full independence as a new country, followed decades of warfare with the Sudan government. During the war the USA had consistently supported the South (nominally Christian but largely animist) against the Islamic north. The fact that Osama Bin Laden had lived in Sudan gave added impetus to American support for the South especially when the pro-American John Garang was leader of the Sudan People's Liberation Army (SPLA). But when Garang was killed in a helicopter crash, support for the new leader, Salva Kiir, wavered and opened the way for the Nuer leader, Riek Machar to challenge for the leadership. The situation was contained but not resolved in a deal by which Machar became Vice President while Kiir held much greater powers as President in the new government.

Machar was never satisfied with these arrangements and refused to disarm his tribal militias. Other tribal groups were also dissatisfied and took advantage of an inexperienced and weak administration. Cattle raiding took place with impunity but it was the discovery of extensive oil resources in the regions along the northern borders with Sudan that raised the stakes and converted local fighting into civil war. The government began to receive substantial advances for the expected production and arguments arose over the division of spoils. Both Kiir and Machar anticipated the possibility of war and used their share of the oil revenues to secure support and buy weapons. Corruption spread through the Ministries in Juba. As a result the process of state-building got nowhere. Services were left to aid agencies. The lack of roads and other infrastructure, inherited from decades of Sudanese discrimination against the south, was not addressed. The people remained extremely poor despite the rapture of independence, formalised by a referendum in 2011.

Neighbouring countries lined up in support of one or other of the rival leaders. Sudan supported Machar and Uganda supported President Kiir. Kenya was less committed, perhaps hoping that whatever the result they would be able to benefit from a new pipeline taking oil southwards instead of the long and problematic route northwards through Sudan. This led Sudan to manipulate the situation to prevent any such bypass of its territory. Sudan appears to have adopted a policy of destabilising the South so that it could exert control over the oil wells lying along the borders.

These events coincided with the Western focus was on the Global War on Terror and the new problems emerging in the Middle East, especially Libya and Syria. South Sudan had little political significance in the West because it posed no threat of Islamic extremism. The peace process was left to the regional powers in the Horn of Africa under the aegis of the African Union but because each of the regional powers had their own interests it made no progress. Only strong pressure from superpowers could have overcome or focused the interplay of regional interests. In Somalia the USA had demonstrated how it could take control in the case of an Islamist insurrection but South Sudan was 'off the radar'.

Direct fighting between forces loyal to the President and Vice-President erupted at the end of 2013 with a sudden attack by Dinka soldiers on unarmed Nuer in Juba. News quickly spread to Bentiu in the northern oil-producing areas and fighting broke out between fully-armed militias organised on tribal lines. Vice President Machar was well prepared for this and counter-attacked quickly. He almost overthrew the President in a rapid military operation but Uganda intervened on the side of the President. Its army drove Machar away from the capital. The war settled into a series of inconclusive battles in different parts of the country and then into general violence that completely disrupted economic activity and services. The war shifted from military encounters to looting of civilians.

After the Comprehensive Peace Agreement in 2005, the UN had established a peace-keeping mission (UN Mission in South Sudan – UNMISS) tasked with monitoring violations of the agreement and protecting the aid system. UNMISS had established military camps in different parts of the country and these now became the refuge for thousands of people fleeing from the fighting and violence. Others fled to less volatile areas and took refuge, if they could, with relatives or in houses where they could pay for their accommodation.

Oil revenues, almost the only source of government finance, were drastically reduced by the war and officials were left unpaid. Many staff in government services continued to work but they received no support or payment from the central government in Juba which had practically collapsed.

With hundreds of thousands of people displaced and in desperate need, a massive humanitarian operation was launched. The situation in South Sudan never captured the headlines but Western countries provided $1 billion per year for aid operations. Agencies were unable to raise much money in direct appeals to the public because attention was focused elsewhere and this was clearly a war. It could not be presented, as agencies always preferred, as an 'Act of God'. In fact this war was particularly difficult to explain in terms that might elicit public sympathy. It was being waged between two egoistical leaders and fought along tribal lines.[134] Without strong public support aid agencies were heavily dependent on funding from Western states. This may explain their unwillingness to apply pressure for a political or military solution. Instead they maintained the fiction of a humanitarian solution.

The global security system had disengaged from South Sudan from the time of the peace agreement in 2006. But aid had poured into the country in significant amounts. The theory was that aid would act as a 'peace dividend' –people would see that peacefulness was rewarded with aid. The problem was that this had little to do with the actual causes of conflict which were, at the high level, the rivalry between Kiir and Machar, and at other levels rivalries between tribes and cattle-herders. The provision of services may have impressed women and children but the reality was that they had no influence over decisions relating to politics and war.

The USA had encouraged the division of Sudan because the South was seen as a Christian bastion against the Islamic north but the power struggle that emerged after the peace agreement had no significant Islamic dimension to it. the international community continued to finance a peace-keeping operation (to the tune of more than $1billion annually) but its mandate allowed for little more than monitoring.

---

[134] For a much more detailed analysis see De Waal (2015a)

When large-scale violence erupted in 2013, UNMISS provided a refuge for people fleeing from violence but did no more. But the deployment of UNMISS and the humanitarian relief operations could be used to support an argument that 'something was being done'.

The situation was very similar to what had happened in Bosnia in the 1990s (see Chapter One) when a pointless and destructive war continued for three years because international geopolitics would not support a military intervention. The same 'solution' of blue helmets and humanitarian aid was applied. Finally the war was ended in a few days by the threat of US air attacks.

In South Sudan, as in Bosnia, aid was ineffective because of the war situation. It was practically impossible to reach the people most in need because they had fled into inaccessible areas. As the war progressed road travel became more dangerous and militias began to 'tax' aid convoys. On the road north from Juba to Bentiu there are now dozens of militia checkpoints taking bribes and payments to allow the goods to proceed further. Humanitarian aid has become a major source of resources for the combatants and the case can be made that it has a serious effect in fuelling the war.

Aid operation agencies have had to rely heavily on airdrops. These are not only ruinously expensive but ineffective and likely to allow 'leakage' of aid materials into the hands of the militias. Short visits by aid staff while the aircraft waits are insufficient to ensure that relief goods reach the right people and nothing can stop militias descending on the people to despoil them of their goods after the aid workers have left. In practice it was impossible to prevent large-scale looting.

Such an aid operation could only have very limited effects but aid agencies continued to put out impressive figures and glossy reports. Closer scrutiny shows that these focus on numbers of people in need and amounts of money spent rather than numbers of people being saved from hunger and distress. In reality, if people survived it was mainly through their own efforts. Over decades of war people had learnt 'survival strategies', such as long and dangerous migrations, but they could not apply these strategies if the level of disruption by war became too great.

While conducting an evaluation of the humanitarian response for the UN in 2015 I was driven to the conclusion that humanitarian aid alone could not be considered an adequate response to the situation. The problem was that an appearance of a humanitarian response, when in fact it could not succeed, was worse than no response at all because it removed the incentive for the global security system to take the situation seriously and intervene.

The war was not inevitable; it arose simply because the rivals could not work together and regional neighbours had made matters worse. [135] It had become an absurd clash of egoistical rivals that was destroying the country. But in the absence of higher level international engagement, the peace process was being run by regional powers with huge vested interests, and some of them with an interest in destabilising South Sudan. As the independent-minded Ethiopian Ambassador in Juba advised me, the only way forward was for the international community to engage much more deeply in the regional peace process.

People in the aid system acknowledged this but the dynamic of their agencies was to focus on humanitarian relief and hope that someone somewhere was doing something about the war. The possibility of individual agencies standing out to focus on the war issue was reduced because humanitarian aid is now rigidly controlled by the UN's humanitarian agencies (OCHA, WFP, UNICEF etc) and their work, as they see it, is humanitarian relief rather than peacemaking, which falls to other parts of the UN. But even the UN Department for Peacekeeping Operations (DPKO) is more concerned with its pointless monitoring missions such as UNMISS rather than considering the issue of peace-making –i.e. imposing peace. This falls to the Security Council which in this case did not regard the case as a priority.

The means of UN control over humanitarian operations is the Cluster system which was introduced in order to coordinate aid. In theory the national government leads the process and a UN agency takes the 'lead' on each sector of response (food, water etc). But in practice the national government steps back, unable or unwilling to cope with the plethora of competing aid agencies, and the UN takes control. Donors have been so enthusiastic about coordination that most of them insist that any agency receiving their help must take part in the UN coordination arrangements. In some cases funds pass through the UN agencies to others.

---

135   See Crisis Group briefing South Sudan's Risky Political Impasse August 2016-
https://www.crisisgroup.org/africa/horn-africa/south-sudan/south-sudan-risky-politi-
cal-impasse

On top of all this the UN then places a Humanitarian Coordinator (HC) who has considerable power to shape the response. Generally the HC is drawn from the aid system and has a strong focus on humanitarian aid. In order to counter this bias the UN has instituted the notion of an 'Integrated Mission' in which the HC takes the lead in drawing together the military, political and humanitarian aspects of the response. But, at least in South Sudan, the HC was primarily concerned with raising funds for the aid system and simply exchanged information with the military and political components of the UN. In the case of South Sudan, this leadership was based in-country and the UN in New York was not much involved. This may have increased the tendency to focus on humanitarian aid rather than the wider issue of international effort to bring about peace. When I raised these issues with the HC and other UN leaders, suggesting a much stronger focus on efforts to bring about peace, I was told that this was not relevant to the evaluation and references to these issues were deleted from the final report.[136]

South Sudan presents an obvious case for implementation of the Right to Protect (R2P) agreed by the UN General Assembly (see Chapter One). The reluctance to consider heavy political pressure or military intervention seems to arise mainly from the fear that as in Somalia, Iraq and Afghanistan it is easier to intervene than to secure lasting peace and stability. This may be true but there are examples of successful interventions in Bosnia and Sierra Leone. The failure to intervene in Rwanda to stop the genocide is now widely acknowledged. The problem is that intervention is not consistent and some interventions (notably Iraq) have taken place without UN sanction. Even though the Security Council is flawed, it is the only system we have to prevent each country from approaching global security in its own way. In the case of South Sudan the key issue is lack of leadership from the UN, allowing the response to the crisis to be dominated by the aid system.

Each of the four countries (South Sudan, Somalia, Yemen and Northern Nigeria) named in the 2017 UN Appeal presents a unique challenge but the underlying problem is war and perhaps we need to reset the global system to acknowledge that the focus must remain on

---

[136] Following deep disagreements I withdrew from the evaluation and a new report was published some months later without my participation. See IAHE (2015)

stopping war. We must not allow an aid system that has an interest in boasting its successes to diminish the determination to stop war. In most cases humanitarian aid does little to help because war destroys the basis on which humanitarian aid works.

# CHAPTER EIGHT

# 'NATURAL' DISASTERS

This Chapter begins with a statement of the main issues and then presents two extensive case studies.

When all else fails, apologists for the aid system refer to saving lives in times of natural disasters. But the aid system fails even at this apparently simple task. In the case of sudden disasters, lives are saved by neighbours and local organisations long before the aid system arrives. In cases of 'slow-onset' disasters such as droughts, people save themselves through their survival strategies. It is generally only a war that prevents them from doing so (they will have experienced droughts over many years and adapted to them) and in the case of war, as shown in the previous chapter, the aid system tends to divert attention away from the need to stop the war and is ineffective in offering relief because the war disrupts and distorts the way they operate.

There is a huge imbalance in the aid response to different disasters. From the point of view of people in need, it is a lottery. Some attract attention for geo-political reasons, and today it helps to be on the right side in the Global War on Terror. Other disaster responses are driven by the public response in Western countries but this is even more haphazard. Some disasters are more appealing than others. This has little to do with their seriousness or the ability of the aid system to do much to help. Photogenic disasters, or disasters for which there are graphic images, lead to 'successful' public appeals while disasters in obscure places without powerful images do not. In high profile cases, the degree of public response dictates the degree of response by the aid system: the response follows the money.

Donor governments use their aid budgets as they wish for most of the time but if the public suddenly becomes agitated then they respond regardless whether the funds are best addressed to the disaster that catches the public eye. In the absence of any objective means of differentiating responses to disasters, the media hold sway and sometimes celebrities are co- opted to reinforce attention to a particular disaster. In comparison with development, humanitarian aid is just as prone to distortions but they come from the public rather than government policy.

A striking example is the Indian Ocean Tsunami of 2004 which attracted a huge Western response because graphic images of Western people affected by the disaster appeared on TV screens in the immediate aftermath of Christmas —on Boxing Day in fact. Those images bore little relationship to the scale of needs and in particular to the ability of aid agencies to do anything useful. The disaster was a spectacular one but the needs were not very great.

Although nearly three hundred thousand people died, most of them died immediately, before the world even knew about the disaster. There was very little that could be done to help the survivors. The disaster struck a narrow coastal belt over a very wide area and the hinterland was unaffected. People only had to run a few hundred meters from the sea to find safety and services that had not been significantly disrupted. Schools and hospitals in interior areas continued to function. Governments were not incapacitated. As soon as the wave subsided people rushed from safe areas to help those who could be rescued and then they turned to the task of burying or cremating the dead.

The population on the coast had been hugely reduced and so it was not necessary to rebuild what had existed before. Some of the survivors found that they had become rich because they inherited large amounts of property and land. Practically all that was needed was tidying up. But within a few days the UK public appeal by the Disasters Committee (DEC) had raised over £100million and a year later the total was £350million. This was far more than could usefully be spent but, under the rules of the appeal, it could not be used anywhere else or for any other disaster within the area affected by the Tsunami.[137]

---

[137]  Vaux et al (2005)

At the same time the Democratic Republic of Congo (DRC) was ravaged by a particularly destructive war. An invasion by other African states had swept across the country disrupting services and communications. Government was largely destroyed. Armed gangs roamed the country and people were forced to flee into the jungle for safety. Disease and malnutrition were rife and people died in very large numbers. Few aid agencies managed to reach the affected areas and they failed to produce any images or descriptions that caught the public imagination in the West. The fact that a war was involved made it difficult for aid agencies to attract sympathy from the public and because there was no 'terrorism' dimension, Western governments also were uninterested. Instead aid agencies withdrew staff from DRC (and other parts of Africa) and sent them to Indonesia, India and Sri Lanka to respond to the Tsunami.

A few aid agencies tried to call a halt to donations for the Tsunami and some even pointed out that the needs of the DRC were much greater but their arguments carried no weight against the tide of public sympathy. DRC was inaccessible to the media and they also had deployed their resources to cover the Tsunami. Because so few aid workers were left in DRC, reports dwindled further. It is difficult to be sure about the number of lives lost in the DRC but the reputable American aid agency International Rescue Committee (IRC) reported that- *'four studies, conducted between 2000 and 2004, estimated that 3.9 million people had died since 1998, arguably making DR Congo the world's deadliest crisis since World War II. Less than 10 percent of all deaths were due to violence, with most attributed to easily preventable and treatable conditions such as malaria, diarrhoea, pneumonia and malnutrition.'* [138]

Aid money could have made a big difference in DRC. People were dying of very simple preventable causes. Medicines and medical care would have made a big difference and saved hundreds of thousands of lives. A massive international effort could have reduced the disaster to a modest crisis. But this did not happen simply because public interest was focused elsewhere and because the DRC lacked political importance. The aid system was completely embroiled in the task of

---

[138]  IRC: Mortality in the Democratic Republic of Congo –An Ongoing Crisis, May 1 2007 https://www.rescue.org/report/mortality-democratic-republic-congo-ongoing-crisis

spending money in the Tsunami countries and did little or nothing to raise the issue of DRC.

In the distant past aid agencies would have used their own money to address a disaster such as in the DRC and then campaigned to draw attention and government funding towards it but although the international charities are now much bigger, they have become very dependent on public appeals and government funding. This arises from their need to use any 'unrestricted' money gathered from the public without a specific designation, to maintain their infrastructure and activities that cannot be financed by appeals or government grants.

Moreover, competition among the international charities has increased and they are more reluctant to challenge public opinion for fear of losing 'market share'. This leads to a 'winner takes all' basis for response to disasters. The disaster that happens to attract public attention drives all other disasters off the agenda of the aid agencies. From an agency perspective there is no 'credit' for tackling a disaster that the public does not recognise. Instead of basing responses on the ability of the agency to do something useful, they are based on the amount of money to be raised and profile to be achieved. Because the public is likely to be confused by the mention of war, there is not only a preference for 'natural' disasters but also pressure to portray man-made disasters as if they were 'natural'. This perpetuates the underlying problem that the public has had little opportunity to learn about the real problems that aid agencies face in trying to match resources to needs. Agencies constantly gloss over problems and make exaggerated claims of success.

In reality there is no such thing as a 'natural' disaster. Although a hazard such as a Tsunami or earthquake may be natural, the way it causes human suffering depends on the political and social circumstances of the area affected. By and large, the poorest people in the poorest countries suffer much more from disasters that have little impact on rich people and rich countries. This may be an argument for international aid in some cases but it is also an argument that even humanitarian aid must take account of social and political realities. There is a great danger that aid will reinforce inequalities and exaggerate the problems that existed before the disaster. Unfortunately the relentless pressure to spend funds fast and to achieve public profile often lead aid agencies into competitive and ineffective behaviour especially in the case of 'mega-disasters'.

The reputation and future fundraising of international charities depends very heavily on their performance during events which capture media attention. Much of their work is low profile and can be managed in a sensible manner provided that there are no biases built into the resources available (as in the case of government grants). But in the case of mega-disasters caution is thrown to the winds. Chief Executives, many of whom lack expertise in disaster response, take over and direct the response with an eye to the agency's profile and fundraising success.

International charities create special departments to address disasters and these departments develop a different culture from the rest of the organisation, priding themselves on speed and quantity of items delivered rather than on depth of understanding, consultation and analysis. Responsibility for the response passes from those who have regularly worked on or in the country affected to those who simply know how to deliver emergency aid. Because of this structural shift agencies are even less able to take account of underlying problems and long- term results. The humanitarian side tends to downplay political aspects of the disaster in order to get on with work quickly and the development side may eventually take back ongoing programmes that cause political difficulties in the longer-term, typically by bypassing and offending the government and local 'partners'.

Although these issues are recognised by many staff working in the aid system, it has proved difficult to do anything about them because the driver is the profile and success of the entire organisation. The aid system is intensely competitive and competition for funding is particularly acute in times of disaster. Levels of cooperation decline and agencies focus on looking good rather than doing good. Logos and flags are used prominently to attract the media and stake out claims to disaster territory. There is a rush to claim places that are easily accessible to the media rather than those where the needs are greatest. The priority for speed is transmitted to aid workers in the form of constant questions from senior managers desperate to impress the media. Disaster response can make a knowledgeable and cautious aid manager turn to a reckless frenzy of spending.

This process usually leads, despite pledges and commitments to the contrary, to the exclusion of the people and governments affected by a disaster from involvement in aid programmes and, consequently a lack of longer-term positive impact. This Chapter presents two examples of this –the 2004 Indian Ocean Tsunami and the 2010 Earthquake in Haiti.

## The 2004 Indian Ocean Tsunami

At first sight the 2004 Indian Ocean Tsunami presents one of the least political of modern disasters. A massive underwater earthquake sent a shockwave across thousands of miles of the Indian Ocean and, as it approached the shore, this wave reared up into a gigantic wall of water that destroyed everything in its path before petering out a few hundred metres from the shore. But even in the case of the Tsunami there were important political dimensions and lack of political awareness by aid agencies led to unintended and potentially harmful results.[139]

The earthquake occurred in the sea off Aceh, Indonesia, and had two critical characteristics. It affected countries that were popular tourist destinations for Westerners, notably Thailand, Sri Lanka and the Maldives. Secondly it happened on 26th December when Western people were replete with celebration and good cheer. Dramatic images showed tourists running from the wave towards their coastal hotels – some making it to safety and others not. Significant numbers of viewers had visited those places, or knew someone who had. Relatives of those affected could be easily interviewed and their stories resonated strongly with the Western public. The nature of the disaster appeared to place it squarely in the 'Act of God' category, free from the taint of politics and war.

The response in the UK was unprecedented- *'The DEC appeal received over £350 million before closing on 26th February 2005. In addition to this, members of the DEC raised substantial amounts directly and via their international networks. This income far exceeded any previous DEC appeal and in fact exceeded the total raised from all DEC appeals since 1988'*[140]

Over 280,000 people were killed by the Tsunami. Although it affected ten countries, the effects were limited to a very narrow coastal strip, in most cases just a few hundred metres. People had

---

[139]  This section is based mainly on Monitoring and Evaluation reports that I wrote for the DEC –see bibliography

[140]  Vaux et al (2005) p14. The total finally reached £392m according to the DEC website

either been killed by the sudden arrival of the Tsunami, which rose up as it hit the shore, or had fled inland and survived. People were helped by neighbours to escape from fallen trees and buildings but by the time aid agencies appeared, a few days after the event, this work was already done. Aid workers arrived with huge amounts of money and far more was being collected. They saw the devastation but it was not entirely obvious what they should do. Even before they arrived most of the dead bodies had been removed by military forces and local volunteers. Those who survived were generally uninjured because they had managed to run far enough inland to escape the wave or find shelter from its massive effects on the coast.

People wanted to trace their relatives and friends but this was not something that aid agencies were well placed to do. It was best done by local people and organisations. The recovery of infrastructure was a responsibility of government and would take time. The only obvious role was to hand out relief goods. Initially agencies brought them by air from outside and then realised that, in the countries most affected –notably Indonesia, India and Sri Lanka- these materials were available locally just a few hundred metres inland. Assessment teams found little to do but they were told by senior managers that their organisation's reputation depended on being seen to do something. One or two agencies, including Plan International, tried to avoid getting involved on the basis that the disaster had not directly affected areas where they already worked. But they simply could not afford to dissociate themselves from the huge outpouring of sympathy coming from their supporters and had to make a sudden change of course, taking staff from other areas of the world to respond to the Tsunami.

It quickly became apparent that the public response would be far greater than the estimated needs but only a couple of agencies, notably MSF and Concern, said so and tried to close off their appeals and divert finds to other causes. In vain they tried to draw attention to the famine and health crisis in the Democratic Republic of Congo but instead, as noted above, staff were taken away from DRC to work Indonesia, India and Sri Lanka.

I had the opportunity to lead a team of international and local researchers evaluating the response of the thirteen international charities receiving funding through the public appeals of the Disasters Emergency Committee (DEC). One of the main conclusions of the evaluation was that the system of public appeals should be reformed. Although aid agencies might consider various criteria including levels of need when deciding whether to launch an appeal, the process was driven by the emotive response of the public. Agencies had no control over the scale of donations and could not divert them for other uses because of agreements with the broadcasters which hosted the appeal on TV, radio and other media. These agreements also stipulated that funds must be used quickly. The evaluation report argued that- *'The donor public should be better informed about how the system works, or might work, as part of an argument for flexibility in donations and setting aside appeal funds for longer-term work to reduce vulnerability and improve the preparedness of the system as a whole.'*

But as the cases of Plan, MSF and Concern had shown it was very hard for aid agencies to resist the will of the people. The public had decided what to do with their money and expected to be praised for their generosity. Even if a group of agencies tried to put the arrangement on a more rational footing just one of them might refuse to join in and could then sweep the board of public donations by claiming that they were the only one able to do anything effective. Among the DEC members there were always several very large agencies that would always want to 'maximize income' and so the issue of finding a rational approach to disasters has never been resolved.

In response to the Tsunami, agencies faced a crisis because they had far more funds than they could reasonably spend within the one year timescale initially stipulated for the appeal funds. The only option was to extend the time period and agencies were able to put forward a strong case because they would have to rebuild houses and this would take time. The broadcasters reluctantly agreed. They expressed a suspicion that aid agencies simply wanted to hold back funds for long term development and this, in their view, was not what the public expected. Nevertheless the surfeit of funds in the case of the Tsunami was so huge that they had to agree to allow spending up to a maximum of three years. In fact reconstruction took a lot longer but agencies were able to overcome this problem because most of them had also received funds directly from the public that did not need to be considered as part of the DEC appeal. These funds were held back to be used in the fourth and fifth years.

At the time of the main Tsunami response in 2005-7 agencies had not yet become used to the idea of cash distributions. Many still thought that people would misuse the money and that goods would not be available. By purchasing items and having them distributed by their own staff wearing agency logos they could gain much more profile and so a huge process of distributing materials took place, and in the judgment of later evaluations, extended for far too long.

The biggest problems arose over rebuilding houses and the process was extremely slow. It proved particularly difficult in Aceh, where so many people had died, to establish which survivors had rights to which plots of land. Elsewhere, governments and local authorities held up plans for rebuilding because they wanted to move people away from the coast, ostensibly in case of a similar event in the future. But nothing like the Tsunami had ever happened before, at least for hundreds of years, and the issue was more a reflection of commercial pressures by those hoping to gain control of the coastal areas, in some cases in order to build tourist hotels. Developers and speculators began to exert an influence, slowing down and complicating processes of decision-making. The DEC Monitoring Report on the effects of the Tsunami in parts of India found that- *'A principal element in the government's strategy for reducing vulnerability is to move people away from the coast... NGOs suspect that the hotels and houses belonging to richer people will be exempt; in effect poor people will be cleared away from the coastline so that it can be delivered for other purposes.'* [141]

Government authorities were quicker than aid agencies to recognise that rebuilding would take many years. In India and Sri Lanka the governments decided to erect large temporary shelters but the aid agencies refused to improve the conditions in these shelters. The agencies argued that these 'barracks' did not comply with the Sphere Minimum Standards but another reason was that the clock was ticking on DEC funds —they must be spent quickly and the only way was in building houses. If the 'barracks' became too comfortable or even permanent the DEC funds would not be spent for many years to come. Because there had been so many deaths, especially in Aceh, agencies were already competing with each other to find people who needed new houses. In a couple of cases model projects were completed and shown to the media but a review for the DEC a year after the

---

[141]   Vaux, T and M Bhatt (2005) *DEC Asian Tsunami Disaster Monitoring Mission: India,* unpublished report p11

Tsunami, nearly all the displaced people were still living in tents or in the 'barracks' erected by government agencies.

The political situation in Aceh was complicated because oil had been discovered some years earlier and this had led to a dispute about the use of oil revenues. This dispute developed into a movement for the independence of Aceh and a guerrilla war which had reached a stalemate by the time of the Tsunami. The Indonesian military forces were viewed with suspicion by many local people both because of human rights violations during the war and because the military had taken possession of forests in Aceh during the war and used their political power to flout rules about felling. Aid agencies were disturbed to find that the military would be the main source of timber for rebuilding houses. This led at least one agency to try to source materials from Australia, leading to further delays in rebuilding. Others simply ignored the political and ethical dimensions of purchasing timber in Indonesia.

The most serious political problems emerged in Sri Lanka where the war between the government and the LTTE (Tamil Tigers) was at its height.[142] Initially the government was satisfied with the aid response because it concentrated in the Sinhalese southern areas of the President's own constituency around Galle. These areas were most easily accessible to aid agencies and were well known as tourist destinations. They attracted large numbers of individual donors who decided to travel to Sri Lanka and hand out funds and materials themselves in areas they remembered from their holidays. Even the bigger aid agencies initially focused on these areas because of public interest. When they turned their attention to eastern and northern areas of the country, the government became suspicious and claimed that there was a political motive to support the Tamil population and the LTTE. This suspicion was increased when aid agencies, faced with problems of spending their funds, argued that Tsunami funds should be used to help Tamils displaced by the war as well as those affected by the Tsunami. Agencies pointed to the fundamental 'needs come first' principle of the Red Cross Code[143] and argued that they could not deny aid to people displaced by the war, many of whom were living

---

[142] Vaux, T (2006) *Conflict Assessment Report, Sri Lanka*, Humanitarian Initiatives unpublished paper

[143] IFRC (1991 and website)

in far worse conditions than those affected by the Tsunami. In effect the agencies were using the same argument that they had failed to use in relation to the DEC appeal in the UK.

By 2006 the DEC was in crisis because funds were unspent and there was little likelihood of spending them even within the three-year period. The DEC decided to allow funds to be used for any needy person in the areas affected by the Tsunami. Later, this was further relaxed to cover entire districts in which there had been Tsunami damage. But the DEC was unable to follow the Red Cross principle that the funds should really have been used to address needs on a priority basis globally.

Aid programmes became embroiled in political issues especially in Sri Lanka where the government made every effort to deter agencies from working in the Tamil areas. Some agencies were singled out for direct restrictions. Agency staff were denied travel permits. None of them could reach into the areas directly affected by the war. Eventually the government issued a directive to all the aid agencies not to work in the east and north but only in the south. This was not fully implemented but the government's influence brought about an overall imbalance in the disaster response towards Sinhalese areas. It would be possible to argue that the Tsunami disaster weakened the areas of Tamil resistance while putting the government in a good light among its Sinhalese supporters where aid was freely available.

The extraordinarily high level of funding for the Tsunami response should have allowed aid agencies to abide by the highest standards but the opposite seems to be the case. Among the principles of the Red Cross Code considerable weight is given to relations with the affected people —a need to consult, to involve them in decision-making, to build local capacity and to treat people with dignity. But these principles were flouted. The DEC evaluation included public opinion surveys among affected people in India and Indonesia and as well as the DEC evaluation there was also a much bigger evaluation process commissioned by donors and the UN under the name of the Tsunami Evaluation Coalition.[144] This also included extensive interviews with affected people. In addition, public opinion research was undertaken

---

[144]  Tsunami Evaluation Coalition (2007) http://www.alnap.org/resource/5539

by the Fritz Institute in 2005[145] soon after the disaster event. This was practically the first disaster in which public opinion research tools were used extensively. There was considerable agreement between the results of the different surveys. They do not make encouraging reading.

Firstly it was found that the role of the aid system was modest compared with that of local people and institutions. The Tsunami Evaluation Coalition found that- *'The disaster response was mainly conducted by the people themselves. Practically all immediate life-saving actions and initial emergency support in the first few days (and weeks in some cases) was provided by local people, often assisted by the wider national public and institutions, including the national militaries.'*[146] Similarly the Fritz Institute found that only around 10% of people in India and Sri Lanka were aware of any international organisations during the first 48 hours.

Secondly there was too much emphasis on foreigners handing out relief materials rather than efforts to work closely with the survivors. The survey for the DEC Evaluation found that- *'people feel the greatest affront to their dignity in not being able to work. A person in one of the camps asked: "If we are to be fed, why can we not do some work?" and the translator for the survey team summed up by saying: "Eight hours of honest work is most difficult to find in humanitarian interventions."'*[147] Opportunities to employ affected people in the disaster response were often overlooked and the work given to contractors. As one person said- *'We can do more and more. Do give us work. We can enlist others. We can sort out problems. We can call people. We can negotiate and trade.'*[148]

Thirdly there was competition rather than cooperation. For example, people complained about a 'tsunami of assessments' in which one agency after another visited the same place and asked the same questions. The DEC survey found that-*'behaviour was competitive with information deliberately withheld from other actors'*. People interviewed for the evaluation said-*'So many agencies came and promised us so much. There was a tsunami of promises but it had no impact on our life. Thank our*

---

[145] Fritz Institute (2005) *Lessons from the Tsunami, top line findings,* Fritz Institute at http://www.fritzinstitute.org/prgHumanitarianImpact.htm

[146] Telford and Cosgrave (2006) p18

[147] Op cit p50

[148] Ibid p44

luck that we did not believe all those promises for long and started shelter building on our own.'[149]

The survivors felt that they had not been properly involved in decision-making. A farmer in Indonesia said about a meeting with an aid agency- 'We *discuss activities*. We *discuss outputs*. We *discuss issues*. *They decide actions*.' The DEC evaluation concluded that the aid agencies had been particularly weak in relation to the Red Cross principles of 'building the capacity of local organisations' and 'involving beneficiaries in the management of aid programmes'.

The same weaknesses were reflected in all the countries of the Tsunami response, strongly suggesting that they result from systemic factors rather than variants between aid managers and aid agencies. The aid agencies have established clear aspirations in the form of the Red Cross principles but do not follow them, at least in the case of mega-disasters, because commercial pressures predominate. Evidence from other opinion surveys relating to high profile disasters confirms this. For example, in relation to the aid response to the Pakistan Earthquake in 2005, the Fritz Institute found that there was '*minimal consultation with those who were affected..... Most households reported that they had no input in the decision-making processes related to the restoration of livelihoods (98%), shelter (98%), counselling and psycho-social care (98%) and food assistance (97%)'.*[150]

ALNAP's State of the Humanitarian System 2012 Report includes a compilation of surveys following high profile disasters in Haiti, Democratic Republic of Congo, Pakistan and Uganda. Around 70% of people said they had not been consulted before aid was distributed. In answer to the question- 'Did the aid group listen and make changes based on your input?' around 65% of people replied 'no' and only 20% 'yes' with the rest as 'don't know'. Only 30% of people felt that aid groups communicated well with the recipients and local communities about their plans and activities. Similarly only around 40% felt that they were able to 'give an opinion on the program, make complaints or suggest changes.'[151]

---

[149]  Ibid p47

[150]  Press Release October 5 2006, Fritz Institute http://www.fritzinstitute.org/ prsrmPR-PakistanEarthquakeSurvey.htm

[151]  ALNAP (2012) p48

The 2004 Indian Ocean Tsunami response was the last case when the DEC commissioned and published a full evaluation by independent researchers. The member agencies were afraid that the criticisms in the evaluations, although accurate, might be taken up by the media and lead to less public support for appeals. The DEC shifted to a process limited to auditing whether agencies did what they had said they would. This left the task of full evaluation to the agencies themselves to manage in their own way. As described earlier in Chapter Four, this allowed agencies to control the evaluation process and ensure that only positive results were published.

The deeper issue is that the gigantic response to the 2004 Tsunami did not save any significant number of lives. The theory that frenetic activity by foreigners in the wake of a disaster helps the affected people is a false one. There may be cases where it does but it is certainly not true in all cases. The negative effects of an overwhelming need to spend an arbitrarily large sum of money are extensive.

A second underlying problem is that a mass of competing agencies are bound to cause inequalities, tensions and resentments among the affected people. Because the system is fundamentally unaccountable, its effects are haphazard and wasteful. The whole response could have been much better handled by governments. India initially refused to accept aid on the basis that it was unnecessary but later gave way because the aid system needed to spend the money. Some aid workers even tried to impose their own procedures and standards on government officials. An aid worker who lectured an Indian District Collector about Sphere Standards was told to leave the District. India, as well as the other main countries, Indonesia and Sri Lanka all had powerful and effective governments with huge experience of disaster response.

The way to tackle biases such as that of the Sri Lankan government at the time of the war would be to negotiate for a pattern of distribution strictly based on needs and then assist the government to make it happen. Any failures by government could then result in international pressure to make the government take more responsibility for the protection of its own people. If the government absolutely refused to deliver aid in Tamil areas then back channels could be found to deliver aid despite the government as had happened during the wars in Ethiopia in the 1980s.

The tendency to ignore and bypass the national authorities is particularly acute in relation to high profile disasters. In a survey conducted as part of ALNAP's 2012 Review of Humanitarian Action, disaster management authorities in national governments- '*expressed frustration with the international system's lack of deference to national authority. They noted a lack of respect for national capacities, customs and sovereignty and an ongoing 'tendency for agencies to bypass national authorities' and to directly engage at local levels... The relationship between donors, non-government actors and recipient states can often be strained.*' [16] The sheer scale of aid operations after such a high profile disaster was overwhelming. In the report quoted above, ALNAP estimated that there were 274,000 staff engaged globally in disaster relief.

A new principle is needed in international aid –not to undermine the responsibilities and accountability of national governments but instead turn all efforts towards making them meet those responsibilities. The aid system is based on a premise that governments in poor countries are unable to cope with the effects of disasters but this is not true. Instead, governments retreat from disaster response, or preparing for disasters in advance because they expect the international relief system to come and do the work for them. It is absurd to imagine that governments such as those in India, Sri Lanka and Indonesia cannot cope with disasters.

Some national governments are much stronger than others, of course, but when we talk about weak and fragile states we really mean those in which the benefits of statehood are narrowly confined to an elite group. They can be perfectly capable of managing sophisticated patronage systems and substantial commercial enterprises but may not want to concern themselves with disasters if they can avoid it. Yet disasters can be an opportunity to strengthen national capacity, unity and accountability. Passing the problem to the aid system simply exacerbates the problems that existed before.

Best of all would be a situation in which systems of cash distribution such as Universal Basic Income or selective variants, managed by the national government, already provided a minimum income for everyone or at least for poor people. The immediate task in emergencies would be to ensure that this continued and it could be adjusted to suit particular circumstances. There would be no need for a distinction between those disasters that attracted Western interest and those that did not, nor the need for a money-driven response dominated by foreign organisations. Arguably, such an approach could be 'sold' to the

Western public and the means found to encourage support for such programmes around the world on a regular basis in support of national governments.

## The 2010 Haiti Earthquake

Similar tendencies and outcomes can be demonstrated in the aid response following the 2010 Earthquake in Haiti. This disaster also elicited a massive international public response. It was presented as a purely 'natural' disaster and there were graphic images available. Haiti is close to the American mainland and Haitians in the USA and Canada played a particularly active role in drawing the attention of the media and raising funds for the disaster. As in the case of the 2004 Tsunami, there was more money available than could readily be used, bearing in mind the limited experience of agencies working in Haiti, the destruction caused by the earthquake and the weakness of the government. But, as in 2004, there was no mechanism to control the flow of resources or to divert public generosity towards situations where more could be achieved.

The number of people killed by the earthquake is variously estimated at between 160,000 and 230,000. The wide variation in estimates reflects a lack of reliable information characteristic of this weak and fragile state. There was no reliable information about where people lived or how many there were in different locations. Government systems for collecting such data were flawed, reflecting a long history of disengagement from the concerns and welfare of the general population. It would have been difficult for the government to collect such data because very large numbers of people lived on land that they occupied illegally or on the basis of informal agreements. In reality, Haiti was run by shadowy figures within and outside Haiti who overtly or covertly manipulated the government around their own ends. Very few of Haiti's 'ordinary' (poor) people owned their own homes. Land and property was owned and tightly controlled by a secretive elite class. The underlying problem was massive inequality between this rich landowning class and the majority of extremely poor Haitians.

There is a greater degree of certainty about the number of people displaced from their homes because they could be counted. The massive figure of 1.5 million people reflects the total destruction of flimsily-built huts and houses, many of them located on the steep slopes of gullies where people were forced to live because the good land was taken by elite groups and too expensive. The tragedy was on a scale comparable with the 2004 Indian Ocean Tsunami but concentrated in half an island in the Caribbean.

When I visited Haiti for the first time in 2009, a few months before the earthquake, I was shocked by the levels of poverty, anger and inequality.[152] The country had been chosen as a case study as part of an analysis of fragile states commissioned by two international charities. Because Haiti is such an extraordinary almost unbelievable case, details of this analysis are attached as an Annex. Haiti has many of the characteristics of the poorest countries in Africa transposed into one of the world's wealthiest regions, just a short distance from Florida. Although I did not take part in the relief operations I undertook a review of the experience for one of the leading international charities and this enabled me to interview staff directly involved and read internal reports. I was shocked for a second time –by the enormous difficulties faced in the international response and the scale of its ultimate failure.

In summary, the history of Haiti is that back in 1798 it had been the scene of a successful slave revolt and seemed to be destined to become a beacon of freedom and equality. But the opposite happened. After the country's independence, France imposed punitive sanctions and demanded reparations which kept Haiti poor for the following century and beyond. An elite Haitian group stepped into the shoes of the former colonial power and inequality began to increase among the victorious former slaves. By the twentieth century, indications of revolution and communism had begun to alarm the USA and led to interventions in support of the brutal Duvalier dynasty of dictators. The USA preferred to have Haiti kept in order by the dreaded secret police, the 'Tontons Macoutes', than risk another socialist challenge as had happened in Cuba.

The Duvalier regimes used violence to suppress civil society especially the cooperatives that had been formed in rural areas to raise farm incomes. Haitians responded by setting up clandestine political organisations with equally vicious gangs. With US support, the Duvaliers kept control by favouring the elite group of Haitian families who kept tight control of the land and practically every aspect of the

---

[152]  Vaux, T (2009)

economy. The work of informers spread a culture of suspicion and distrust. Civil society was reduced to evangelical church organisations that competed with each other and drew support by offering an educational alternative to the disastrous state education system.

The democratic system of governance and reaction against the Duvaliers opened up possibilities for the people to re-assert their influence over politics. Jean-Baptiste Aristide, a former priest, became President promising to lead a progressive government. But in ways that remain clouded in secrecy the USA and elite Haitian families were able to destabilize and undermine his regime. This resulted in widespread gang warfare, especially in the capital, Port-au-Prince. The USA financed a UN 'stabilisation' mission, MINUSTAH which arrived in Haiti in 2004 in order to prevent further descent into violence and anarchy. The mission succeeded to an extent in reducing gang violence but President Aristide lost popular support and was forced out of the country under pressure from the USA and France.

The new series of Haitian leaders proved to be ineffective. They were unable to make progress (assuming they wished to do so) in reconciling the interests of the exploitative elite class and the majority of poor people. Because of Haiti's instability there was very little inward investment. High levels of unemployment exacerbated the problems of violence creating a vicious spiral of economic collapse. The only viable businesses focused on import and export, together with smuggling of drugs and weapons. Because much of their activity was illegal, these businesses had an interest in weak government and instability. Conditions were so bad in Haiti that most elite Haitians emigrated to Canada and the USA although some of them continued to manipulate the situation. They successfully used their influence to prevent the emergence of stable pro-poor government.

This shadowy elite retained ownership of large tracts of land and, not having to witness the results of exploitation, became even more vicious as absentee landlords. In the urban areas, especially Port-au-Prince, poorer Haitians rarely owned the land on which they lived but instead paid rent to the absentee landlords. The situation was scarcely better in the rural areas where lack of investment and the deliberate destruction of cooperatives and peasant movements over many years kept Haitians very poor and caused a steady migration to Port- au-Prince.

At the beginning of the twenty-first century Haiti was unique within the Americas. No other country came close in terms of failed human development. 76% of the Haitian population, some 4.4.million persons, lived on less than $2 per day and 56% on less than $1 per day. The country was characterised by widespread violence, dominance of gangs, smuggling of weapons, inequality, failures of governance and extreme poverty. It was almost impossible to conduct business legally and no system to prevent illegality. Haiti occupied a position almost at the bottom of Transparency International's Corruption Perception Index. In 2007, it was in 177th place, ahead only of Iraq, Somalia and Myanmar.

On 12th January 2010, Haiti was struck by an extremely severe earthquake, centred on Port- au-Prince. Because of migration from the rural areas, the population of the city had increased from an estimated 732,000 in the 1980s to around three million by 2008 (although nobody really knows).[153] Most people had moved into slum settlements but elite groups retained ownership even of the steep slopes of ravines and hills. As more and more people came to the city, they settled in the most dangerous places. Because they could be evicted without notice (often under pressure from gangs and hired thugs) people built houses for short-term occupancy without regard to safety. Many were constructed out of waste materials found on rubbish heaps. When the earthquake struck, these structures collapsed, sometimes crushing the people underneath. Of the homes destroyed by the earthquake, it has been estimated that 86% were built after 1990.[154]

The problems that emerged were not about relations among poor Haitians (who responded positively as neighbours always do in times of disaster) but the utter disregard shown by the wealthier classes and the ability of the wealthy elite to undermine and limit the actions of government. According to Mark Schuller who conducted studies in Haiti before and after the earthquake-[155] *'Neighbours helped one another*

---

[153] Dupuy, A (2010) *Disaster Capitalism to the Rescue: the international community and Haiti after the earthquake,* NACLA Report on the Americas 43/5

[154] Etienne, Y (2012) *Haiti and Catastrophes: Lessons not Learned* in *Tectonic Shifts: Haiti since the earthquake, Schuller M and P Morales eds* Kumarian Press, Sterling

[155] Sculler, M (2012) —see bibliography. This section on Haiti after the earth-quake draws heavily on this source.

*out of the rubble, pulling out dead family members and sharing emergency rations. Makeshift clinics were set up in the middle of the street, where people slept side by side, middle class and 'pep la', Haiti's poor majority. Committees sprang up, making lists of household members, those dead, injured or handicapped, elderly, infants and pregnant women. They also shared water and pots to store it, foodstuffs, medicines and first-aid materials.... The life-saving contribution by Haiti's people was immediate and significant but went without recognition or compensation by the Haitian government, foreign agencies or the media.....' (p175)*

Government was undeveloped and under-resourced even before the disaster but its offices and infrastructure were obliterated by the earthquake. Port-au-Prince housed nearly all Haiti's administrative functions as well as NGO offices, banks and industry and nearly everything was destroyed. This made it extremely difficult for the aid system to operate. There was no significant experience of disasters either in government or NGOs. International charities were poorly represented in Haiti. Many had decided that although Haiti was extremely poor they did not want to run operations in the Caribbean Region which was generally rich. Typically, Haiti was visited occasionally by agency staff from outside and there were very few international staff who resided in Haiti and learnt about the country.

Added to this, the earthquake killed staff of the aid agencies and destroyed their offices. Local staff were so traumatized or concerned with their families that they could not work, especially in the early stages of the response. As a result the aid managers leading the aid response mostly came from abroad and had very little knowledge about the country.

Most of the poorer people spoke Creole rather than French which was the language of the educated elite but quite a number had acquired some knowledge of French. But many of the new international arrivals did not know French and therefore looked for English-speaking local staff. This made them dependent on elite Haitians who had travelled to the USA and Canada. These persons might not be seriously committed to the interests of poor people and because of the strong social divisions in Haiti they might not even know anything about the lives of ordinary people but they were in a strong position to influence the aid effort. English was the language mainly used in aid coordination meetings and this further excluded local voices and NGOs.

Because the earthquake had created spectacular images published in the media, funds came pouring into the aid agencies. Competition and commercialization took precedence as the aid system moved into gear. The agencies had to act quickly or at least be seen to act quickly. Goods were put on planes before the assessment whether they were needed. Agency T-shirts and logos appeared in Port au Prince and aid workers began to fan out looking for places to place their flags. Because of public expectations in the West, plans were drawn up hastily but agencies soon found that they faced immense difficulties in implementing even the most basic kind of response, such as food distributions, because there was so little infrastructure. Bogged down in the detail of distributing relief goods, agencies failed to step back, organise consultations with the people and find ways to work in this unusual environment. In a typical case[156]-'*The initial outline plan for the response was agreed within a couple of days of the earthquake on the basis of assumptions and general knowledge. Although a more detailed plan was later developed for fundraising purposes, there was no thorough re-appraisal of strategy and focus, taking into account the assessments and reports made in the meantime. The Real Time Evaluation (in May 2010) finds that-* 'No consolidated assessment document with key findings and conclusions was ever prepared'.

Even when they were forced to acknowledge the existence of these problems agencies failed to develop strategies to tackle deeper issues, such as inequality and land ownership. Wealthy Haitians exploited the situation. They refused to make land available for relief camps without payment and agencies were so affronted by these demands that they placed relief camps in unsuitable remote locations. This made people move away from their home areas and reduced the chance of restoring incomes through work.

The lack of consultation and negative effects of decisions by aid agencies led to increasing tensions. Aid workers found that Haitians were quick to find out what was happening and vocal in their complaints. Information about the immense resources available through international appeals and promises made by aid agencies spread rapidly through the ubiquitous mobile phone system. Haitians knew exactly

---

[156] Name of the agency withheld because it would be unfair to single out one organisation when practically all did the same

how much money was available and what the agencies were claiming to do. They complained when they did not receive their due.

In the intense heat of this competitive international response, with the media watching every move and equating effectiveness with speed, aid managers competed for high profile and easy locations, such as on the road to the airport. Other areas were completely neglected, adding to the complaints coming from the people. Relations reached a crisis point after the outbreak of cholera in October 2010. This outbreak had spread from Nepali soldiers in the UN stabilisation force, MINUSTAH. The epidemic killed 6,300 people and infected 240,000 by the end of August 2011.[157]

Cholera spread rapidly across Haiti because of a general lack of clean water and sanitation. Only in a third of the relief camps was there a designated agency responsible for the toilets. Only around 15% of the camps had any NGO responsible for water.[158] A year after the earthquake, 40% of displaced persons did not have access to water and 30% did not have toilets of any kind. Despite a Sphere Standard that a toilet should not be shared by more than 20 persons, in a sample survey the average was 273.[159]

By November 2010, nine months after the earthquake, a million people were still displaced from their previous homes. In fact the disaster response never recovered from these initial failures. Around $13bn had been pledged by bilateral donors and multilateral agencies immediately after the earthquake but according to the UN Office of the Special Envoy for Haiti, only 50% of these pledges ($6bn) were disbursed by 2013, three years after the earthquake.

Time photographer Gael Turine, who made many visits in the aftermath of the earthquake and returned to Port-au-Prince for a final review five years after the earthquake, concluded- *'When you walk around the country's capital Port-au-Prince, you still see half-destroyed buildings around town. The wounds are still here, and everyone says that they're living in worse conditions than before...When you look at the history of humanitarian relief, there's never been a situation when such a small country has been the target of such a massive influx of money and assistance in such*

---

[157] Schuller (2012) p172

[158] Schuller (2012) p188 drawing on WASH Cluster reports

[159] Ibid

*a short span of time. On paper, with that much money in a territory the size of Haiti, we should have witnessed miracles; there should have been results.*[160]

Lack of local knowledge and staff together with competitive behaviour and huge imbalances in the spread of services made this a particularly ineffective aid response. The UN 'Cluster' coordination system did not properly involve the government. Many aid staff, influenced by their local contacts in the Haitian elite, simply discounted the government because of its supposed corruption and ineffectiveness. But when given the chance officials sometimes did well. Government staff found ways of working even in the notoriously violent slum area of Cite Soleil, which had been avoided by most aid agencies. With leadership from government officials, Water and Sanitation (WASH) was fully covered by February 2011 when most other areas had totally inadequate coverage.

The government never really got a chance to show what it might do. The majority of aid from donors went to the UN and international charities. In a detailed study of the response, Mark Schuller concludes- *'Donors' neo-liberal ideologies and prejudices that favour private voluntary (organisations) that have little accountability to crises-affected populations have kept the one institution that has the responsibility and public accountability, the Haitian government, both national and local, from being able to respond to the crisis.*[161]

The worst problems were faced by people living on land which elite groups wished to re- occupy: *'Consistently, humanitarian agencies bowed to pressure not to provide services on private land, thus allowing Haitian elites and middle classes to assert property rights.*[162] The earthquake response presented an opportunity to challenge the power of Haiti's elite. Well- informed local offices of aid agencies could have worked with government to ensure that shadowy claims of land ownership and demands for rent were set aside in the interests of the people. But the international appeals took over. The political aspects of the disaster were ignored, the national government was pushed aside, and local

---

[160]   Time Magazine January 2015: http://time.com/3662225/haiti-earthquake-five-year-after/

[161]   Schuller (2012) p192

[162]   Schuller (2012) p189

organisations were marginalised. Little effort was made to consult with the affected people.

Among the international charities, Oxfam was unusual in at least recognising the underlying issue of inequality- *'Many Haitians have told Oxfam that the first thing that needs to change is the inequality in Haitian society; that exclusion is pervasive in education and government at all levels. Wealth and power have always been concentrated in the hands of Haiti's small political and commercial elite.'* [163] Oxfam pledged to focus on making the government accountable to the people by encouraging the people to be more active citizens- *'Every Haitian must become an active citizen: have the information they need to enable them to make informed decisions on their future, and work together with the government to rebuild the country.'* [164] But Oxfam did little to put this approach into action and in any case the analysis wrongly implied that the problem was the government rather than the elite groups that manipulated and weakened the government for their own purposes.

From an early stage Haitians complained that the aid effort lacked transparency and accountability. This issue was taken up in a study by the Center for Democratic Governance (CFDG) based in Washington- [165] *'Three years after the quake, we do not really know how the money was spent, how many Haitians were reached, or whether the desired outcomes were achieved... We found that about 94% of humanitarian funding went to donors' own civilian and military entities, UN agencies, international NGOs and private contractors... Detailed financial reports and rigorous impact evaluations are hard to find. There are some exceptions, but most organisations only publish case studies or other descriptions of their work; negative outcomes or failures are almost never documented. Of the thousands of projects being run in Haiti, we found only 45 organisation or project-level evaluation reports at the end of 2011. A total of 23 reports do not have specific project data and only four have any specific detail about how the money was spent.'*

---

[163] Oxfam GB (2010) Haiti: *A Once in a Century Chance for Change*, Oxfam Briefing Paper 136

[164] Ibid

[165] CFDG Senior Fellow Vijaya Ramachandran and Policy Analyst Julie Walz summarizing the full report in a blog for The Guardian

The government of Haiti became increasingly vocal in its demands for transparency and accountability from the aid agencies and frustrated that instead they were blaming the government- *'It is a contradiction that the Haitian government is asked to improve transparency when the international aid community itself fails to provide adequate information to the public. Pierre Erold Etienne, director general of the Haitian finance ministry, said: "[The] real problem is that we do not have or, I should say, we have only very little overall information on aid … We are required to be transparent. We publish the financial information relevant to the execution of our budget. All we ask is for the same transparency from our donor friends, which should help both us and them.... It is very hard to achieve good outcomes when we cannot determine who received the money and how it was spent. Haiti received an amount almost equal to its gross domestic product, but several hundred thousand people remain in tent camps set up in the aftermath of the quake. Port-au-Prince still lacks good roads, electricity and safe drinking water. Transparency is a critical step towards better project design and implementation in Haiti and other poor countries.... We can and should do a better job of helping people to regain control of their lives in the aftermath of disaster or conflict.'*[166]

With $20billion available, the aid response scarcely restored the conditions that existed before the earthquake and certainly did not 'build back better'. People were left just as vulnerable to disasters as before. In October 2012 the tail of Hurricane Sandy touched Haiti affecting only a small area and a limited number of people. Because there were no measures to evacuate people or mitigate the effects of the storm, 104 people were killed and 15 people remained missing. The same hurricane hit 24 States of the USA with full force affecting many millions of people but because of good preparation, warning and rapid evacuation only 131 people were killed.[167] In Haiti's well-organised neighbour, the Dominican Republic, just two people were killed by the hurricane.

Haiti was just as vulnerable when Hurricane Matthew struck on 4 October 2016, killing 546 people according to official reports and creating Haiti's worst humanitarian crisis since the 2010 earthquake. The UN reported 1.4 million people in need of humanitarian aid,

---

[166] Ibid
[167] Wikipedia: Hurricane Sandy

800,000 requiring urgent help and 150,000 displaced. Communication networks and public infrastructure were out of service and there were reports of attacks and looting of aid convoys. The spread of cholera (never wiped out after the 2010 outbreak) intensified further.[168]

With practically unlimited funds, the response to the Haiti earthquake should have been a great deal better. It should have laid the foundations for employment and development, tackled inequality and reduced the risk of future disasters but it did none of these. The government and local NGOs were marginalised by the 2010 international response and did not increase their capacity to handle future events. Nothing was done to overcome Haiti's underlying problem of inequality.

The roots of failure can be traced back to the way in which disaster aid is configured. Small local disasters in which aid agencies may have the ability to do something useful are underfunded and huge resources are focused on those that hit the jackpot of media attention. Because of public perception that speed, scale and the presence of expatriates are the marks of a successful response, even the agencies which know better are reduced to a lowest common denominator of frenzied but pointless activity. The agencies cannot afford to oppose this because their general reputation rests on the profile they achieve at these times of media blitz and they know that by the time the failures become apparent media attention will have moved elsewhere. A conspiracy to de-politicise disasters fuels the arguments for speed, scale and expatriates. The result is highly beneficial for the aid system but much less so for the victims of disasters and its overwhelming tendency is to marginalise the national government.

The response to 'natural' disasters might actually benefit from a little more of the 'securitization' agenda that overwhelms the aid response in Afghanistan, Iraq and Somalia. In Haiti the tendency for chaotic relief operations to strengthen the position of elite groups and weaken government may have led to more smuggling of weapons and drugs across the Caribbean region. This was the issue that I had

---

[168] Crisis Group update report on Haiti October 2016 https://www.crisisgroup.org/crisiswatch?utm_source=Sign+Up+to+Crisis+Group%27s+Email+Updates&utm_ca mpaign=c4e24c0b53-crisiswatch_2016_11_02&utm_medium=email&utm_term=0_1dab-8c11ea-c4e24c0b53- 359780625#haiti

researched for the UK government back in 2008 concluding that gangs based in Haiti were a serious threat to other Caribbean countries especially Jamaica- '*Political instability in Haiti has created new opportunities for transnational criminal networks and the increased movement of criminals to and from Haiti and drug and arms trafficking.*'[169]

In the case of the 2005 Pakistan earthquake, referred to earlier, Pakistani expert Ahmed Rashid writes- '*The devastating earthquake that hit northern Pakistan on October 8, 2005, did much to revive the militant groups and provide them with a new role.... Seventeen extremist groups that were either on the UN list of terrorist organisations or banned by the Pakistan government were reactivated as Islamic NGOs.*'[170]

The dominance of the aid system, and its uncontrollable binges in times of high profile disasters, could be regarded as a threat to global security. The dangers of fuelling the war in Sri Lanka have been alluded to above. This is simply not a good way to run global affairs.

---

[169] Vaux T and A Harriott (2008) *Small States Big Problems: Strategic Conflict and Security Assessment – Caribbean,* unpublished paper commissioned by DFID

[170] Rashid (2008) pp292-3

# CHAPTER NINE

# POVERTY REDUCTION

# WITHOUT AID

I went to India as a Field Director for Oxfam in 1976 and lived in Gujarat until 1980. I returned in a similar role based in Calcutta (now Kolkata) from 1982 to 1984. During my time in Gujarat I first encountered the Self Employed Women's Association (SEWA) based in Ahmedabad, the Gujarat State capital.

One of the main criticisms of Western aid (see Chapter Four) is that it turns local NGOs into contractors who do what aid managers want rather than what they or the people want. The Self Employed Women's Association (SEWA) refuses to be a contractor. It is a union of working women and its mandate comes from the members. SEWA has been strongly influenced by the Gandhian principle of self-reliance, and has kept to this principle regardless of many temptations to rely on outside help, including (with one major exception to be examined later) help from government. It accepts some foreign aid but only on its own terms and normally in response to a need expressed on its website.[171] Self-reliance is a primary objective of the union as well as a principle. SEWA measures its achievement against the self-reliance of members and the organisation rather than against other considerations such as the results of specific projects.

---

[171]  http://www.sewa.org/about_us.asp

When I started working in India in the 1970s labour unions and cooperatives in India were widely discredited because of corruption and the dominance of elite leaders. I once heard cooperatives characterised as 'a good time for the Chairman'. Unusually, SEWA has scrupulously followed the lead of its members and it has developed as a functioning democracy. Significant questions are always debated among the members and normally settled only on the basis of overwhelming consensus. Although the impetus for SEWA came from a small group of intellectual and elite women, their objective has been to develop leadership from within the union and to ensure that every member is involved in decision- making. This is unusual among locally-based organisations, partly because they tend to reflect the social structures around them and partly because reliance on aid empowers the elite leadership which controls access to foreign resources.

SEWA began in the 1960s as an offshoot of the biggest textile union in India, the Textile Labour Association (TLA) which had been established by Gandhi in the 1930s. Gandhi promoted self-reliance as a defence against colonial dominance. Famously he refused to wear imported cloth and to pay taxes on salt as demanded by the government. Gandhi preferred to wear homespun (khadi) cloth and, in one of his most telling acts of defiance, gathered salt from the edge of the sea and challenged the colonial government to arrest him. Gandhi recognised the value of the Indian textile industry (even if it did not make khadi cloth) as a challenge to foreign rule and as a symbol of national self-reliance. By the 1930s cotton from India was no longer sent to Lancashire to be processed and then sold back to Indian people at huge profit. Indian companies had now taken over most of the mills but Gandhi wanted the workers to have meaningful lives and a fair share in the profits.

In its heyday up to around the 1960s, the TLA helped to bring about cohesion among the workers and mitigated tensions between Hindu caste groups as well as between Hindus and Muslims. Religious tension had been a major source of violence especially around the time of the partition of British India in 1947. The collapse of the Indian textile industry in the 1960s, caused by failure to compete with new technologies and cheaper goods from the Far East, led to a rapid reduction in the workforce. The leaders of the TLA failed to handle the crisis fairly. They favoured some groups rather than others and became closely associated with specific politicians. The TLA lost its reputation as an honest broker and came to be regarded as a tool of politicians.[172]

Women played a limited role in the textile mills (most of the employees were men) but the cuts fell particular harshly on women. The dominant cultural ideal in urban Gujarat, which Gandhi himself had promoted, was that married women should focus on the family while the men went out to work. The employers and the TLA agreed that women should be laid off first. But in many cases their husbands and other family members were also laid off and poverty spread throughout the communities clustered around the (now dormant) mills. In many cases this led to depression and violence on the part of men, especially against women who were still employed or had found a means of earning money outside the textile mills. In general women proved to be more adaptable and many turned to 'self employment' for survival.

Some women continued to do the same jobs for the textile industry but without the security of being employees. For example, they moved materials and machinery but were paid per load rather than on an employment basis. In this context, 'self-employment' denotes a high degree of insecurity and poverty. Typical roles include running small stalls on the streets, making cheap items, daily work on building sites and working as domestic staff without written contracts. The basic idea of SEWA was that it would increase the bargaining power of such women by helping them to be self-sufficient rather than dependent on employers.

Ela Bhatt, a highly educated Gujarati woman from a high-caste family, had been one of very few full-time women employees of the TLA, working in the legal department. She was deeply committed to Gandhian thinking[173] and increasingly believed that the TLA was no longer following the essence of Gandhian thought, especially that it was not focusing on the poorest or 'last' person (the Gandhian principle of *Antyoday*). She became critical of the union, especially of its treatment, or rather abandonment, of women.

---

[172] Varshney (2002) pp 232-4

[173] Except his views on women perhaps. See bibliography for her books and books about her.

While working for the TLA, she spent much of her spare time studying the living conditions of women providing self-employed labour for the mills and became more and more alarmed as the effects of retrenchment spread. Women were forced to take on more and more, work longer hours and to accept roles that were harmful to their health and safety. She watched women carrying enormous loads on their heads; others pushed heavy handcarts or worked at home for many hours making items that sold for a pittance. She noted that the women handled dangerous materials and faced great risk of injury. They were unable, in many cases, to provide safe conditions for their dependent children and usually unable to send them to school. Following cultural norms, it was women who had to bear the responsibility for care of children and elderly relatives but now they also had to work very hard to make money as well as continue these other roles. It was widely considered shameful for men to take on domestic tasks and, with the sensitivity arising from mass unemployment, this was unlikely to change. SEWA focused on boosting the income of women, knowing that in most cases this would increase their influence and status at home.

Ela Bhatt (widely known as 'Elaben'[174]) felt that the self employed women working for the mills should remain within the concern of the TLA union but the officials disagreed. She helped the TLA to create a 'women's wing' to support the remaining female employees but the TLA leadership gave little active support and eventually she decided to go it alone, leaving the TLA and organising a separate union of self-employed women. After leaving the TLA she took the opportunity to travel in other parts of India, studying the problems faced by self-employed women.

She found that exploitation by middlemen was very common. One of the main reasons why women were vulnerable was that they lacked their own basic tools and working capital. Typically, women who kept small stalls would take a loan at the beginning of the day and return it with, ten or twenty per cent interest at the end of the day. The middlemen took the profit from those who manufactured goods at home. Women running stalls on the streets ('street vendors') were

---

[174] The suffix 'ben' is used throughout the union, and more widely in Gandhian circles, meaning 'sister'

often harassed by the police demanding money and taking whatever they wanted from the stall. They were vulnerable to illness because of unhealthy and risky work but could not afford to take time off because in many cases they lived from hand to mouth. Many women fell into debt because of a crisis such as a sick child or theft of their belongings. These debts could mount up until they were caught in a poverty trap, held by money-lenders in a kind of bonded labour or slavery.

As Ela Bhatt put it- *'To be poor is to be vulnerable. The condition of being poor, of being self-employed and of being a woman are all distinct yet interrelated states of vulnerability. Poverty makes one become a chronic victim of forces beyond one's control. With every misfortune, problems compound, leaving one increasingly powerless and setting in motion a spiral descent into starker poverty. Only work, a steady source of income, and asset ownership can break one's fall.'*[175]

Ela Bhatt's researches and widespread consultation with working women pointed towards savings, however small, as the means of reducing risk and leading towards self-reliance. SEWA members were expected to save something every day and 'activists' (*aagewans*) made a daily round to collect the savings and find out if the member had any problems or issues to discuss. The process of saving promoted a sense of unity and self- reliance and the 'activists' helped to bring women together and provided opportunities for mutual support. Savings were used mainly to promote and protect livelihoods as the centre of all other activity.

One of Ela Bhatt's first involvements was with the Ahmedabad 'street vendors' who sold vegetables outside the city's main market. She organised a protest against harassment by the police but the city's leaders failed to respond. They regarded the women as a nuisance and shopkeepers wanted to have them removed from the market because they sold goods cheaply. They made the police evict the street vendors. But the vendors had been encouraged by Ela Bhatt's interest and were determined to take a stand. They returned to the market, defying the police, and organised further protest demonstrations. The vendors received considerable support from the public (probably because the women sold vegetables very cheaply) and the authorities backed down. But when public attention was turned elsewhere the officials and police

---

[175] Bhatt (2006) p23

evicted them again. SEWA sought the voluntary help of sympathetic lawyers and took the case through the courts eventually reaching the Supreme Court in New Delhi which came down in favour of the street vendors. The Court ruled that they had the right to occupy traditional positions and carry on their trade. This judgment applied not only to Ahmedabad but to the whole country. It seemed to be a great victory.

SEWA celebrated but no political party was willing to take up the issue in the Indian Parliament and pass the legislation needed to confirm this right into law. The Supreme Court judgment was challenged in several cases around India and the street vendors in Ahmedabad had to fight more court cases and threats of evictions.

Around this time, Ela Bhatt was invited by leading political figures to become a member of the Rajya Sabha, the non-elected upper house of the Indian Parliament. She was advised that she might be able to put forward a private member's bill in support of street vendors if she gave her support to a political party. This was the track that many civil society leaders, including many Gandhians, had followed in the past but Ela Bhatt had noted that it nearly always resulted in compromise of the interests of poor people. The people simply became vote banks and the leaders did what the party wanted rather than what the people wanted. Elaben decided to participate in the Rajya Sabha as an independent member but this meant that she had little political influence; the necessary law was never passed. Ela Bhatt later observed- *'This is the price one pays for keeping one's distance from all political parties; but we would not have it otherwise.'*[176]

The example of the TLA had been a salutary one for SEWA. By giving its support to a single political party the TLA had created enemies outside and factions within the union that eventually destroyed it as an organisation acting for poor people. SEWA went on to become stronger and bigger but its influence on national legislation and political change remained limited.

In its early days SEWA leaders were optimistic about achieving change through 'citizen action' but later fell back on self-reliance. SEWA took up a number of protests, campaigns and demonstrations but over the course of time the members found that in the Indian context at least, it was extremely difficult to achieve lasting results.

---

[176]  Bhatt (2006) p89

There might be an appearance of success but in the end the political system blocked significant progress. Ela Bhatt described three levels of challenge for women trying to achieve permanent 'rights'- *'As I see it, injustice has three faces. First, there is the face of injustice that the women see for themselves –that of the direct exploiter. That face may be a hard-hitting policeman, a cold- hearted employer, or a vicious contractor. The system that supports the direct exploiter is the second level of injustice, which includes government agencies and the legal structure. The women do not see it as readily until they gain awareness..... All this exploitation is made possible by injustice at the third and highest level –that of policy and law-making......'*[177]

The three levels reinforced each other, making it extremely difficult to achieve lasting change. SEWA was often successful in dealing with the first level, the open hostility of direct opponents, but it had much more difficulty dealing with what lay behind. The problem was that the power of the middle and upper elites was hidden and the way it operated inaccessible to poor people. They might concede one point and then find ways to punish poor people. Manaliben, a self employed woman who became President of SEWA, made the observation- *'Where I have dealt directly with employers through meetings and negotiations they have brought some positive results. But in court cases, workers have mostly lost. Or they may have received some compensation or favourable orders, but ultimately they have lost their job.'*[178]

Ela Bhatt turned her attention to building up the membership of SEWA and making it fully representative of the members. The leadership of educated elite people including Ela Bhatt gave way to leadership by elected members of the union who were themselves poor working women. Instead of engaging further in the parliamentary process, SEWA now focused on fostering self-reliance. This was not simply a matter of expanding services and gathering resources but of developing leadership from among the members. In her early researches, Ela Bhatt had found that there were some women who had innate leadership skills and that these skills had often been developed through their experience of being self employed and responsible for family finances

---

[177]  Bhatt (2006) p69
[178]  Bhatt (2006) p78

and harmony.[179] She now withdrew from formal leadership and focused on bringing forward such leaders from within the union. The policy proved to be effective and SEWA entered a period of rapid expansion in terms of numbers of members, participation in decision-making and spread of activities.

I first encountered SEWA in 1978 when I was the new Oxfam Field Director in Western India based in Ahmedabad. At that time SEWA membership in Gujarat was just 730 women.[180] I had heard about SEWA and visited them in order to see if they could make good use of Oxfam's help. At that time Oxfam had very few fixed policies or preferences and it was mainly up to its local representatives to identify and respond to requests coming from local organisations. The only significant condition was that Oxfam's aid should help the poorest people.

At that time Ela Bhatt was still in the process of diversifying from work associated with the textile industry. She had been studying the work of women who made quilts out of scraps of waste cloth from the textile mills. These 'patchwork quilts' were not fashion items but the cheapest type of bed-covering available for the poorest people. They were made out of rags including shoddy used to clean machinery. The rags had to be sorted and cleaned before being stitched together. A group of women had come together to do this, joined SEWA and started a savings programme.

The women were well aware that the traders who bought their products made most of the profit and they proposed to form a cooperative to buy the raw materials directly from the mills and sell the finished *chindis* (quilts) to the public. My arrival was timely because the cooperative needed an injection of working capital. They did not yet have enough from their own savings and, although funds could have been found from elsewhere in the SEWA network, my offer of help from Oxfam provided a simple and convenient way forward.

At the time I left Gujarat in 1980 all this seemed to be working perfectly but more than two decades later when I returned to Ahmedabad (to evaluate responses to the earthquake in 2001) I discovered that the story of the *chindi* workers had been long and

---

[179]   For SEWA's approach to leadership see especially Rose (1992)
[180]   SEWA Annual Report 2013

involved. With the capital provided by Oxfam the women had purchased cloth and set up a production unit but the merchants realised that this would challenge their power and so they offered to pay a higher rate for all *chindi* workers in the city if the women would continue to work under the old system. SEWA recognised that a small production unit was a limited step when thousands of women were involved in the trade. SEWA agreed to close the cooperative and accept the offer of higher pay for all workers in the sector.

But once the *chindi* workers had closed their cooperative, the merchants went back on their promise. SEWA then approached the Labour Office to have *chindi* work recognised under Minimum Wage legislation but the traders failed to come to the meetings and undermined the negotiations. They began to single out SEWA members and deny them work. After many more discussions and problems, an agreement was signed with the Labour Commissioner but it was not properly implemented or enforced. It was only an intervention by the national Finance Minister (through a contact of Ela Bhatt) that brought about payment of *chindi* workers at the official minimum rate. But even this lasted only for a short while. SEWA was ready to go on fighting but the collapse of the textile industry led to shortages of raw materials and most of the *chindi* workers were forced to find other occupations.[181]

Despite such setbacks SEWA's membership in Gujarat had grown from just 730 when I first met them to over 200,000 members.[182] Its scope now included a much wider range of industries and occupations. SEWA had built up a set of social projects that were beginning to amount to a comprehensive welfare system. Engagement in these new activities often came about in response to a problem or a crisis. If a member had trouble saving money or repaying a loan, SEWA would identify the underlying cause through meetings and sometimes through short research processes. This would lead to a decision whether something should be done to reduce this type of risk for all members. For example, members discussed the issue of childbirth as a threat to livelihoods. They suggested that all members should make a small additional monthly payment to insure against this risk. The pooled fund was used to provide daily wages when a member was unable to work.

---

[181]   For a fuller description see Bhatt (2006) pp58-79
[182]   SEWA Annual Report 2013

Members also raised the issue of childcare and this resulted in SEWA running nursery schools —not with the primary objective of educating children but in order to protect the livelihood of the mother. Health was another reason for loss of livelihood. In India basic government services should be free but this is not really the case and visits to government health institutions often involve huge amounts of wasted time and it may also be necessary to pay bribes for services. Many members preferred to go to private doctors because their treatment involved less time off work and was often more effective. SEWA decided that its most useful role would be to buy medicines in bulk and sell them to the members cheaply, leaving them to use private or government doctors as they wished. The second step was to form a cadre of 'barefoot doctors' and 'barefoot midwives' who visited members to give advice on preventive health, family planning etc. By gradually adding more and more programmes to address the risks faced by members, SEWA built up what has become today India's largest comprehensive contributory social security scheme for workers in the informal sector, now known as the Integrated Social Security Programme.[183] It was not planned as a comprehensive system but has evolved because each time a new risk was identified a new element was added to the protection system.

The basis for all activity is saving. SEWA has set up its own Bank in order to safeguard members' savings and lend it out for productive ventures initiated by the members, usually on a personal basis. The SEWA Bank also manages funds intended to insure members against risk such as childbirth. The insurance role of the Bank expanded in response to the many and varied risks experienced by very poor people. The biggest of all was the threat of disasters arising from floods, droughts and violence, for which SEWA developed a special scheme in the 1990s. Members had put forward proposals for an insurance scheme which would provide enough to live on in the early days after such a disaster and also a cash grant to replace essential materials. SEWA's initial programme had been based on the tested formula of small contributions from a large number of members to create a central pool.

But the amounts were relatively small and it was unclear how SEWA could address a really large and widespread disaster. SEWA

---

[183]  Dayal (2001)

tried to work with the government, which at that time was putting pressure on insurance companies to provide cover for very poor people. SEWA developed a scheme by which an insurance company agreed to underwrite an agreed level of compensation payments for those members who chose to join. SEWA's role was to collect the contributions and verify the damage in relation to claims. This was not too great a task for SEWA because it already had a cadre of 'activists' who visited each member regularly.

Widespread flooding in 1998 had shown the limitations of the scheme. Although SEWA made the assessments within two days of the disaster, the company took many weeks to make the payments. The purpose was to protect livelihoods in the early days after a disaster and the scheme was not much use if payments arrived late. SEWA took back responsibility for the scheme and underwrote the risks with its own assets, notably the capital of the SEWA Bank. Over time, SEWA hoped to expand the scheme to such a scale that a disaster in one area would be spread across a much wider membership. But not all members had agreed to join the scheme and when the earthquake occurred, SEWA was left vulnerable.

On January 26th 2001 the Western areas of Gujarat were struck by a severe earthquake. I returned to Gujarat soon afterwards to monitor and later evaluate responses to the earthquake by the international charities that had received funding through the Disasters Emergency Committee (DEC), the UK-based fundraising consortium.[184] After I had written the DEC report I was asked by SEWA to review its response to the same disaster.[185] This provided an opportunity to compare the different approaches and the relationship between SEWA and the international charities.

The Gujarat Earthquake had become international headline news. As many as 20,000 people had died, most of them crushed to death in the collapse of ancient stone buildings. It is estimated that 167,000 people were injured and 339,000 homes were destroyed.[186] The

---

[184] Disaster Mitigation Institute et al (2001)
[185] Published as Vaux, T and F Lund (2003) *Working women and security: Self-Employed Women's Association's response to crisis,* Journal of Human Development Vol 4, No 2 July 2003
[186] http://earthquake.usgs.gov/earthquakes/eqarchives/year/2001/2001_01_26.

earthquake occurred at a time of day when children had just arrived at school and were practicing for Republic Day parades. Fortunately this meant that many were out in the open rather than in their classrooms. Less fortunately many mothers with young children were still in their houses and it was the collapse of traditional stone houses with heavy timbers that caused most of the deaths and injuries,

The area worst affected was far out on the Western borders of Gujarat, adjacent to Pakistan. Kutch is a dry area, almost a desert, inhabited mainly by small farmers relying on a mixture of herding animals and growing crops when there is enough rain. In relation to SEWA's insurance scheme it was fortunate that the city of Ahmedabad, with the greatest concentration of SEWA members, was not much affected by the earthquake. In the Western areas where the effects were worst, SEWA had only recently started to enrol new members and the number of members in the insurance scheme was small. SEWA was able to meet all claims, making quick assessments in the days after the earthquake so that members could quickly start earning money.

Even on the day of the earthquake, SEWA members travelled beyond their villages to find out what had happened to other members and collect insurance claims. This was possible because the buses continued running, perhaps because the drivers did not immediately understand what had happened. Within hours of the earthquake, SEWA members had contacted each other not only in their own communities but across the whole area. This, together with the insurance payments, gave a huge boost to SEWA membership in the region.

While insurance payments were still being made, attention turned towards the crucial issue of income from work. Other than farming, the main livelihood activity for women in the disaster area was embroidery. This was a traditional skill in the region that was now being used as a source of cash income by selling the goods further afield. Embroidery from the Kutch region was beginning to become famous among collectors in Gujarat and internationally. Pieces of broken mirror were sewn into brilliant patterns that flashed in the bright light of the desert. Embroidery was used mostly in women's clothes but also, to a lesser extent by men, and to adorn prize animals.

---

php, accessed on October 2, 2014.

Before the earthquake SEWA had begun to put production of embroidery items on a cooperative basis by providing materials and buying finished products for sale in Ahmedabad but now many more women wanted work and existing members wanted to earn more in order to replace their losses. Other occupations had been lost in the confusion following the disaster. Aid agencies were beginning to arrive in the affected areas but they were focused on giving out relief items rather than helping people resume work. SEWA members decided to rely on their own efforts as they had done in disasters in the past.

By the evening of the day on which the earthquake happened, a team had arrived from SEWA's main office in Ahmedabad about two hundred miles away. The question asked by local SEWA members was *'Have you brought us work?'* Discussion focused on expanding the embroidery business so that every member could achieve an income sufficient to cover immediate needs and start to rebuild their home. When the team returned to Ahmedabad, materials for embroidery were ordered in bulk but the sales side of the operation presented a challenge. Normally each member produced whatever they wanted and received payment for each item sold. In order to provide an assured income for a far greater number of members, production would have to be standardised.

Members were asked to copy generic patterns and the manufacture of items was divided into different stages and processes. On this basis, the number of women earning from this work increased rapidly. Within four weeks of the earthquake, all 20,000 members in the area were working and being paid but many more women from a much wider area now wanted to join SEWA. The union policy had always been to expand in order to achieve greater self-reliance and so the new members were welcomed and invited into the embroidery programme. Before long, the number of member/embroiderers rose to nearly 80,000.

Production ran far ahead of sales. Stocks began to accumulate in Ahmedabad and SEWA's advisers in its cooperatives and other institutions concluded that a wider market would have to be found. Designers in Mumbai volunteered to create fashion clothes using the traditional embroidery skills but adapting the colours and designs to the market among wealthy people in Mumbai. SEWA embroidery became a fashion success and spread to other cities of India and abroad.

SEWA described its response to the earthquake on its website and invited offers of help from aid organisations but made it clear that this would only be accepted in support of what it was already doing. But there was no response from the aid system. Typically, aid agencies preferred to develop their own programmes based on their own assessments of need. They then looked for local NGOs to do what they had decided. This approach was not acceptable to SEWA. The outcome was that SEWA received no significant help from aid organisations until, after several months, a German organisation offered to subsidize reconstruction of a small number of houses.

Part of the reason for this lack of interaction may have been that SEWA moved on a different timescale from the aid agencies. Even from the start its focus was on livelihoods and cash distributions from the insurance scheme were its only venture into providing relief aid —and in that respect the members were free to use the cash as they wished rather than receive items that they might or might not need. The aid agencies were preoccupied with a relief phase and, driven by an excess of funds, lasted longer than was necessary. By the time they turned their attention to livelihoods, typically two or three months after the disaster, SEWA had fully developed its programme and found ways to finance it.

The earthquake had not necessarily destroyed the pots, pans, clothes and blankets of the people but the relief programmes of the aid system were designed as if they had. People who were asked whether they wanted such items might naturally reply in the affirmative. Relief work had to be presented in a spectacular way and so goods were unnecessarily air-freighted from donor countries even though practically every item could be purchased in India more cheaply. Even Oxfam, usually one of the most careful agencies, rushed to air-freight bottles of mineral water which could easily have been bought at roadside shops in Gujarat, helping the local economy.

Agencies deployed hundreds of expatriate staff, also quite unnecessarily. There were plenty of skilled staff in India and many NGOs capable of running aid programmes. In Gujarat, the Gandhian tradition of voluntary public service had been particularly strong but NGOs found that they were being bypassed. The DEC evaluation report concluded that agencies would have done much better if they had deployed fewer international staff and instead developed more effective partnerships with local organizations.[187]

Because SEWA programmes were designed by the members they were different from those designed by aid agencies. In the case of housing for example, SEWA did not simply introduce earthquake resistant methods (as many aid agencies also did) but focused on making the house suitable as a workplace for women. SEWA also challenged the prevailing custom that the house was the property of the man by giving ownership to the woman. This addressed the risk of women being evicted from their house as widows if their husband died.

The housing project put SEWA in a position to influence the large-scale house reconstruction programmes being developed by the government. Engineers had been drafted into Gujarat from all over India in order to assess the damage to houses and identify people who would qualify for new houses or for help in repairing old ones. Many of the engineers proved to be ineffective either because they were unfamiliar with the work or because they were tempted to take bribes to modify their results. SEWA agreed to take over the process and deployed its own experienced staff and engineers. Ela Bhatt became a member of the high level State organization overseeing the response to the earthquake.

A good relationship with the State Government (at that time) enabled SEWA to put forward a plan for a large-scale programme to mitigate the effects of drought in the arid areas affected by the earthquake. The State Government was very cooperative and worked with SEWA to secure finances from IFAD and the World Bank.

SEWA's experience of the original grant for the *chindi* workers shows that foreign aid can have modest but positive effects if it is given in support of what local people and organizations have already identified as the needs. The timescales of aid agencies are likely to be much shorter than that of a locally-rooted NGO and they may not be around to follow through on all the problems and issues that arise later but provided that they boost the self- reliance of the local organization this may not matter. The problem is that as aid agencies became larger they became more prescriptive and made local organisations follow the aid agenda rather than their own. This undermined the voluntarism,

---

[187]   Disaster Mitigation Institute et al (2001)

honesty and credibility of those organisations and left them less able to help when problems and issues arose later.

Today the aid system likes to project itself as taking a lead in the kind of work that SEWA does in organising people and challenging authority but aid agencies do not have the patience and persistence to stay with 'partner' organizations and pursue the same issues over many years. A current Oxfam publication about this process of proceeding 'from poverty to power' features the work of SEWA[188] but does not mention that Oxfam's links with SEWA were broken in the 1980s and even in disasters such as the 2001 earthquake, SEWA received no offers of help from Oxfam.

Like most other agencies, Oxfam now sets global priorities and looks for organizations to implement them ('partners') rather than offering long-term support to the same organizations for whatever those organizations choose to do. Because priorities are in a constant state of flux, with radical changes every few years, local organizations must either accept a role as contractors or find their own solutions and struggle, as SEWA has done, to achieve self- reliance. Increasing dependence on donor government finance has made this worse because donors also change policies rapidly.

Although Oxfam and other aid organizations recognize the need for poor people to be empowered, they cannot cope with the huge timescales, constant grind and low profile of the actual process. Ultimately this is not so much because they do not recognize the problem themselves but because they have to raise funds from people and organizations that do not. The aid system cannot reform itself. It is time for it to step back and concede the lead to organizations such as SEWA.

---

[188]  Green (2008) pp162-3

# CHAPTER TEN

# FREEDOM FROM FEAR

In this book so far, poverty has been defined largely in terms of income. This is useful to understand the spread of poverty globally and the trends of increase or decrease. The book has also cited a number of cases where poor people use income to purchase services such as health and education from the private sector. They do so because states often fail to provide these services in a form that is accessible to poor people and with results that poor people consider worth the sacrifices they have to make. In both the Nepal and India case studies, even quite poor people are shown to turn towards the private sector when governments fail. The provision of services by governments is extremely important but in considering the challenge of extreme poverty, incomes take precedence both in the analysis and in the solution because people can choose freely what to do with them.

But the predicament of very poor people is not limited to physical want. People also need security and the poorest people, as several case studies have shown, are the most vulnerable to various forms of disaster but particularly the effects of violence. Accordingly the notion of Human Security, which provides the theoretical basis for this book, strives towards not only 'freedom from want' but also 'freedom from fear'.

This correlates to an extent with the notion, reflected in Oxfam's fundamental mandate for example, that our aim should be to reduce poverty and distress. But distress is slightly different from fear and more difficult to address, as I shall show later.

Compared with poverty, 'freedom from fear' is a difficult concept and often gets left out of the discourse about aid and poverty. Arguably, 'freedom from want' should lead to 'freedom from fear' because, as people acquire a degree of wealth, they can use it to purchase security and to exert an influence that protects them from harm. In the last resort this is true and takes us back to the central importance of income as the practical means to achieving Human Security.

But fear is an integral part of the experience of poverty because poverty equates closely with vulnerability and that means risk and risk causes fear. This Chapter sets out to explore the nature of the problems as they affect poor people in order to clarify what should be our concerns when thinking about poverty in the broad sense. In particular it explores the issue of geopolitics as a cause of fear and the inability of conventional aid to address this problem.

A DFID policy paper 'Preventing Violent Conflict' published in 2006 points out that violent conflict is a prominent cause of poverty-'The costs of violent conflict are enormous. It is not only the obvious and immediate toll on lives and property. Development is a victim too. During the 1990s, half of the countries where life expectancy, income and education went backwards had experienced violent conflict. Of the 34 countries furthest from reaching the Millennium Development Goals (MDGs), 22 are in the midst of –or emerging from- conflict.'[189]

With the 'easy wins' against extreme poverty already made in China and India, the problem is now concentrated in areas of conflict. Paul Collier has called violent conflict 'development in reverse'.[190] In my own experience I have found that poor people can cope remarkably well with poverty but their lives become unbearable in the case of violent conflict. The most extreme type of suffering is experienced by those who lose what is most dear to them, especially their families. This is a reason why my experience in crisis situations such as South Sudan leads me to focus on stopping the war rather than trying to ameliorate the poverty.

Unfortunately the aid system, instead of focusing on the role of donor governments in causing or perpetuating wars, has come to operate on a hypothesis that poverty causes violence and that this can take the form of armed conflict and also terrorism. One of the arguments used for increasing aid budgets is that this will reduce

---

[189] DFID (2006) *Preventing Violent Conflict,* Policy Paper, DFID London

[190] ActionAid (2011) p27

terrorism. This is profoundly wrong and even if the result is less aid, it should be challenged.

My conflict studies in a score of different countries consistently conclude that poverty is at most a minor contributory factor to violence. It is not the anger of poor people that starts wars but the greed or ambition of elite leaders who then choose to exploit the vulnerability of poor people as the means to achieve their ends. The poorest people lack the means, including time off from the struggle for survival, to initiate violence. As in the case of the artisanal miners in the DRC, described in Chapter Five, poor people are so constrained by the struggle to survive that they cannot take the risk of plotting to overthrow states or even engage in local violence. As shown in the case of self-employed women in India (Chapter Nine) poor people literally live from day to day. The dollar they earn one day has to be earned again on the next day because otherwise they and their families will starve. But a widespread misunderstanding of poverty now makes poor people an object of fear —the mob likely to come and attack the houses of the rich. This is not a good reason for perpetuating the aid system.

Violent conflict can be usefully modelled as an interaction of 'Greed', meaning unchecked pursuit of elite interests, and the 'Grievances' of poorer people.[191] In practically all cases, conflict analysis shows that the 'Greed' elements predominate and the Grievances of the people are largely irrelevant. Conflict studies point time and again towards failures in governance because of the dominance of certain elite interests. By implication, the way to improve global security is to focus on the Greed elements in order to restrain them from exploiting poor people.

This is valid at all different levels right up to civil wars, as in South Sudan today, or even the geopolitical competition that has caused disaster in much of the Middle East. These 'Greed' elements will very often be found to have links into the establishment of aid-giving countries, as in the case of arms sales that have exacerbated human suffering in Yemen. This may be an inconvenient truth but it has huge implications; instead of aid programmes we need global politics and democracy that holds powerful governments to account. People in richer countries should be campaigning against any activity of their own

---

[191] See Berdal and Malone (2000)

governments and societies that causes fear and want. Aid has become a diversion, making the unacceptable acceptable.

This lesson was impressed on me repeatedly during the 1990s when I managed Oxfam humanitarian programmes in the Former Soviet Union. When the opportunity to break away from the USSR was seized, countries did not naturally divide into convenient units. The USSR had deliberately mixed people together and moved them about. As a result war broke out in Georgia, Armenia, Azerbaijan, Chechenya, Tajikistan, Moldova and elsewhere. Hundreds of thousands of people were displaced and entire populations were plunged into darkness and cold when gas, oil and electricity supplies were cut off. From one of the most stable and prosperous parts of the world, these parts of the USSR were plunged into chaos, social tension and political upheaval.

People fled from areas where they had become a targeted minority. Others were impoverished in ghost cities with no food or heating. When I visited the region in 1991, people were angry with me for coming to offer aid. In some cases I was literally chased away as soon as I started talking about food and water and clothes. People felt insulted that I could so much belittle the loss of family, identity, nationality, pride and security by offering a few crumbs from the tables of those who were unaffected and, very likely, did not understand. I learnt to listen more patiently as people described exactly how they had lost their families and many times I left the room with a guilty feeling as a person burst into tears or erupted in hysterics. It was not a happy time. I realised that the aid solution I had come to offer was no use. It could not restore the past, stop the ongoing violence or offer hope for the future. I had seen distress and realised that I could not help.

The suffering and distress in the former Soviet Union was simply a by-product of Kremlin strategy. Initially conflicts erupted because people in different areas and different ethnicities tried to establish control for their own group, excluding others, but the Kremlin quickly realised that there was an opportunity to destabilise and control these regions of the 'near abroad' as Russia had done in the past. The theory was that countries on Russia's borders might be tempted to secede or at the least make links with Russia's enemies. The way to stop them was to make them weak and dependent on Russia. Provoking war between this group and that was the means to do so. Under the USSR, supply of oil, gas and electricity had always been centrally provided and controlled. It was easy to switch off the lights in distant capitals such as Tblisi, Baku and Yerevan. The suffering that resulted had no ideological content. It did not reflect rival views or even rival interests. It was simply a mark of man's inhumanity to man.

The poverty that emerged almost overnight in Russia's near abroad' was different from the dominant Western stereotype derived from Sub-Saharan Africa and the Indian subcontinent. Lack of heating can be a killer just as much as lack of food and water. At the time of the collapse of the USSR, people might still have enough to eat but they suffered great distress because they had recently enjoyed a high standard of living and the sudden decline into poverty was a shock. In addition, people lost their identity as citizens of the USSR. In many cases, their identity was further reduced and transformed by civil war. They were narrowed down from being citizens of a proud superpower to being unrecognised members of a tiny enclave that had broken away from another tiny entity. People did not know who they were.[192] Nationalism and various forms of extremism flourished. Russia itself was a victim of terrorist attacks emanating from its 'near abroad' notably Chechenya.

As the countries that broke away from the USSR tried to stabilise, Moscow could pull the strings of destabilisation, provoking separatist movements, controlling migration for work in Russia, threatening to stir up trouble or send in the troops if its neighbours did not comply and cooperate. As Russia became more stable it developed sophisticated strategies to curb the tendencies of these countries to turn towards Europe and NATO. When Azerbaijan developed its oil resources and made direct links with Europe, Russia encouraged its pro-Russian neighbour Armenia to wage war over the disputed territory of Nagorno Karabakh. Russia used control of oil pipelines through Armenia to manage the situation in its own interests. When Georgia proposed an alternative pipeline, Russia stirred up trouble along its path and made it clear that it could stop the pipeline any time it wished. Although the period of active conflicts lasted only a few years, none of them was resolved. In each case dismembered states and huge displaced populations left uncertainty and fear because in each case the war might resume at any time. A recent report by Crisis

---

[192] See Vaux (2001) Chapter Seven

Group predicts that the war between Azerbaijan and Armenia over the disputed territory of Nagorno-Karabakh is about to resume.[193] Meanwhile for nearly twenty years hundreds of thousands of people have lived in camps, displaced during the war in the 1990s and unable to go home or start a new life, held as pawns for when it might prove convenient to restart the war.

In Georgia also around a quarter of a million people are still displaced from their homes in Abkhazia and South Ossetia.[194] Immediately after the collapse of the USSR, the Georgian President Gamsakhurdia declared independence for Georgia but in doing so coined the patriotic-sounding slogan 'Georgia for the Georgians'. This may have meant 'not for the Russians' but this was interpreted as a threat by all those in Georgia who were not ethnic Georgians, especially the Abkhaz and South Ossetian people living in the northern territories adjacent to Russia. Fearing that they would be oppressed by the 'Georgians', and given assurances of support from Russia, the Abkhaz and South Ossetian peoples seceded. With Russian help they were successful in repulsing Georgian efforts to recapture these territories but could not achieve recognition by the UN.

Having fought for 'independence' they found they had little choice but to be dependent on Russian protection and control, in effect becoming part of the Russian Federation. But Russia did not want them to flourish so much that they might ever make a claim to full independence. Russia blocked their efforts to secure international recognition and fielded a 'peacekeeping force' ostensibly to monitor the supposed peace agreement in the breakaway territories but in reality as an army of occupation.

Similarly, Russia took advantage of the war between Armenia and Azerbaijan to strengthen its military presence in Armenia, adjacent to its long-time regional rival Turkey. These measures gave Russia the chance to reassert its military power in the southern Caucasus region and limit the advance of EU and NATO influence. It also opened the

---

[193] Nagorno-Karabakh's Gathering War Clouds, Crisis Group Report June 2017 https://www.crisisgroup.org/europe-central-asia/caucasus/nagorno-karabakh-azerbaijan

194 Vaux, T (2003) Strategic Conflict Assessment, Georgia http://www.human-security.org.uk/downloads/GeorgiaSCA.pdf

way for further expansion, including a return to influence in Eastern Europe and finally into Syria, taking advantage of the civil war. In all these cases, Russia had an interest in perpetuating weak states that were beholden to Russia.

Western aid agencies took on the task of dealing with the humanitarian consequences of conflict in the Southern Caucasus. Oxfam and others provided help, using finance from Western governments, but there were no possible solutions to these humanitarian needs – or rather the Russian interest would not allow a peaceful solution. Gradually aid agencies had to withdraw and leave national governments to do the best they could.

Russia created a political stalemate which it could continue to control. Governments in the region could do very little because of the explosion of nationalist sentiment that followed independence. Exiles from the secessionist territories of Georgia, especially from Abkhazia, opposed any peace settlement short of complete reassertion of sovereignty. With Russian forces now preventing any Georgian counter-attack (or so it seemed), this led to a situation in which displaced people could neither return to their homes in the breakaway territories nor find new homes because the government's stated claim was that it would recover the lost territories.

One of the characteristics of secessionist territories is that they operate outside the law and so become a focus for smugglers who have no interest in stable governments and uncorrupted states. The breakaway territories became havens for smuggling cheap oil and cigarettes from Russia which were traded into Georgia across a border that had to remain porous because, from the Georgian government perspective, the new territories did not exist. This trade enabled leaders in the secessionist territories to become rich and strengthened their resolve not to negotiate. Worse still, Georgian politicians also began to benefit from smuggling and lost the determination to resolve the underlying problem. Huge inequalities emerged. Politicians made a fortune out of smuggling, the people directly affected by the wars became poorer and poorer while the majority of the population could not advance as a nation economically or politically.

Georgian politicians turned for help towards the EU and NATO and received expressions of sympathy but no offers of military assistance. Frustration in Georgia and increasing public dissatisfaction with corruption linked to smuggling led eventually to a change in government. Under President Saakashvili there was less corruption but the pressure from nationalists continued and eventually persuaded the President to respond intemperately to Russian provocations. A Georgian attempt to recapture South Ossetia by force was easily repulsed by Russian-backed forces. These forces then entered Georgia and imposed a humiliating climb- down by the President. Russia emerged in complete control.

A similar scenario was played out following the collapse of the USSR in Moldova, adjacent to Ukraine, where the pro-Russian northern territory called Transdniestria seceded and developed a profitable industry smuggling cigarettes, oil and weapons from Ukraine and Russia. The political authorities in Moldova benefited from this trade and allowed the situation to continue. They made a fortune and did nothing to help the thousands of people displaced by the secession of Transdniestria. Once again aid agencies stepped in to help with the consequences. In the hope that Moldova might one day join the EU, development assistance was provided but Russia's stranglehold on trade and the corrupting effect of smuggling undermined the economy and Moldova has become by far the poorest country in Europe. Its poverty has disqualified it as a potential member of the EU. Once again Russia has achieved its aims.

Western efforts to promote peace-building between the peoples in the separate entities met with little success, not because ethnic hatreds were insurmountable but because Russia ensured that these efforts could not succeed. In Georgia, local peace-building was expected to support diplomatic discussions being held sporadically in Minsk. With support from the UK government, civil society organisations were brought together from Georgia, South Ossetia and Abkhazia to discuss issues of common interest but the Minsk process went nowhere and so there was nothing for civil society groups to work on.

By the end of the 1990s aid managers, especially in DFID, recognised that the only possible way forward was much less direct. They turned towards developing civil society and democratic governance in each entity separately with the tacit aim of limiting the influence of nationalists who still promoted violence. Research from the Balkans had given a strong indication that this would be more effective than conventional attempts at peace-building. After the NATO intervention in Kosovo in 1999 and the end of Serbian control, huge budgets had been allocated for peace-building. This often took the form of cultural and sporting events to bring together the victorious Kosovars and the remaining Serb minority in Kosovo. CDA found that the results of were superficial and ultimately pointless.[195] People could be tempted to attend such events and might behave in a friendly manner towards each other but there was no significant change in attitudes. Back at home, the pressure from more warlike and antagonistic elements was too strong. Efforts to promote peace were likely to be portrayed as treacherous and anti-national.

Instead the study found that work to develop civil society within each community separately had a much more significant impact. It enabled people who wanted peace to develop the skills and organisations through which they could limit extremism. Democracy within each community could contribute to peace by promoting moderate voices. Transparency and accountability were much more effective than conventional 'peace-building'.

In Moldova, Georgia and other post-Soviet countries, DFID turned towards general processes for the development of civil society rather than dialogue between opposing sides. Somewhat belatedly this reflected George Soros' analysis of the situation in post-Soviet Europe and his work through the Open Society Institute.[196] The big advantage for George Soros was that he was independent of Western political influence. He used his own money. Whatever DFID or the UK Foreign Office did provoked a suspicion from the Russians that it was not about poverty reduction or good governance but about drawing countries into the ambit of Europe and NATO (which it was). Accordingly even the people involved in these exercises were a little suspicious of the ulterior political motive and the aid effort did not trigger new dynamism in civil society. People did what they were paid to do.

Soros worked in a different way, simply supporting activists across the region rather than designing programmes. Initially he supplied basic equipment such as laptops and photocopiers and later offered communications and research support for citizen activism. Soros had

---

[195] CDA Collaborative Learning Projects (2006) The organisation was created by Mary B Anderson of 'Do No Harm' fame
[196] Soros (1998)

little time for aid agencies as I found when I visited him in London around 1995 in order to find out whether he might be willing to support Oxfam's work in the region.

The Open Society Institute (and affiliates) became a central focus for critiques of governance in many countries across the region. Its relentless focus on transparency and accountability to the people was a persistent limitation to those governments that were inclined towards autocracy and secrecy. The Institute directly challenged the political culture that had developed under the USSR, Yugoslavia and other Communist countries. Reactions have become more extreme in the last few years. Russia expelled the Soros affiliate in 2015. Belarus and Uzbekistan have also banned his organisations. In Macedonia a 'Stop George Soros' campaign was launched by embattled politicians. Soros continues to make news across the region (as in the recent case of Hungary's efforts to close the Central European University established by Soros in Budapest. By contrast the work of aid agencies has been abandoned and forgotten.

Soros's work could be described as focused on 'freedom from fear'. For many people living in former Communist states there was a fear that the old systems of autocratic governance, secret police and repression of civil society would re-emerge. These fears were increased when nationalist forms of government emerged, using the old techniques of generating fears of foreign influence as a deliberate tool for control. For those in the near abroad there was the added fear arising from the aftermath of unresolved conflicts. They could go back to war at any time. There was also the fear of Russian meddling. Although Western aid could be used in a general sense to support civil society, this could add to the suspicions of governments that foreign interests were involved, as indeed they were. This made them susceptible to government pressure and also pressure from within the West not to upset diplomatic relations, whereas Soros could not be accused of representing any state. Indeed, ever since Soros denounced George W Bush over the Iraq war, he has been a target of Republican attack including a recent letter from secretary of state Rex Tillerson criticising USAID for collaborating with the Soros organisation in Macedonia (the Open Society Foundation).[197]

---

[197]   *Public Enemy Number 1*, The Economist May 20th 2017

The problem with Western aid is that it reflects Western political interests and preconceptions. With its rubric of good governance, it often prejudged what the people themselves might want to do. Soros' approach was different because it was simply empowering citizens in relation to their governments but leaving them entirely free to develop a focus and plan of action. The Open Society Institute in each country acted independently of any central control. Its reports became one of the very best sources of information about the region.

The point to be emphasised here is that the aid system could not have done what Soros did. It was tied into projects that made it dependent on national governments and Western donors. Here and there it might offer support to citizen activists but the whole point of citizen activism is that it arises from the wishes and interests of the people. The aid system today cannot cope with bottom-up activism. It neither has the independence nor the timescale.

The Open Society Institute has continued to work in support of citizen activism in East Europe and the Former Soviet Union since the 1990s. Its approach has evolved but not changed. It studiously avoids being aligned with any political party. Its experience mirrors Ela Bhatt's 'three levels' of obstacles to poverty reduction in India as presented in the previous Chapter. SEWA's experience shows that it is not difficult for working women to save money, organise and overcome immediate problems but their progress is limited when they come up against traders who exploit their hidden influence on government. Here Soros goes a step further by exposing these influences (the Open Society) and he supports organisations that challenge power at the national level.

SEWA could not reach to the national level, firstly because the system at that level was controlled by elite interests and secondly because SEWA was vulnerable to counter-measures by government. This was demonstrated in 2002 when, having joined with the State government in a large development project after the earthquake, SEWA was caught in a dilemma when the State Government failed to control 'communal riots'. SEWA leaders were well aware that top politicians had allowed the 'riots' (read pogroms) to continue unchecked for several days but the members decided that the union should not be put at risk. SEWA's criticisms were muted but even so the State Government abruptly closed the development project leaving SEWA with large debts.

This reflects the dilemma of any organisation, including aid agencies, that try to combine citizen activism with other types of work. In the last resort they keep silent at crucial moments because they need to deliver aid, run projects and pay their staff. The Soros approach is particularly appropriate in Eastern Europe and the Former Soviet Union because there is no real need to run the more conventional projects aimed at poverty reduction. Countries have recovered sufficiently from the collapse of 1990 to ensure minimum living standards. People displaced by earlier wars are kept alive, at least, by their governments.

A recent analysis by the Crisis Group of the situation in Ukraine concluded that the best way to resolve the problems and limit Russian expansion was to improve the transparency and accountability of the Ukraine government in Kiev. [198] According to this report, Russian advances have been held back only because there was insufficient support even from pro- Russian groups in other parts of Ukraine. However, the popularity of the Kiev government is deeply marred by corruption and unless this is challenged from within Ukraine, the local population may decide not to support Kiev and allow further Russian advances.

In some parts of the world, the power of dictators cannot be challenged even by brave and independent organisations such as the Open Society Institute. This is typically the case in some Middle Eastern countries that happen to be dominated by Islam as their main religion. The region is also characterized by national borders, laid down after World War I, that do not correspond to ethnic and religious identities. The combination of factors has led to war and war has created the conditions for terrorism to arise.

My concern here is to argue that terrorism arises from fear rather than poverty. At the simplest level, terrorists are not usually drawn from the ranks of the very poor except in cases where they are instruments of others from more elite sections of society. Studies of terrorists, such as one of suicide bombers, bear this out- *'None of the suicide bombers —they ranged in age from 18 to 38 —conform to the typical profile of the suicidal personality. None of them were uneducated,*

---

[198]  Crisis Group Briefing: *Ukraine —military deadlock, political crisis* December 2016 https://www.crisisgroup.org/europe-central-asia/eastern-europe/ ukraine/b85-ukraine-military-deadlock- political-crisis

*desperately poor, simple-minded, or depressed. Many were middle class and held paying jobs. Two were millionaires.'[199]*

For example, the terrorist attacks in Dacca in Bangladesh in 2016 were carried out by students from wealthy and influential families who, as in so many cases of terrorism, appear to have had no idea that their sons had been radicalised. Nevertheless, ever since 9/11 I have come under pressure when conducting conflict analyses to examine a possible link between Islam, poverty and violence. The assumption appears to be that very poor Muslims are likely to turn to terrorism and therefore should be under special surveillance.

In the dozen or so conflict studies I have conducted directly for DFID[200] I found no case in which poverty has a direct causal relationship to terrorism (or violent conflict). For example, a study in Pakistan conducted for DFID in 2008 found that-*'The relationship between poverty and conflict is complex. Underlying poverty, especially in the form of youth unemployment, probably contributes to instability in a general sense but political exclusion is probably the stronger driver of instability.'* [201] Similarly the study concluded that- *'It is tempting to see terrorism as springing from poverty and illiteracy. But, however undesirable these are, they are not the root causes of political violence. Many terrorists are of middle-class or privileged origins and well educated and those who support them are likely to be more educated than their fellow citizens.'*[202]

As in conflict studies in many other countries, unemployment was indicated as an underlying cause of grievance among poor people but not as a direct driver of conflict. Extreme poverty is associated with a very high degree of vulnerability and risk. Poor people are reluctant to take on the further risk of engagement with terrorism and violence. At the extreme level of poverty, survival becomes an all-consuming task.

The causes of violence and terrorism are more likely to be found in factors relating to inequality and exclusion and this is where they have to be addressed. In Pakistan, as my 2008 study showed, political circumstances rather than poverty have created the conditions for

---

[199] Ibid

[200] Mostly using the Strategic Conflict Assessment method —see DFID (2002)

[201] Unfortunately the full report on this 2008 study contains sensitive information cannot be published

[202] Elsworthy and Rifkind (undated) Kindle

violence and terrorism. For decades Pakistan has suffered from alternating cycles of democracy and military rule. Politics in Pakistan suffers the same problems of patronage and elite rivalry that have already been described in relation to other states. The democratic stage of the cycle degenerates into political wrangling and neglect of governance, causing widespread frustration opening the way for a military takeover which briefly ensures stability but then fails to address issues of governance and development and becomes embroiled in fruitless and destructive internal conflicts. In recent years support for Pakistan as part of the Global War on Terror has made it more difficult to make shifts in the cycle or tackle problems peacefully than it was before.

Instead of, in a sense, blaming poor people for violence and terrorism, it may be better to look at the wider national and international political dimensions. According to a report by the Independent Human Rights Commission of Pakistan the security situation worsened because of military activities along the Afghanistan border carried out in Pakistan's role as an ally of the West in the Global War on Terror-'*Military action in Balochistan and the Waziristan agency cost grave loss of life. Still more disturbing was the callousness with which citizens were made the targets of bombs, missiles and bullets used against them by the armed forces. Such actions were generally justified on the grounds of national security interests and the war on terror.*'

Poverty is not a significant factor in all this. Nor does violence alone turn people towards terrorism. It appears that the problems arise from a combination of factors including loss of identity and sense of injustice. The violence by the army in Balochistan and Waziristan undermined the power of tribal leaders and left them disaffected. Traditional social structures began to disintegrate. This allowed radical extremist movements, notably those that had already developed in Kashmir, to extend their influence —into the Swat Valley, for example.

Counter-attacks by the military displaced large numbers of people into camps in the Peshawar area where they could easily be radicalized. The spread of weapons and explosives from Afghanistan provided ready means for further violence. It is not hard to see how extremism could spread and it is unnecessary to blame poverty or poor people. On the contrary the fault lies with political leaders both national and international. The Pakistan study notes that- '*Western military force has tended to worsen Pakistan's internal problems. National pride has been wounded by the country's association with the USA, which is widely perceived as biased against Islam.*' In other words, the Global War on Terror itself can be viewed as the source of terrorism.

The Pakistan report for DFID ended with an argument that although poverty reduction was desirable it was desirable for itself rather than as a means to reduce violence. If DFID wanted to reduce violence and terrorism in general then it would be better to look towards the UK's political involvements and in particular the unquestioning Western support for the military regime. The study was abruptly terminated.

The mechanism by which political exclusion in Pakistan turns towards terrorism is religion. My 2008 study in Pakistan concluded that- *'Nationalists and tribal leaders have found it increasingly difficult to negotiate with the state, especially after the Global War on Terror. Politicians remain clamped within the narrow confines of patronage systems. Those that do not win a seat in government do not take up responsible roles in opposition but plot to discredit their political rivals. All this opens the way for extremism, and in Pakistan extremism is most easily focused around religion.'*

Religion can link poverty to terrorism but this is not a spontaneous process but one that is cultivated by extremist religious leaders. The means of exerting influence over poor people is partly through sermons and partly through Koranic schools. In the absence of good government schools, poor people send their boys to *madrassa* (Islamic) schools and it is here that they are manipulated towards violence and terrorism. Among the poorest families a common motive for sending their boys to *madrassas* is simply that they will get something to eat. The schools vary in their range of studies but generally focus on rote learning of the Koran. This provides only very limited chances of employment, and then only in religious establishments. In that way, Koranic schools tend to produce frustration but it is the frustration of thwarted intelligence rather than the angry reaction of poverty.

Despite the Koran's injunction for each person to take responsibility for their own life, this type of teaching suppresses questioning and encourages blind loyalty to religious leaders. Such leaders select the statements from the Koran that suit their purposes, including harsh versions of Sharia Law, hatred of other religions and the glories of *jihad.*[203] Pakistan's troubled political history has encouraged religious

---

[203] In the Koran jihad mainly refers to a process of cleansing the soul. See Jalil (2014)

extremism and this has been exploited by wealthy Islamists from Saudi Arabia and elsewhere.

Unfortunately, Western prejudices and misunderstandings have not only led to an association of terrorism with poverty but also a direct link to Islam as if Islam made terrorism inevitable. Even though there are many other forms of terrorism affecting the West (e.g. fanatics with easy access to guns, neo-Nazis etc), in most cases Islam is the immediate suspect and this is creating a vicious cycle in which Muslim people are angered by the way they are treated and, in extreme cases, turn towards violence.

In my studies for DFID and other agencies after 9/11 there was constant pressure to check out the role of Muslims as possible causes of violence. In Nepal and Mozambique, for example, I was asked to give particular attention to this issue even though the Muslim populations are very small and have no significant relevance in relation to conflict. Islam is not in a good position to defend itself because it has no central authority or spokesperson and it is easy enough to find someone with extreme views who purports to speak for all Muslims. The right of each person to interpret the Koran in their own way is a fundamental tenet of Islam and so Muslim people are unwilling to criticise what others are saying or refute the most egregious assumptions being made by non-Muslims.

Islam is also vulnerable to misinterpretation because the Koran was written at a time of considerable violence and contains verses that are easily open to the charge that it sanctions violence. It was progressive in relation to the extremely limited cultural confines of its time and region of origin but can easily appear conservative in relation to modern times, especially in the West. The Koran is very clear in its opposition to aggression and only sanctions the use of violence for defence but some Muslims have picked out the few verses that appear to contradict this view. The biggest misfortune for Islam is that it happens to be the dominant religion in some of the world's most repressive dictatorships, especially in the Middle East, and it is these countries that attract attention rather than the much more moderate forms of Islam practiced in Bangladesh and Indonesia, for example.

The reasons for the spread of dictatorships in the Middle East owe a great deal to post- imperial settlements that have created unrealistic borders and unstable countries. The existence of huge oil reserves in many Islamic countries of the Middle East has made the West unusually tolerant of human rights issues. Many of the dictators maintain power by force with Western backing. But instead of blaming the imperial past or the dictators or arms sales, the West blames Islam. Desperation and a sense that the West plays a hypocritical role in the region, may prompt some people to turn to terrorism.[204]

This general prejudice has opened the way for a more specific prejudice that directly affects the aid system. This is the view that Islam leads to the oppression of women. A glance towards Bangladesh and Indonesia would show that this is not a reasonable proposition but it has been the source of huge tension among aid workers, especially in Afghanistan. In reality, the limited expression of women's rights in Afghanistan has much more to do with the historical and cultural context than it does with Islam. But by characterising it as an issue relating to Islam the West has reduced the likelihood that recent advances will be sustained.

Just before the 9/11 event, I visited Afghanistan to evaluate a livelihoods project for the international charity, CARE.[205] The custom of the time was for aid workers to travel into Afghanistan by road from Pakistan and wear Afghan clothes, not so much as a disguise but as a form of respect for local custom and to avoid being provocative either to the Pakistan border guards or to the Taliban who then held power in Kabul. While driving across the city in a local taxi, a Talib ('Islamic scholar' but probably only a student of a *madrassa*) stopped the car and reached inside to test the beard of the driver. If hair showed through his fist the driver would be allowed to pass. Otherwise he might face chastisement of some kind. The Talib looked doubtful at the tiny amount of hair showing at the end of his fingers but was about to let the driver go. Then he looked at me and noticeably hesitated. I guessed that he had no orders what to do about foreigners.

For a moment he looked perplexed but then he noticed a cassette tape in the player. He reached across the driver, pulled it out and unravelled the tape from inside the cassette before throwing it to the ground. All tapes and all forms of music were banned. As we drove on the driver spat out of the window. 'Idiot' he said. It made me realise that the fanatical form of Islam espoused by many of the Taliban was not at

---

[204] See Jalil (2014) notably Chapter Eight
[205] For CARE

all acceptable to ordinary people. They would not defend the Taliban's ban on short beards and tape recordings but it is easy to imagine that if the West asserted a right to short beards and tape recordings, the Taliban might cite verses from the Koran that turned the issue into a religious one. Even moderate and sceptical Afghans such as my driver might then come to the defence of the Taliban.

'Mission creep' is the root of all evil as far as the Global War on Terror is concerned. The Western military intervention after 9/11 was intended to kill or capture Osama Bin Laden and close down Al Qaeda but the Taliban (an amorphous collection of nationalists and Islamists) had acted as his hosts and felt obliged to honour a commitment that is very fundamental to the Afghan culture. When US forces began to target the Taliban as well as Al Qaeda (which consisted mostly of foreigners) the Taliban presented themselves as defenders of both Afghanistan and Islam. From a war on terror the mission quickly became a war on Afghanistan and on Islam.

Western forces and spokespersons took far too little care to lessen this risk and made the situation unnecessarily worse.[206] One of the most sensitive issues in Afghanistan was (and remains) the status and role of women. This had been a cause of difficulty in Western relationships with Afghanistan for many years. I had come across this sensitivity in 1989 when I visited Afghanistan at the time when the USA was using and developing the *mujahaddin* in a proxy war against the Russian-backed regime based in Kabul. There was no possibility of air travel and travel into Afghanistan from Pakistan was dangerous because of the threat of Russian airstrikes. Vehicles moved slowly along tracks that were little more than heaps of stones, stopping at least five times a day for prayers. At that time the West was all in favour of Islam because it provided a motive for opposition to the godless Russian communists.

It was very unusual to see a woman and I never spoke with a woman during the entire visit. A woman who ventured out of her house would be covered at least in a headscarf but even so I was warned not to look in her direction. On arrival at a house the men-folk (only) assembled in the guest quarters but food was served by

---

[206] A similar mistake had been made by the British in their dealings with Afghanistan in the nineteenth century with fateful results The story of the Afghan Wars of 1839-42 is wonderfully told in Dalrymple (2013)

boys and men only. Women never made an appearance. I came to understand that these customs were particularly rigid in Pushtun areas. They had evolved over centuries of instability and conflict and had little to do with Islam except that Islamic customs had evolved in a similar context. As described by Ahmed Rashid- *'Situated on the crossroads between Iran and India, Central Asia and South Asia,, and Central Asia and the Middle East, Afghanistan has been a gateway for invaders since the earliest Aryan invasions from Central Asia into the Indian subcontinent more than six thousand years ago.'* [207] The constant threat of violence and use of rape as a strategy to undermine opponents led to heavy restrictions on the role of women. These were reinforced during the period of the US-backed *mujahaddin* and even more so during the following years when anarchy and civil war prevailed.[208] The main factor affecting the role of women was not Islam but security —and US interventions had made matters worse.

The south of the country had developed a cultural code known as Pashtunwali[209] in which women were romanticised. Women could be the subject of elaborate love poems but remained confined within their huge fortified compounds. All this had very little to do with Islam.

During the 1990s my role with Oxfam included oversight of emergency activities in Afghanistan.[210] The Russians had departed after heavy losses and Kabul was under the control of the Taliban which had stepped forward to stop the spread of violence by warlords. There was a crisis because Oxfam had taken responsibility for a project to rebuild one of the main installations providing water to the city. It had been badly neglected during the time of the warlords and the Taliban had no capacity or inclination to undertake its reconstruction. Lack of clean water was the cause of extensive disease and deaths in Kabul, especially from diarrhoea. The work was 'life-saving' and had been put forward as an emergency project.

Oxfam's local representative insisted that women should be consulted about the project both as a matter of principle and also because women would be the main collectors and users of water.

---

[207]  Rashid (2008) p6

[208]  Povey (2004) p173

[209]  Pashtuns are the largest single tribal group in Afghanistan.

[210]  This experience is described in more detail in Vaux (2001) Chapter Five

Under Taliban rule, men were not permitted to interview women. Oxfam wanted to employ female staff for this purpose and as a matter of principle. The Taliban refused without giving a reason and Oxfam stopped work on the project. Oxfam went so far as to discourage any other agency from taking it up because this would reduce leverage on the Taliban to take a more flexible approach towards women. To cut the story short, the water supply project was never started.

This caused some controversy within Oxfam. An external review pointed out that lack of clean water from this project would have led to around 1,800 cases of severe diarrhoea per year and a considerable number (perhaps hundreds) of deaths. The review questioned the wisdom of trying to influence an organisation such as the Taliban which had never shown any sense of responsibility for providing services. The issue was particularly difficult for Oxfam because at that time there was an influential lobby at the HQ in Oxford seeking to make gender rights and the representation of women a much higher priority. The Afghanistan water supply had become a test case. Managers refused to step down and the matter was left unresolved.[211]

The reasons for the Taliban's position are not clear but might be as much based on Pashtunwali as on Islam. Arguably a way forward could have been found by focusing on the safety and security (in the current context) of the women involved rather than on the precepts of women's rights, Pashtunwali and Islam. Instead the dispute became a confrontation in which the Taliban may have perceived that Pashtunwali and Islam were being challenged and tested. On Oxfam's side the issue was perceived as one of women's rights. There was never going to be agreement.

When I visited Afghanistan again in 2001, I came across a way of working with women that was acceptable even to the Taliban. The provision of assistance to widows is explicitly encouraged in the Koran. At the time the Koran was written and in many parts of the world today, widows can be identified as a group that often suffers extreme poverty. This arises because in many societies women lack property rights and, if they become widowed, they can be instantly ejected

---

[211] In 1999, a gender focus became well established in Oxfam but senior managers re-affirmed the principle that humanitarian needs should take precedence except in the most unusual circumstances —indicating that Oxfam did not ultimately uphold the earlier decision.

from their house and made destitute. Because of this cultural context, widows are, almost by definition, the poorest of the poor. For widows in Afghanistan almost the only option may be to turn to prostitution and this could result in punishments from the Taliban. By providing food and other assistance to a large group of the city's widows, CARE addressed a serious problem and did so within the cultural constraints of the time and place.

In Western aid circles, 'feeding widows' is likely to score very low in relation to more ambitious projects that involve cultural, social and political change. The ability of aid to focus on 'root causes' (in this case it might be the question of property rights) is a great strength of the aid system. But the assumption that developing and transforming other societies is a Western prerogative is under increasing question, especially because aid has been so closely tied to the Global War on Terror. Poor people and countries are increasingly suspicious about Western aid. Arguably the right to bring about transformative change has been lost because it has been so widely abused.

CARE's office in Kabul was run by a well-known Pushtun leader who was openly critical of the Taliban but knew how to handle them. By showing respect for culture and custom when needed, he was able to open the way for work with widows. But if the project with widows were to become the basis for wider change and social transformation, the aid agency would have to step back. There would be no sanction from Afghan culture or Islam. The lead would have to come from the women themselves and foreign funding would be more likely to limit progress rather than increase it.

Aid cannot flourish when it rides on the back of foreign invasion and cultural antagonism. After the US-led forces had secured control of the cities and some towns, an array of aid agencies arrived to do their work and, as the Russians had done before them in the 1980s, introduced the norms of Western culture including girls' education. One of the successes cited in the early years after the intervention was an increase in girls' education.[212] But it remains to be seen whether this momentum can be sustained. Can it escape the taint of association with a foreign invasion? The same was done by the Russians in the 1980s and no result was left behind.

---

[212] For an example see Gill (2016) p68

The current state of turbulence in Afghanistan is likely to continue because it is simply an episode in a much longer regional and superpower conflict. For decades Afghanistan was the the focus of 'The Great Game' between the empires of Britain and Russia. More recently it has been the focus for rivalry between Iran, Pakistan and India –all countries that are vastly more powerful. In particular, Pakistan has made it a top priority to limit India's influence in Afghanistan. This led to overt and covert support for the Taliban that has whipped up religious fanaticism and instigated terrorism.[213]

The relative success of aid in Nepal, described in Chapter Six, was possible because the rival regional superpowers, India and China had adopted a 'hands-off' approach for fear of provoking the other -Nepal was not significant in the Global War on Terror and so Western aid was relatively free of political constraints. The same can be said about aid during the Cold War, especially in Sub-Saharan Africa –it was relatively free from superpower involvement. But there is no 'hands-off' in the countries involved in the Global war on Terror. Aid has been squeezed out of an independent role. Unfortunately the countries of the Global War on Terror are so high profile and the international interest so strong that aid has perhaps been wiped out globally.

Poor people depend for their security on patronage systems and other forms of group identity. Very poor people may have little to offer in return except the ability to take up arms on behalf of the patron. But this is not to say that poverty leads to violence. It simply makes poverty a tool for those already committed to violence. By implication, the aid system should not be attacking poverty but attacking those who mobilise poor people around violent ends.

The theory that less poverty will lead to less violence may underpin recent increases in aid budgets but it represents a misunderstanding of poverty. In my studies it usually turns out that the Grievances correspond directly to the Greed and are reactions to it. The driving factor in conflict is the unchecked pursuit of elite interests. This is more likely to happen in weak states and other states may perceive an interest in perpetuating this weakness. The instability of patronage systems in much of Africa, for example, is exacerbated by regional neighbours, as in the recent case of South Sudan.

---

[213]  Rashid (2008)

If extreme poverty was reduced the price of recruiting very poor people into violent causes might go up but this would not prevent those processes from happening. The real drivers of conflict are very powerful indeed. Leaders controlling African states not only want to enjoy the benefits of power but fear serious repercussions if they lose power. Now that China has scored an 'easy win' against extreme poverty it may seem that the remaining problems will be solved on a similar timescale of a couple of decades. But this will not be the case. The remaining problems reflect poverty traps such as the one that the West has created with its Global War on Terror. African wars present another kind of poverty trap but the factor that makes them particularly persistent is their regional and international dimension. They cannot be resolved because of external interference.

Much of the extreme poverty in India results from the deliberate efforts of elite groups to undermine the bargaining power of poor people and to punish them for any assertion of rights. As described in the previous Chapter, women who organised themselves to earn more for their work were excluded from markets by wealthy traders. These traders were able to mobilise support from officials and ultimately attempts to secure permanent rights were counteracted by the influence of elite groups at the national level. Faced with an intractable situation, SEWA pursued a policy of self-reliance. Similarly, as recounted earlier, a group of landowners in Bihar blinded labourers who demanded higher wages. For decades the landowners were protected by politicians and only recently have processes of democratic change brought about improvements. This change did not come from below, or from the efforts of aid agencies, but from realignments of elite interests at the top. The persistence of extreme poverty in India, despite rapid economic growth, reflects the depth of the poverty trap.

The reason why the remaining problems of poverty will prove so difficult to overcome is that elite and powerful groups benefit from poverty. At the national level, regional and global powers prefer to have weak and impoverished allies that are dependent on them, rather than strong, independent and wealthy states. This particularly applies to states that are caught up in regional and superpower rivalries. It was the ultimate cause of many of Africa's 'tribal' wars over the last decades. It is the reason why Nepal stays poor and it is a reason why Afghanistan will never be stable and rich. Somalia and South Sudan are victims of regional rivalries in the Horn of Africa –and so on. Such high-level rivalries thrust some countries into perpetual poverty and within those countries some groups are caught in particularly weak positions, as for example the Bantu tribes of Somalia. In such cases, poverty is intractable and those of us concerned to eradicate it must turn away from 'root causes' and simply deal with the consequences.

The World Bank has pointed out that the remaining problems of extreme poverty are not limited to the obvious cases, notably India and Sub-Saharan Africa.[214] Poverty in other countries, not generally characterised as poor, can take extreme forms both because inequality creates poverty traps and because to an extent poverty may be regarded as relative to the general state of society. The $1 a day type of definition is useful as a starting point but i becoming less useful as poverty becomes focused in 'pockets' that may not show up in national statistics. Poverty of the persistent, intractable kind found in 'poverty traps' may also be regarded as a more serious focus for concern because it is unlikely to go away unless something radical is done –and yet the factors that create these traps are likely to be beyond the scope normally associated with aid.

---

[214]  World Bank (2016)

# CHAPTER ELEVEN

# WHERE HAVE WE GOT TO?

World Bank data show that the number of people experiencing extreme poverty has reduced by around half in the last three decades and is now well under a billion people. This progress is mainly attributable to the efforts of a single country, China, and to a lesser extent India. The countries that have received most aid do not demonstrate such progress and so we can conclude that the role of aid is marginal. Economic growth is a considerably bigger factor although it does not necessarily ensure that poor people benefit.

Leaving aside India's shameful persistence as home for a third of extremely poor people (268 million out of around 800 million in 2011), extreme poverty is now concentrated in Sub- Saharan Africa, which is home to more than half of them-[215] *'Sub- Saharan Africa is not actually going backwards. Its absolute poverty rate has fallen from 54% in 1990 to 41% in 2013. But because Africa's population is growing so quickly –by about 2.5% a year, compared with 1% for Asia- and because the poverty rate is declining only slowly, the number of poor Africans is higher than it was in the 1990s. With more destitute inhabitants than any other region, sub-Saharan Africa now drives the global poverty rate.'[216]*

In addition there is the issue of fear and insecurity which affects a similar or larger number of people, although the figures are less reliable. The challenge of measuring 'freedom from fear' has never been satisfactorily addressed. Estimates for numbers of people living in

---

[215] World Bank figures quoted in The Economist April 1st 2017 pp55-6
[216] Ibid

insecurity can be based on the total populations of fragile states, as in Paul Collier's book *The Bottom Billion.*[217] The World Bank Development Report 'Conflict, Security and Development' in 2011 includes a wider range of causes of insecurity and reaches a higher figure- *'One-and-a-half billion people live in areas affected by fragility, conflict, or large-scale, organized criminal violence.'* [218] But this is not all. As the Bank has recognised, poor people experience fear in countries that fall outside these definitions. The concept of Humanity implies that the insecurity and fear of the people of North Korea, living under a government that rules by fear, should be a matter for our global concern regardless of the poverty that also exists in that country. There is a danger that the attempt to measure insecurity could result in a reduction of moral scope, and in particular a focus on civil wars and criminal violence rather than the violence perpetrated by states.

Thirdly there is the trend detected by the World Bank and others that increasing inequality is creating conditions for people even in richer countries that could be described as extreme poverty even though they are not defined by an income of $1-2 dollars a day.

Over the years since World War II the aid system has been the main focus for response to problems of global poverty but the aid system has grown in scale but reduced in usefulness. It is now simply an arm of Western governments and serves its own institutional purposes rather than the needs of poor people. Quite rightly, national governments say that it is time for them to take the lead and the responsibility. Although the 2005 Paris Agreement can be seen simply as a way to leverage resources that national governments can do with as they wish, it is the only viable way forward. The buck has got to stop with the leaders of poor countries. Increasing the aid budgets simply increases the problems of patronage, undermining local organisations and taking away responsibility from national governments.

It is tempting to step back and wait for poor nations to take up their responsibilities, take control of the UN and find ways to make the Security Council more effective. That is the right way forward and trends point in that direction. But the basis of my concern over the last forty years has been the concept of Humanity and it does not go

---

[217]  Collier(2007)

[218]  World Bank (2011) Overview p1

away. I have become more conscious that what concerns me is not the poverty and distress of distant people but the fact that my own country and lifestyle contribute to it. That is where the focus should now shift and it makes me think that the behaviour of our own government and society is what we are responsible for rather than poverty and distress globally.

The problem is that the dependence of the aid system on our government and the prejudices of our society make it unable to address this problem. Its criticisms of arms sales to Saudi Arabia are muted by the need to get government grants. Its determination to stop wars such as in South Sudan and Syria is diluted by the desire to run big aid programmes, obtain access to difficult places and generally become bigger than the next agency. In the next steps forward the aid industry is more likely to be a hindrance than a help.

Turning to more practical steps, it is important to distinguish our concerns relating to extreme poverty and insecurity from the concerns of those who have made aid an instrument for other purposes, notably Western security, trading interests and general 'soft diplomacy'. Those objectives will continue to be served anyway. The problem is that aid has been co-opted to support them and this has discredited the core of the system including even the basic objective of eradicating extreme poverty. We should keep sight of that simple aim and then ask what needs to be done without assuming that aid is the answer.

A clear conclusion arising from this book is the need for a global welfare system that guarantees a minimum income for poor people and possibly for everyone. Aid might have a very modest role in supporting this but it is up to national governments to take the lead and aid to support what they choose to do. Secondly there is a need to revive the Right to Protect (R2P) concept and reshape global arrangements to ensure that extreme poverty and human suffering are treated seriously rather than as adjuncts of national policy. Russia may always have shown cruel disregard for the people affected by its obsession with controlling the 'near abroad' but this does not mean that other nations should follow the same track. On the contrary they should unite to limit and shame Russia and any other country that disregards Humanity.

Poverty in general is not a matter for acute moral concern nor does it matter that one country bullies another. Some people are poorer than others and by living uncluttered lives without the plague of endless choices they may be quite happy. Bullying among nations is part of the global order, just as it is in the playground. The point at which an outsider feels drawn to think and respond is when these behaviours cause distress. This triggers a set of questions. How am I involved? What influence do I have? This may take us down the track that Florence Nightingale, Eglantyne Jebb and Edith Pye followed when, before founding big institutions they spoke truth to power.

The international charities still purport to speak truth to power but it is a distorted truth, told with an eye to government grants, public appeals and institutional growth. They have too much baggage. Instead the lead is now being being taken by light-footed entrepreneurs in the social media and campaigning organisations that have no institutional interests. In so far as the international charities try to move in the same sphere, they confuse and corrupt it.

## Human Security

We need to rethink the notion of poverty and expand it into Human Security, recognising that vulnerability and violence are an integral part of poverty and a significant reason for our concern. Although this is an extremely valid and useful concept it has suffered from abuse. It first came into the consciousness of mainstream aid agencies through the 1994 UN Human Development Report[219] which noted that 'security' has *'for too long been interpreted narrowly: as security of territory from external aggression, or as protection of national interests in foreign policy, or as global security from a nuclear holocaust. It has been related more to nation states than to people.'*[220] The UN set up a Commission on Human Security which published its report in 2003[221] and put forward the notion that it could be expressed as the achievement of 'freedom from want' and 'freedom from fear'.

To make matters worse, the concept of Human Security has been muddled up with the interests of institutions and Western donors. Firstly, UN Secretary-General Kofi Annan extended the notion further by adding 'freedom to live in dignity' which was even more difficult to measure than 'freedom from fear' and implied a considerable widening

---

[219] This report is credited to Pakistani Foreign Minister Mahbub ul Haq working in association with Amartya Sen

[220] Op cit

[221] Commission on Human Security (2003)

of the concept. Secondly different UN organisations institutionalised the concept of Human Security into their own mandate. Each one developed its own frameworks and principles and this caused confusion and rivalry across the UN.[222] Thirdly, donors muddled the term with their own concerns about Western Security. In Canada, Human Security was co-opted as an opportunity to extend the notion of Western security to local level.[223]

A UN Trust Fund for Human Security was set up following the World Summit in 2005 but it has too many purposes, including peace-building in conflict situations, climate change and climate-related hazards and sudden shocks that might lead to insecurity such as the global spike in food prices and the global financial crisis.[224] Secretary-Generals have continued to argue that the Fund can address threats that have both local and global dimensions but the Fund has lacked support and the concept itself lost traction especially after the Global War on Terror and the co-option of the security agenda around Western interests. It is still a useful way of looking at the issues but difficult to apply in practice.

Although the concept of Human Security enabled the UN to link its work on global security to human development, reflecting the terms of its Charter, the UN was never able to overcome the difficulty that these 'freedoms' can only be assessed subjectively. They depend on the way a person feels about their circumstances rather than a categorisation based on income, services etc. The implication was that only the people themselves could decide if they had achieved Human Security. In theory this would have put poor people in charge of the process for achieving Human Security globally but so far this implication has not been taken up. Perhaps it is time to do so. A way of doing so would be to ensure that whatever steps are taken by national governments to achieve Human Security, a system is in place to establish whether the

---

[222] Jolly, R and D B Ray (2006) *The Human Security Framework and National Human Development Reports: A Review of Experiences and Current Debates,* IDS, Sussex. See also Kaldor, M (2007)

[223] Maclean, S, D Black and T Shaw eds (2006) *A Decade of Human Security – global governance and new multilateralisms,* Ashgate

[224] Report of the Secretary General: Follow up to General Assembly resolution 64/291 on human security, April 2012

people are satisfied. This might be a functioning democratic system or opinion surveys or citizen activism to enable poor people to express their views. Otherwise we shall simply see a re-run of top-down aid processes in which poor people have things done for them rather than take control.

## A Recap of Aid History

The fact that the best conceptual basis for aid does not actually drive it is a telling point and reflects the reality that aid serves a range of different purposes. During the Cold War, aid was used to support allies and as a carrot to attract the people living in the enemy's client states. This led to a Golden Age for international charities because political biases and controls were limited. The West wanted to impress and the USSR did not join in the game. At that time aid agencies could claim a degree of neutrality in humanitarian operations and, while they relied on active public support, they could claim a degree of independence from government donors. But over time the agencies grew and their internal interests became paramount. Also, the global media became more focused on sensational events, limiting public involvement with disasters to huge, pointless binges. Competition within the media and among the aid agencies accelerated this process.

Meanwhile the Western ideology of the Cold War, already developing into neo-liberalism, took the dorm of Structural Adjustment Policies, an early version of the 'austerity' programmes of today. The effect was to smash patronage systems and open the way for violent conflict.

Then came the Global War on Terror and the co-option of aid around the Western security agenda. Economic growth driven by globalisation enabled some poorer countries (Bangladesh for example) to make significant improvements in human development and considerable inroads into extreme poverty. But the return of nationalism based on individual states now threatens globalisation and may slow down the development of states such as China that have been in the lead in eradicating extreme poverty. African growth is already starting to slow and the continent may prove to be exceptionally vulnerable to the new trends.[225] This does not bode well for the chances of eradicating

---

[225] *Clouds over a Continent,* The Economist June 3rd 2017 p48

extreme poverty. Concern for the poorest and most vulnerable people may seem a luxury as people all over the world struggle with increasing inequality. Everyone may come to regard themselves as poor.

Nationalism and the pre-eminence of national self-interest are not simply Western phenomena. Indeed, these phenomena in the West provoke counter-reactions in other countries and may cause a narrowing of national identity. The rise of Hindu nationalism in India is a case in point.

Aid as a means to reduce poverty was a concept that arose from public concern in the West especially when images of global poverty were unexpected and shocking. This coincided with the benign neglect of aid during the Cold War. But Western governments now use aid actively as a tool for their policies and this makes it a focus for suspicion among other states including those on which aid is focused. The negative effects of aid in bypassing national governments and NGOs are becoming more apparent and those governments and NGOs are becoming more vociferous in their criticism. The claim by aid agencies to make a direct link with the people is spurious and comes too late. It looks like an attempt to perpetuate their control. But national governments and NGOs already recognise aid as a threat and have decided to take back control.

There is nothing that aid agencies can do about this. There are no reforms that are fundamental enough to alter the current dynamics. The political economy of aid agencies is dominated by Western governments and their own interests. There is no sign that non-Western governments are willing to step forward and take control of the aid machinery. They are pursuing their own approaches outside the aid system, as Turkey has done in Somalia (Chapter Seven). Although agencies have formed international networks they are still managed and operated from a small group of Western countries and highly influenced by those countries.

There are other reasons to conclude that the time for aid has passed. The argument that current deficiencies can be overcome by a 'final push' with huge amounts of money (the Sachs-Bono thesis) makes no sense when we consider that aid has as much likelihood to do harm as to do good.[226] In particular aid flowing through the institutions that

---

[226] As shown by Deaton (2013) and others

have created poverty strengthens those institutions and allows them to continue to create exclusion and poverty. In extreme cases, such as in Rwanda before the genocide, aid leads to violence.[227]

Aid has not been successful in addressing political crises and wars. Indeed, aid has often provided an excuse for lack of political and military engagement as in the current cases of South Sudan and Syria. By exaggerating its own importance the aid system diverts attention away from the need to end unnecessary suffering by whatever means.

## Alternatives to Aid

Citizen activism has developed in poorer countries because of the availability of better communications, especially social media. But the aid system is likely to hinder rather than help. If it sets the agenda, it marginalises local organisations. If it fails to consult with local people, as in the case of the ban on rare minerals in DRC, it can damage their interests and inadvertently increase the level of violence. By employing local people and organisations it turns them into contractors, takes the initiative from them and commercializes the expression of Humanity.

The problem at the heart of these risks and deficiencies is that aid works top-down rather than bottom-up. The challenge is to reverse the polarity of power relations and this will not be done simply by more consultation with poor people, leaving the decision-making and control of resources in the hands of the aid system and its backers. In fact, the aid system cannot reform itself because that also would be a top-down process. The reform must come from below and need not be predicated on the assumption that the aid system will be a significant part of the answer. Poor people, NGOs and national governments will need to think up something better. The time when Humanity was the exclusive concern of Western people has passed. Humanity is everyone's concern and the way is open for initiatives to come from people within China, India, Sub-Saharan Africa and everywhere else.

SEWA, as described in Chapter Nine provides an example of the kind of initiative that is already happening and will eventually replace aid. There were just 730 SEWA members when I first visited them in 1978 but by 2013 there were more than a million SEWA members in

---

[227] Uvin (1998)

Gujarat alone. SEWA has now spread across India, reaching a total of two million members.[228] This is a wonderful example of eradicating poverty by a bottom-up process but SEWA recognises that it can only go so far before meeting obstacles in the form of resistance from elite interests. For SEWA to overcome the fundamental inequalities and injustices of India there will need to be wider citizen activism from Indian people within India and abroad. India may lack the fixed ideological commitment that has led to huge advances in China but is a relatively open society and can generate its own momentum for change. In the long run that may prove to be a better trajectory than China's which involved terrible suffering during the famine of 1958-61 when, in the name of the Great Leap Forward, Mao caused the death of tens of millions of poor people. It is not a case of the China model being better than the Indian model but that each country and each part of that country may need to take the lead in its own way.

Instead of the old rivalry between capitalism and communism there is now a rivalry between those who favour open societies as the way forward and those who rely on determined political groups that sacrifice transparency in order to have the freedom to take massive steps. Both systems have shown extremes of success and failure. Societies that are apparently open can allow populists to manipulate ordinary people and take advantage of the limited time that they can afford to give, or are willing to give, to governance. But modern technology tends to favour open societies and deeper forms of democracy. It may just take time.

For observers in Western countries attention may need to shift away from aid towards our relations with poorer countries, the effects of globalisation and the recent indications that Western national interests may come to take precedence. Those of us concerned with Humanity may have an influence on this issue even though we may no longer regard direct interference in poor communities as relevant or helpful.

### India's attempts to abolish poverty

The eradication of extreme poverty in China and India is related to their economic growth which has been considerably boosted by

---

[228] SEWA Annual Report 2013

globalisation. Both countries rely heavily on international trade. But the results of growth in terms of poverty reduction vary widely between different countries. Despite very high levels of economic growth, India's development results are not only worse than China's but worse than those of its poorer neighbours.[229] With an annual per capita growth rate of around 5% over the last two decades, India has become richer than many other South Asian countries but it has fallen behind in terms of human development indicators including child mortality and life expectancy.[230] India has become richer than Bangladesh (in per capita income) but the child mortality rate in Bangladesh, which was 24% higher than India's in 1990, became 24% lower by 2009.[231] India's record on child nutrition is particularly appalling and this reflects a lack of education and status among women. A key underlying reason why Bangladesh has moved forward is *'a pattern of sustained positive change in relation to gender relations'.*[232] Women's participation rate in the workforce in Bangladesh is almost twice as high as in India.[233]

Dreze and Sen find that- *'India has a unique cocktail of lethal divisions and disparities. Few countries have to contend with such extreme inequalities in so many dimensions, including large economic inequalities as well as major disparities of caste, class and gender.... India seems to be quite unique in terms of the centrality of caste hierarchies and their continuing hold on modern societies...'*[234]

India presents a challenge not only to those who believe that economic growth will eliminate poverty but also to those who believe that democracy and citizen action will achieve the result but in a different way. Poverty has been practically eliminated in some States, notably Kerala, but not in others, including Gujarat. There are huge differences between the performance of different States. At State level India presents some of the best development results in the world as

---

[229]   Dreze and Sen (2013)

[230]   Dreze, J and A Sen (2012) *Putting Growth in its place,* Outlook India www.outlookindia.com

[231]   Ibid

[232]   Dreze and Sen (2013) p59

[233]   Ibid

[234]   Op cit p213

well as some of the worst. The differences appear to lie in the different elements of the 'cocktail' that Dreze and Sen described above.

Independent India has avoided the mass deaths from famine that characterised China's path to development and also the colonial period[235] in India. Parliamentarians use the threat of famine as a way to castigate their opponents. But the problem of persistent hunger has remained. India has some of the worst figures for malnutrition in the world. Sen observes that- *'India's overall record in eliminating hunger and under-nutrition is quite terrible..... Judged in terms of the usual standards of retardation in weight for age, the proportion of undernourished children in Africa is 20 to 40 per cent, whereas the percentage of undernourished Indian children is a gigantic 40 to 60 per cent.'*[236]

Persistent hunger is particularly shocking because India holds gigantic food stocks- *'If all the sacks of grain were laid up in a row, this would stretch more than a million kilometres, taking us to the moon and back'.*[237] These food-stocks cost a great deal to maintain but do nothing to help poor people. Most of the food rots away before it can be used. The food mountain results from the practice (as in the USA) of buying crops from farmers at a guaranteed minimum price. This benefits rich farmers who dominate the political system and do not want food to be put back onto the market because it would depress the prices they might receive for the rest of their crop. Whereas the USA decided to send the food abroad as aid, India has no overseas food aid programme. In India the obvious solution was to distribute the food to poor people but lobbyists have used every possible argument to prevent this.[238]

The problem is certainly not lack of government programmes and pledges to help poor people. Programme after programme intended to abolish poverty[239] has been developed but the majority have failed or yielded only limited results. In the 1970s, when I first arrived in

---

235  Over four million people are thought to have died in the Bengal Famine of 1942-3 –see Sen (1981)

236  Sen (2005) p212

237  Ibid

238  Sen (2005) p213

239  The slogan 'Garibi Hatao' (abolish poverty) was one of Mrs Gandhi's favourites in the 1970s

India, the State of Maharashtra launched an Employment Guarantee Scheme (EGS) as a permanent guarantee of work at a minimum rate of pay (cash or food) in order to prevent starvation. This was extended to other States but it was applied patchily according to the political situation and availability of resources.

Faced with the likelihood of defeat in elections in 2004, the Congress Party made a manifesto commitment to introduce a national programme along the lines of the one in Maharashtra. Congress unexpectedly won the election and passed the National Rural Employment Guarantee Act in 2005. It became a legal requirement for the government to provide a hundred days of unskilled work on public works programmes in return for payment (at a very low rate). In theory this Act alone should have been enough to prevent hunger but it caused massive political controversy in India. Elite interests undermined the scheme by inserting a clause requiring suspension of programmes in the event of any corruption. Since corruption is practically impossible to avoid in the Indian context, the programme was curtailed in some areas. Dreze and Sen consider that it has been generally effective but would be further improved by better accountability to the people.[240] At the time of writing, the programme remains in the political balance, strongly opposed by powerful elite interests.

As with all such schemes there is a huge difference in implementation in different parts of the country. A study showed that even within the north (where pro-poor programmes face most opposition) performance was much better in Chhattisgarh State (which is generally one of the best in reducing poverty and vulnerability) than in Uttar Pradesh (one of the worst).[241] The difference appears to stem from differences in the political composition of the State Governments. The Chhattisgarh government includes strong pro-poor elements which make serious efforts to inform the people about their entitlements and encourage public pressure.

The government clamps down on corruption and, although it loses some support from elite groups it draws significant electoral support from poor people. But in Uttar Pradesh (UP) there has been

---

[240] Dreze and Sen (2013) pp199-205

[241] The Economist, November 17th 2012, *Development in India –a tale of two villages*

political instability for a long time and levels of corruption are much higher. The programme has been much less successful. It all depends on the mathematics of political support, the machinations of political manipulators and the strength of lobbies especially those supported by elite groups. It is not so much a matter of the power of civil society as the power of elite lobbies. This is because, in general, elite lobbies have much greater control over politicians than civil society does.

The stakes and risks for civil society can be very high. Activists in India who directly challenge the political establishment, such as novelist and environmental campaigner Arundhati Roy, can face a backlash from elite groups, using the courts and threats to protect their interests.[242] Civil society may be forced to team up with political parties and get drawn into violence.

## Cash Distribution

India's technological advances have opened up new possibilities both for greater public awareness about corruption and the role of elite lobbies and also for making programmes more effective. More than a billion fool-proof identity cards have been issued and these now offer an opportunity to make direct cash payments to huge numbers of very poor people. In 2012 the Government of India announced the launch of a cash transfer programme which would put $58 billion into the bank accounts of 90 million households.[243] This would make it the biggest programme of its kind in the world. The government has made plans to extend it further in the form of a Universal Basic Income (UBI) for every citizen.

This is extremely controversial and there are already signs of significant compromises with elite interests-'*There is now a proposed amount: 7,620 rupees ($113) a year. Equivalent to less than a month's pay at the minimum wage in a city, it is well short of what anyone might need to live a life of leisure. But it would cut absolute poverty from 22% to less than 0.5%.*'[244]

---

[242]   In February 2016 Roy was accused of criminal contempt of court for speaking out on behalf of a detainee https://www.theguardian.com/books/2016/feb/02/pankaj-mishra-arundhati-roy-hindu-nationalists-silence- writers-india

[243]   The Economist November 17th 2012 p58

[244]   The Economist February 4th 2017 pp66-7

Opposition to the plan is ostensibly focused on issues of cost but may really reflect a fear that poor people receiving the UBI would not be forced to work for a pittance or else starve, as happens widely today. Richer people are worried about losing their source of cheap and exploitable labour. Lobbyists are mobilising every possible argument against the proposal and the government already shows signs of back-tracking. Faced with the objection that India's billionaires would also benefit from the programme, the government is looking for ways to reduce coverage from 'universal' to 75%.[245] In response to a claim that the country cannot afford the scheme, the government proposes to pay for it by recycling funds from nearly a thousand existing welfare schemes which will be scrapped, including those that offer subsidised food, water, fertiliser and much else. There is a danger that the old programmes will be scrapped and then the new one is blocked or forgotten.

The Economist concludes hopefully that- *'The idea will not go away. It may seem folly in a country home to over a quarter of the world's truly poor to give people money for nothing. But it would be a swift, efficient way to make it home to far fewer of them.'*[246]

It is possible that discussion about UBI is simply talk intended to collect votes from poor people on the basis of promises and hopes. There are also some more genuine concerns. There is a danger in focusing only on incomes that services such as health and education will be neglected, although as shown in the Chapter on SEWA, even very poor people may prefer to use private services, if they have the money, rather than state-run services. The advantage of cash-in-hand is that each poor person can make up her own mind. But this could give government an excuse to reduce state services that are essential, such as emergency care.

SEWA's experience is that income from livelihoods is absolutely central to survival but poor people also want to reduce the fear of disasters of many different types. Over the years SEWA identified these risks and put in place social insurance mechanisms such as protection against loss of work through childbirth, illness and climatic disasters such as floods. In some cases the income of members is enough to

---

[245]  Ibid
[246]  Ibid

cover the costs but when risks are more catastrophic, collective forms of insurance are needed. SEWA members use a mix of government and private services, notably in the case of health, making the best balance they can between cost and loss of earnings.

SEWA members even regard education as a kind of insurance for the future. If their children are educated the family will have a better chance of resisting exploitation and will be better able to interact with government. The more effective government services are the more the members will use them. There can be different models but the essential point is that people should not fall below a minimum level. Since it is impossible (and highly inefficient) to identify and respond to the millions of risks that poor people face, the role of the state is to underwrite this minimum level and to support those, such as widows and disabled people, who may have no other source of income. For those that work, it might only be fully useful when they face a new threat. But in this way UBI can be seen to support 'freedom from want' in those cases where people are incapacitated and 'freedom from fear' in relation to the risks associated with working at the lowest-paid levels of the economy.

India can well afford to take on the responsibility for UBI but a new international aid system with new institutions might be able to support and underwrite such a programme in other countries that might be less capable of managing it for themselves. The ideal arrangement might be to have a global pool from which states wishing to undertake UBI programmes could draw. This could be run on lines similar to programmes of the World Bank, with terms of lending or grants adjusted against results and the ability to pay back. It could even be run by the World Bank.

## The Role of the Aid System
But at a global level the lobby most likely to oppose UBI is the aid system itself. The institutional interests of the aid system are sharply opposed to programmes such as UBI because they remove the reason for the existence of an aid system. There is no need for policies, guidelines, priorities, consultations, fundraising, child sponsorship or anything else. Poor people decide for themselves how they use the cash they receive and the responsibility lies squarely with the authorities. There is likely to be a role for civil society in monitoring the programme but this will

be at local and national level rather than international. The danger is that the aid system may try to co-opt UBI as an element of the aid system and seek to take control by endlessly pointing to limitations and failures on the part of national governments.

My reason for being sceptical is not only that UBI obviates the need for an aid system but that, in the one circumstance where it might seem that the aid system still has a role, in times of disaster, the aid system has dragged its feet and generally delayed the introduction of 'cash distributions'. The last mission I undertook for Oxfam before leaving in 2001 was a review of the alternatives of food aid and cash in Ethiopia and Kenya[247] The report concluded that-

*'Food aid has many practical disadvantages. It takes time to deliver and offers only limited survival options unless exchanged for cash. If recipients of food aid choose to exchange food for cash at the same time (as usually happens) the exchange value drops. It is commonly estimated that 50% of food aid is sold soon after delivery. There is a strong argument in favour of using cash-based solutions or mixing cash-based and food-based solutions.'*

This was by no means a new proposal. Criticism of food aid had been mounting over many years. Oxfam published a book setting out the disadvantages in 1984[248] drawing on Amartya Sen's 1981 studies showing that famines are caused by lack of entitlement rather than a decline in the availability of food.[249] Sen's case studies showed that food was always present even in famine areas or it could be drawn in by traders. The obstacle was not lack of food but the inability of people to obtain it.

Through the 1980s and into the 1990s food aid lobbies such as the WFP and farmer lobbies in the USA and EU defended the use of food aid as a primary response to disasters. The idea of cash distributions, the obvious response to Sen's analysis, remained practically unheard of and only began to be taken seriously when pressures in favour of food aid eased off. Facing overwhelming criticism, the EU pulled out of food aid in the 1990s leaving the USA as the main supplier. CARE USA, one of the main agents delivering American food aid, withdrew from its role as channel for US food aid. Analysis of the negative effects, notably the depressive effect on local food prices and consequent impoverishment

---

[247]  Vaux, T (2000)
[248]  Jackson, T (1984) *Against the Grain*, Oxfam Publications
[249]  Sen (1981)

of farmers, seemed to make it impossible for food aid to continue but the farmer lobby in the USA was too powerful. No administration would take the risk of cutting that the farm subsidies that resulted in excess production and the need to 'dump' food in other countries.

The lobbies stalled any progress by calling for more and more research to demonstrate the success of cash distributions and drawing on the prejudice that poor people were likely to waste them. In 2000, the Overseas Development Institute (ODI) in London published a comprehensive criticism of food aid.[250] Nevertheless US food aid remains one of the main components of humanitarian action even today –the power of farmer lobbies is considerably greater than the influence of poor people whose incomes are reduced.

Cash distributions offer a particularly good way of addressing poverty because they leave the power of decision-making in the hands of the recipient and the recipient generally knows what is best in their own circumstances. This reflects SEWA's focus on livelihood incomes above all else. Other problems can be addressed so long as there is a basic income. It is the same argument as for UBI.

There are many powerful demonstrations of the positive effects of cash distributions. During a period of populist ascendancy in Brazil under President Luiz Inacio Lula da Silva ('Lula'), the Bolsa Familia (family stipend) programme provided poor families with a monthly stipend. The only significant condition was that their children attended school and were vaccinated. Over a decade the poorest people increased their incomes by seven per cent a year. Remarkably in the Brazil case this happened at a time when the incomes of the wealthier people stagnated. As a result, Brazil managed to lower its world inequality ranking from second to tenth.[251] Rates of school attendance and vaccination also increased hugely.

The Ethiopian government initiated a programme of cash distributions, the Productive Safety Net Programme (PSNP), in 2005. This has proved very effective in averting famine in Ethiopia during the Horn of Africa Crisis of 2011 (see Chapter Seven). The programme continues even in normal times in order to protect pastoralist livelihoods from vulnerability to droughts and fluctuations in food prices. People are provided with

---

[250]  Ed Clay (2000) *Food Aid –Time to Grasp the Nettle?*, ODI London
[251]  Green (2008) p11

cash or food[252] to help them through the difficult period and avoid having to sell animals. If additional support is needed to address a widespread crisis, the Risk Financing Mechanism (RFM) allows the PSNP to be scaled up. The programme was developed by the government with financial (and food aid) support from Western donors and technical support from international charities, notably Save the Children.

In the 2011 Horn of Africa Crisis, the Ethiopian programme performed very well. It provided support to 9.6 million people in the programme areas and a further 3.1 million outside.[253] The additional support was mobilised within six weeks which, according to representatives of the Donor Coordination Team relating to the PSNP, 'easily outperforms the humanitarian system in terms of verifying needs and disbursing resources for the response to be delivered through government systems.'[254]

International charities only began to use cash distributions on a significant scale about a decade ago. The reports have been consistently positive and in 2015 the ODI in London teamed up with the Washington-based Center for Global Development to issue a comprehensive report reviewing all the available research-[255]

'This evidence is compelling: in most contexts, humanitarian cash transfers can be provided to people safely, efficiently and accountably. People spend cash sensibly: they are not likely to spend it anti-socially (for example, on alcohol). Especially when delivered through digital payments, cash is no more prone to diversion than in-kind assistance. Both women and men often prefer cash, local markets have responded to cash injections without causing inflation and it has generated positive impacts on local economies. Cash supports livelihoods by enabling investment and building markets through increasing demand for goods and services. And with the growth of digital payments systems, cash can be delivered in increasingly affordable, secure and transparent ways.' p8

---

[252] This has become about because food aid was offered rather than because it was regarded as desirable in the original plan

[253] Hobson, M and L Campbell (2012) *How Ethiopia's Productive Safety Net Programme (PSNP) is responding to the current humanitarian crisis in the Horn*, Humanitarian Exchange, No 53 February 2012, ODI London p9

[254] Ibid p10

[255] ODI and CfGD (2015)

This report repeated the findings that had been made a decade earlier in reviews of the Ethiopian programme. It found that progress had been surprisingly slow and that cash-distribution was still regarded as experimental and risky by many agencies. The ODI/CFDG High Level Panel found that-

*'The humanitarian system is organised into clusters that focus on the provision of particular goods and services (such as food security, health, or sanitation, water and hygiene). Cash transfers, which enable beneficiaries to choose for themselves what they want to buy, fit uneasily within this structure. These institutional arrangements limit the system's ability to provide unrestricted cash transfers. Left to its own devices, the humanitarian system may gradually increase the use of cash transfers, but progress will be far too slow. Change will be inhibited not by lack of willingness on the part of the staff of humanitarian agencies but by the institutional architecture within which they operate.' p8*

The aid system has an interest in opposing cash distributions and will slow it down rather than speed it up. As a result it is national governments such as Brazil, Ethiopia and now India that are leading the way. This is not to argue that the issues are simple. There are some rare cases in which food aid or other forms of delivery may be more effective, or (more importantly) preferred by the people concerned. In India there has been much debate about replacing the Public Distribution System (PDS) or 'fair price shops' with a cash distribution scheme.[256] In some areas people showed a preference for the 'fair price shops' because the shops made items easily available without the need to travel to markets. But in the majority of areas, people preferred cash. The crucial factor was whether the 'fair price shops' functioned effectively. If they did, then people found them preferable because they removed the need to travel in order to make a purchase. For poor people the cost of travel and loss of working time can be crucial but the difficulty was that they had no way of ensuring whether a shop was run effectively or not. Since this issue is rooted in the deepest problems of elite dominance in India. The best overall approach is likely to be cash distribution on the basis that it is very simple and therefore easier to control.

---

[256]  Dreze and Sen (2013) p211

The ODI/CFGD report concludes that- *'Donors and aid agencies developing humanitarian responses should routinely consider cash transfers as the 'first best' response to crises. The question that should be asked is 'why not cash?' The onus would then be on agencies that want to provide in-kind assistance or vouchers to explain why it is needed in a particular context.' (p23)*

## Why Aid?

Perhaps a more fundamental question is 'why aid?' Arguably the whole responsibility for Human Security is best left to national governments and the peoples of poor nations. Even in the case of selective use of cash distribution in disasters it should be possible for governments to initiate programmes and to do so in a way that would be much fairer than the selective and arbitrary projects of aid agencies. The key to efficiency is to make the scheme as widespread as possible so that methods of selection can be avoided and monitoring put on a rigid universal basis.

Governments do not rate themselves simply on their economic performance or good governance. There is a concept of national pride that makes them support the national football team and deflect criticism from other nations. A reason why China and India will continue to address extreme poverty is that it is a national disgrace. It may also help to bring poor people within the purview of taxation and increase the national wealth but a key way to ensure effort may be a process that pours international shame on those countries that allow extreme poverty to persist. In this regard global citizens may have a campaigning role.

## Self-reliance as an alternative to Globalisation

Ela Bhatt of SEWA offers an alternative or rather an ultimate form of resistance to globalisation.[257] Exploitation by elite groups and the sense of disempowerment that comes from decisions taken far away by unknown people can be reduced by narrowing down our relationships to 'hundred-mile communities' in which goods are traded over much smaller areas and people are more intimately connected with the goods, people and environment in which they live. There might still be

---

[257] Bhatt (2015)

inequality but richer people would see the effects of their actions and have to take responsibility for them. This might include responsibility for the eradication of extreme poverty and distress.

This was the basis of the Poor Laws in England from Medieval times until the beginning of the nineteenth century. The wealthier people in local communities had the responsibility to ensure that no person was destitute and to help them with cash in time of personal crisis or wider disaster. It was only later that the Victorians introduced the idea that people could not be trusted with cash and instead must work for their living, doing what the government wanted rather than what they wanted to do for themselves. The result was the workhouse. Aid has reinvented the workhouse as a global space in which people must work on 'projects' and, if given food, must work for it.

Although hundred-mile communities may be Utopian, there is an important implication for a global welfare system. It will need local participation. If UBI schemes are run from central government offices and do not involve local people then it will become a bureaucratic nightmare in which poor people cannot find their way and lose out because they cannot cope with the system. If the answer lies in involving other citizens at local level then this takes us back to the fundamental problems of distortions caused by the self-interest of elite groups and the unfairness of patronage systems. But this should not be an objection to the attempt. The world can easily afford to eradicate extreme poverty and there should be no excuse for failing.

## Alternatives to the Aid System

The fundamental weakness of the aid system as it exists today is that it lacks independence. The most effective initiatives in the last two decades have not come from the aid system but from independent initiatives mostly sponsored by rich entrepreneurs. As shown in the previous Chapter, the work of George Soros' Open Society Institute has been far more effective in Eastern Europe and the Former Soviet Union than that of either Oxfam or DFID. It has created institutions and momentum within the region whereas what Oxfam and DFID have done has come and gone with no lasting effect.

Another example is the campaign against tropical diseases and in particular against Neglected Tropical Diseases (NTDS) -diseases such as lymphatic filiarisis. The campaign against NTDS is all the more remarkable because these diseases generally affect small numbers of the poorest people, rather than the population as a whole, and there is no source of profit for the Western producers of medicines because, as part of the campaign, the medicines are given free. The governments of the (generally poor) countries involved have given full support. The Democratic Republic of Congo now finances many of the elements itself. In 2015 the pharmaceutical industry gave away 1.5 billion drug doses for nothing.[258] The process has been brought together and supported by the Gates Foundation drawing on the wealth of some of the world's richest people.

The aid system has also engaged in campaigns to eradicate tropical diseases but because it has to raise the funds it is inclined to give itself too much prominence and this tends to make national governments disengage. This is not simply a matter of style but reflects the fundamental problem that the aid system has to distort reality in order to function. For people such as George Soros and Bill Gates this is not a consideration and so they can work on a more equal footing with other 'partners' notably national governments and, in this case, the pharmaceutical industry. By contrast, international charities criticise pharmaceutical companies to attract public attention and then take money from them when given the chance. As Peter Gill records a single aid manager, Justin Forsyth, ran a campaign against Glaxo Smith Klein (GSK) while with Oxfam and then transferred as Chief Executive to Save the Children where he sought and accepted substantial funding from GSK.[259] This kind of thing has not only undermined the credibility of international charities in their home countries but makes national governments and civil society regard 'partnerships' involving international charities with scepticism. Gill, who wrote a glowing account of Oxfam's work in the 1960s[260], laments that *'tie-ups with industry, hard-core advertising, more and more funding from government: this is the modern aid charity at work.'*[261]

Nevertheless I remain a committed supporter of Oxfam as the best of the international charities in my experience. Oxfam has been tainted

---

[258]  The Economist April 22nd 2017 pp53-6
[259]  Gill (2016) p250
[260]  Gill (1970)
[261]  Gill (2016) p251

or compromised by competitive pressures but it would be very difficult for any single established organisation to stand out against the trends of commercialization and control by Western governments. These are the dynamics of international charities today and some succumb more than others. They do good work but they are compromised. Behind every appeal for humanitarian aid lies a tendency to avoid the more difficult challenges of confronting power with truth. Behind the ongoing work to support organisations all over the world lies a tendency to colonise them. I recommend everyone to continue working for and supporting such organisations but not to allow them to stand in the way of new trends and a radical realignment of the aid system.

# CHAPTER TWELVE

# WHERE DO WE GO
# FROM HERE?

W hat is Trumped-up aid?
In the words of the UN Secretary General reporting to the General Assembly- *'There is considerable frustration with the international aid architecture. It is seen as outdated and resistant to change, fragmented and uncommitted to working collaboratively, and too dominated by the interests and funding of a few countries. There is frustration about inequity in the aid system, with so many people suffering in crises that receive little aid or attention, and frustration on the part of neighbouring communities or countries that open their homes or borders with little support. There is wide frustration that the responsibility to respond politically and financially to human suffering is not shared by all.*[262]

Clearly there must be a great deal wrong with the current system for the UN Secretary General to make such a statement. The last sentence could be interpreted to mean that the USA and a small group of Western countries take on a disproportionate responsibility for the aid system and that the answer is more money from more countries. This would be a mistake because the fundamental problem with the aid system is that it represents the interests of the USA and close allies but not many others (*'dominated by the interests and funding of a few countries'* as the Secretary General put it).

---

[262] UN General Assembly (2016)

Trumped-up aid is the type of aid designed to suit the giver rather than the receiver. President Trump has cut US aid for family planning because he does not like it even though, according to the Guardian newspaper, his decision amounted to a death warrant for women around the world.[263] Such aid is only marginally concerned with poverty and distress. It reflects personal and national prejudices and interests. The aid system is essentially the USA-centred system that has emerged since World War II and is not only funded by the USA and its allies ('the West') but deeply embedded in an American world view. Much of it is located in New York and Washington. So long as other countries concurred with the general idea the aid system was acceptable but the Global War on Terror and now the isolationism, nationalism and sheer eccentricity of President Trump have discredited American leadership. In a smaller way, the UK has also been diminished by giving way to anti-European and anti-immigrant pressures.

Western aid now appears particularly unsuitable and outdated. Other countries are unlikely to shore it up or share the costs and they may want to see something completely different. This makes the present a good time to consider radical change. Neither the USA nor the UK seems likely to cling to the old aid system to the bitter end and President Trump has already shown signs of wanting to dismantle it.

Political economy studies are not supposed to make recommendations but instead make predictions of what will actually happen based on an analysis of the interests and mandates of the elements in a political system. Such studies assume that people and organisations will follow their interests rather than their statements of aspiration, principle, hope etc. This is rather a gloomy approach but one that is appropriate in relation to an aid system that is now very self-interested and also riddled with contradictions and confusions. It has many different purposes some of which conflict with each other. If it is to serve the national interest of a donor country then very likely it will not serve the interests of very poor people. If it is to be the 'soft diplomacy' or 'force multiplier' wing of Western interventionism then its purpose is political. There can be no talk of impartiality and neutrality.

---

[263]  I these modern *How one of Trump's first acts signed death warrants for women all around the world* The Guardian 22 July 2017

The decline of the aid system is the inevitable result of a long period of institutionalisation after World War II combined with the increasing use of aid as an instrument of Western political and security agendas. The agenda of reducing poverty and distress has become little more than a way of selling aid budgets to the Western public. Although the need for change is obvious, the aid system itself has become the main obstacle to change. Just as turkeys cannot be expected to vote for Christmas so aid agencies cannot be expected to vote for cash to be put into the hands of poor people nor do they wish the process of development to be taken away from them by national governments and civil society. They want to continue with projects and programmes that have had no discernible effect on poverty in the past and are unlikely to do so in the future.

Faced with criticism the aid industry asks 'what would you like is to do then?' and uses the response to justify new funding –climate change being the latest one. The aid system itself can be viewed as a large contracting company that will do whatever it is asked so long as the payment is right. The aid system does not change the world. It changes itself to suit the flow of resources.

In the last resort the aid system will raise the issue of poverty reduction. Even donor governments prefer not to let go of an argument that provides them with popular support and a large slush fund to pay for ventures such as the Afghanistan and Iraq invasions. The aid system will talk endlessly about poverty reduction but when the budget has been secured or the O.7% GDP target accepted, they will use the money for whatever they want.

Well-meaning politicians who believe that more money means less poverty will continue to pump up budgets while also insisting that 'overhead costs' must be reduced. This makes aid a harmful activity. The notion that aid is just a matter of providing enough money leads to massive waste and does more harm than good. It has no problem about perpetuating patronage systems because they mirror the aid system itself. They are a means to keep poor people quiet, pursue elite interests and give greater opportunities to those in charge.

This is not going to last much longer. The pace of change in the governments that not so long ago were referred to as the 'Third World' is very rapid. Although the Global War on Terror has destabilised the Middle East many countries in Asia have made dramatic advances in the war on poverty. African governments have stabilised after a long period of post-colonial and Cold War conflicts. These governments are in a position to take the lead. Similarly, local organisations are reacting against control by 'handlers' from the aid system. Some have learnt useful lessons from the aid system but now they are ready to pursue their own course, shaking off the charge that they represent a 'foreign hand' and a foreign way of thinking. Especially in economies that are growing steadily, they should be able to find the means to be self-sufficient. The aid system holds them back.

Because so much of the current global turmoil arises because old values and belief systems are under threat, the engagement of local people, organisations and national governments is more important than ever before. The process of development from now onwards can be managed by those who understand the cultural and religious context in which poor people live. They can fight battles within Islam, for example, rather than the pointless and destructive battle between Islam and Christianity.

China and India have taken huge steps forward in the eradication of extreme poverty. The next steps will be to ensure that the remaining 800 million extremely poor people have access to a minimum daily income as a matter of right. The challenge is to prevent elite groups from opposing such an aim on spurious grounds. If that can be done then the rest of the development process will follow without too much effort. When the polarity of power has been reversed to the point that very poor people are no longer desperate and vulnerable, they will gradually assert greater control over their lives and then will be less under the control of elites. The problem lies in the first step and this depends mainly on leaders in poor countries.

Although many of the leaders in poorer countries have been in place for a long time this does not mean that they ignore changing trends outside and inside their countries. The question is how the incentives stack up. Today's leaders have rather more interest in democracy than in the past because time and technology have made the people better informed. Education has spread slowly but it is beginning to have an effect. Leaders may be swayed by the argument that there is political capital to be gained by winning the hearts and minds of very poor people. Some have already had experience of cash distribution programmes. They can see that it could be put on a national basis. The man at the top may find this a useful way to undermine potential rivals. It all depends on the political balance. Just now, India is right on that point of balance and it can go either way.

A global agreement to promote a minimum income, resources from richer countries all over the world, scrutiny at all levels and public information can all help but in the end much will depend on political calculation. The best thing the aid system can do is step aside and stop confusing the issue with projects that help small groups and divert attention from the central issue.

A time of international turmoil is one in which change with regard to poverty may be easier. This is a good time to think about the global order that has been with us since World War II. What should be let go and what should be grasped and defended at all costs? Among the latter I would name the sets of principle established after World War II (UN Charter, Conventions, Declarations etc) but not the institutions that have grown up around them. These are now too 'Western' and they alienate people from different traditions and political backgrounds. In my experience, the UN organisations are welcomed for their money but their ideas are treated with suspicion.

It may be time to shift power from the UN Security Council to a wider role for the General Assembly. It may be time to conclude that many of the post-war institutions, as in the case of the Marshall Plan, have served their purpose and should be superseded by structures that are more genuinely global. Somewhere along the line our common sense of Humanity should preserve and define a sense of responsibility towards the poorest people and where it does not, then others from all around the world should be ready to name and shame. Poverty eradication needs to shift from being a Western aim to being a global one.

To be specific, I hope that national governments will move forwards with Universal Basic Income (UBI) programmes or variants that they decide are appropriate for their circumstances. I hope that they will use such programmes as the basis for Disaster Risk Reduction, ensuring that no-one is so poor that they are vulnerable. During disasters, governments will use the same mechanism, perhaps with larger payments, to enable people not only to survive but also to recover and rebuild their lives. The technology of unique identification, communicating money and communicating information make this easily possible.

It will not be easy to address the remaining problems of extreme poverty but at least the aim is clear. The issue of addressing fear is both complex and ill-defined. The first point is that fear should not be addressed by offering food and water. This is a distortion that has become commonplace because the aid system is geared entirely towards humanitarian response rather than addressing the fundamental causes of fear. If there is a war the primary objective, reflecting the UN Charter, is to stop the war.

The principle of Responsibility to Protect, agreed by the UN General Assembly, provides a good basis for global action to prevent or limit fear in situations where the national government appears to be failing. With the USA withdrawing from global leadership but still the world's biggest military power, rules of intervention need to be shaped that amount to more than a reaction to the last episode and emanate from a much wider group of nations. Intolerable situations such as South Sudan's war between rival 'big men' should not be allowed to destroy the lives of millions of people when a tiny fraction of the world's determination and arsenal could bring it to an immediate stop.

Although regional neighbours may have an interest in intervening, they also have other interests and, as in the case of South Sudan, they may even have interests in perpetuating the war. The problem of 'regional intervention' has yet to be satisfactorily addressed. With declining confidence in the Security Council, following the obsession of some members with the Global War on Terror, there may be scope for other groupings of nations to address these issues.

Much has been learnt from failed 'humanitarian' interventions over the last decades and we should now be able to reach agreement on minimal levels of security just as we have minimum levels of income so that such risky ventures are at least placed on a common footing. This might involve calculating the numbers (or proportion) of people living in fear as a trigger for intervention. The issue could best be addressed by peer groups of nations rather than being assumed to be a Western prerogative. The UN Security Council needs to find ways to be more flexible in allowing others to take up issues which are not the concern of permanent members.

The most important role for the world's better-off citizens is to restrain the evil that their own country does, such as selling arms to governments that behave outrageously or using destabilisation as a tool of foreign policy. Similarly, international charities should ask themselves whether they can stand up to their government at the same time as taking large amounts of money to do what the government wants. One option would be to leave the analysis of conflict to organisations such as Crisis Group that do not have to modify their findings to take account of their aid programmes. Another option would be to become much more transparent about the constraints on telling the full truth.

Cash in the hands of poor people is an answer to many of the problems relating to extreme poverty. But better still would be cash in the hands of poor women because that would give the greatest chance of the money being used wisely for the greater good of all members of the family.

Some countries may be able to select people for cash distribution programmes successfully but as soon as there is a chance for elite groups to manipulate the programme, the poorest people are likely to lose out. In the case of disasters, cash distributions should become the norm but this will not work if the aid system takes charge and different agencies apply different approaches with different people. National government must take charge under the scrutiny of its own people. Charity and civil society may still have a role in identifying and helping those who fall out of the system –perhaps because they are incapable or unwilling to go through whatever process is required for them to benefit from cash distributions.

As Alex de Waal has recently demonstrated[264], even states that can be regarded as fragile are not so weak as they seem. Patronage systems are being replaced by a business approach and Presidents such as Museveni in Uganda and Kagame in Rwanda operate as Chief Executives running countries as business enterprises. In these modernising African states the people are generally supportive because the 'business of power', as de Waal calls it, creates jobs and boosts the whole economy. Money is no longer siphoned out of the country into Swiss bank accounts but reinvested locally. Such governments would be perfectly capable of running UBI programmes. The late President Zenawi in Ethiopia was one of the first African leaders to launch such a programme more than a decade ago. It is true that such programmes can be used to strengthen patronage systems but only if they are

---

[264] De Waal (2015)

selective and this forms a powerful argument for UBI rather than selective cash distribution.

The spread of mobile phones even among very poor people has opened up new possibilities. Cash distributions through mobile phone networks have operated even during times of war, as in the case of Somalia. But there is scope to link up the use of mobile phones to achieve 'freedom from want' to the related aim of achieving 'freedom from fear'. Mobile phones are a source of information and information is a basis for security. Mobile phones have helped women in vulnerable situations to reduce the risk of sexual assault. The phone can also be a tool of accountability. In the case of the 2010 Haiti earthquake, people made use of mobile phones to keep each other informed about possible evictions by landlords and also to find out about their entitlements from the aid agencies. They then put forward demands and criticised the agencies when spending fell far short of the sums collected through appeals.

Mobile phones regularly enable Somali pastoralists to exchange information about grazing lands. Relief operations in Somalia would scarcely have got off the ground without mobile phones to transfer money. People affected by the 2004 Tsunami disaster in Indonesia telephoned relatives in Sri Lanka to warn them to keep away from the sea.[265] Mobile phones and websites play an important role in George Soros' promotion of the 'open society' in Eastern Europe. Many of SEWA's working women have mobile phones to increase their safety and efficiency.

The spread of education, especially among women, offers the chance to make much greater use of mobile phones not only for information and handling cash but also as a means of security. UBI itself is a way of reducing vulnerability because poor people, and women in particular, will be under less pressure to take excessive risks. Cash in hand can be used in various ways to enhance security but access to a mobile phone is a second important step. Cash distribution and mobile phone together constitute a path to Human Security. Making mobile phones available to very poor people is a simple and inexpensive step (compared with the paraphernalia of aid projects) and might be one in which the aid system could help. That way everyone will be happy.

---

[265] IFRC (2005)

# HAITI ANALYSIS

*Based on 'Aid and Fragility' a report for CARE and ActionAid dated May 2009 and updated after the 2010 earthquake*

Haitian society is highly unequal but the quality that gives Haiti its explosive character is socio-political exclusion. Although the appearance is very different, Haiti has a social system not so very different from the caste system in India. There is an invisible 'glass ceiling' through which certain types of people cannot pass. Education plays a key role but exclusion also follows language, skin colour, wealth and place of origin. There is a deep divide between Creole speakers in the rural areas and elite French-speakers in Port-au-Prince and other cities. The coveted French-language private schools are concentrated in the cities, while the (Creole) state schools operate in rural areas. Private school and French are the paths to advancement. Elite groups discount and undermine the government and rely on private services to maintain their standard of living. Only 30% of the health system is public, and 72% of the population does not have access to any kind of health care.[266] Privatisation exacerbates and reflects a profound social division which manifests in huge disparities of wealth and power.

The elite class manipulates government through patronage systems. Government Ministries become patronage networks and a change of Minister is likely to be followed by a change of staff throughout the Ministry. With Haiti's rapid change of governments and pressure to

---

[266] ICG (2009) p7 based on figures from the Ministry of Planning

accommodate different political interests among the elite group, this has led to constant change, uncertainty and government ineffectiveness.

Per capita GDP has been falling steadily over the last 20 years and is now around half its former level.[267] Economic decline has been particularly severe in the agricultural sector, with rural areas now deeply impoverished.[268] Youth unemployment is extremely widespread. About 60% of Haiti's population is below the age of 24 and there is a very high proportion of 15-29 year old youths relative to the total population. This adds to the propensity towards violence. Despite the presence of the UN Stabilisation force, MINUSTAH, nearly 60% of people in the metropolitan area (Port-au-Prince) stated that they were unsafe, compared with just 15% in the rural areas.

When there is a possibility to do so, Haitians emigrate, especially to the USA and Canada. Remittances from family members abroad are an important part of the economy, enabling people from rural areas to migrate to the urban slums, seeking better prospects. The political influence of the diaspora played an important role in bringing about a massive response to the earthquake especially from the USA and Canada.

Although jobs are scarce, many poorer people pin their hopes on education provided by churches or NGOs on concessional terms. This turns the churches and NGOs into major providers of services and the state has, in effect, withdrawn.[269] According to the World Bank, 92% of schools are outside the state system and they are not regulated by the state. The notion of citizenship is hazy. Many people have no birth certificates and no document of citizenship. It is expensive for people to register as citizens, and many choose not to do so. This was one of the reasons why it was difficult to estimate the numbers killed by the earthquake.

Organisations of peasants and urban workers have been repeatedly smashed by paramilitary groups and gangs, working for the elite class. The 'Tontons Macoutes' under the Duvalier regimes were particularly

---

[267]  World Bank (2006) pi

[268]  It is estimated that 75,000 people migrate from the rural areas to the cities every year –ICG (2009) p7 based on a USAID study. In total there are 100,000 new job-seekers in the cities each year –World Bank (2006) piii.

[269]  Non-state schools comprise 92% of all schools –World Bank (2006) p44

vicious but the phenomenon persists today. During Aristide's period of more radical politics, youth gangs were created to counter-act the elite class but have ended up just as dangerous and uncontrolled as the gangs they sought to destroy. In recent years, the focus of violence has shifted from the rural to the urban areas, and especially to Port-au-Prince. In 2006 nearly 60% of people in the metropolitan area felt unsafe compared with just 15% in the rural areas.[270]

But despite all this, there remain some important forms of social mobilisation. Village people continue to form voluntary groups for house-building and for clearing fields, as they have done for generations. In the urban slums, surveys have found a strong presence of community organisations to tackle issues such as sanitation, water, healthcare, education and even electricity.[271] Parent Teacher Associations (especially in the non-state sector) are reported to have fostered community participation, encouraged transparency and tackled issues such as insecurity.[272] Peasant associations and women's unions appeared to be strengthening at the time of the earthquake.

The risks attached to any kind of social activism are high, especially for women. Throughout Haiti's violent history, rape has been used, especially by elite groups, as a method of terrorizing women and undermining resistance. It has been estimated that 85% of the victims of violence are women and 89% of the perpetrators are men.[273] Over half the women in Haiti are thought to be victims of violence and 16% victims of rape.[274] Not only the police but also local communities are thought to take a very negative attitude, with widespread stigmatisation and isolation of rape victims. Nevertheless women have been successful as entrepreneurs in urban areas, often achieving incomes higher than men's.[275]

---

[270] World Bank (2006) p32

[271] World Bank (2006) pvi

[272] World Bank (2006) p46

[273] MINUSTAH (2007) *Les femmes, actrices ou victimes de la violence armee,* www.minustah.org

[274] MINUSTAH (2007) *Centre Multimedia: Dialogue autour du theme de la violence aux femmes* www.minustah.org

[275] World Bank (2006) p12

The UN peacekeeping force MINUSTAH directed its efforts towards suppressing the urban gangs and succeeded in controlling them in the notorious Cite Soleil area of Port-au-Prince.

But by the time MINUSTAH was deployed the character of some of the gangs had changed. There was increasing public sympathy for the gangs inside urban slums because they represented, to an extent at least, vigilante protection against violence by groups from outside. Some of the gangs (and mafia godfathers) are still seen as a political force representing poor people and, in the absence of the state, they act as the local government, providing services including education, health and welfare support.

Before the earthquake, levels of aid to Haiti were already high on a per capita basis, especially if the costs of MINUSTAH are taken into account. In 2009, Haiti was the second highest recipient of Canadian aid after Afghanistan. Pressure from Haitians abroad is a significant reason for this. Governments in the region have an interest in limiting Haiti's role as the Caribbean centre for drug-trading and smuggling of weapons. Neighbours also fear the possibility of a decline into even worse levels of violence in Haiti, as happened in the past.

By the time of the earthquake Haiti had become dependent on aid at all levels. Its security was provided by MINUSTAH and 60% of the national budget was funded by donors. The government was extremely weak- 'Haiti has virtually no government machinery of its own. Political instability has encouraged politicians to grab whatever they can quickly. The government has become adept at producing strategies and policies that promise positive change but in reality these strategies are designed to extend patronage networks or create new possibilities for corruption. Donors avoid funding through government because of corruption and then, bypassing the state, support projects that undermine any semblance of Haitian leadership.'[276]

Donors have not fully recognised the dangers of making NGOs the main service providers and ignoring the responsibilities of the state. Radical elements of civil society complain that NGOs undermine political movements intended to reform the government but some NGOs justify their existence (and funding) precisely because of this. They claim to be creating 'peace', although of a very limited kind.

---

[276] From the unpublished report cited at the head of this Annex

NGOs receiving foreign aid have undermined the state by paying salaries much higher than those in government and drawing away capable staff. By using grand vehicles they created demand for similar lifestyles among officials, and this fuelled corruption. Officials developed deep dislike of NGOs because they flaunted their wealth and also because some of them deliberately exposed the failures of the state. All this made it difficult to develop a dialogue between government Ministries and NGOs. Even before the earthquake, Haiti had become known as the 'Republic of NGOs'.

Numerous reports have shown that aid to Haiti has been copious but ineffective.277 If channelled through NGOs it undermined the state. If channelled through the government money was wasted through corruption and patronage systems. The weakness of the state was exploited by businessmen associated with the elite groups. They mined and quarried without restraint and cut trees, causing huge damage to the environment. Landslides and floods have become more frequent and more devastating. Poor people are extremely vulnerable to disasters such as cyclones and floods.

---

277 Canada's 2004 review, for example, is titled 'A Decade of Difficult Partner-ship'. The World Bank and UNDP reached similar conclusions

# BIBLIOGRAPHY AND REFERENCES

Adedeji, Adebayo Ed (1999) *Comprehending and Mastering African Conflicts –the search for sustainable peace and good governance*, African Centre for Development and Strategic Studies/ Zed London and New York

African Rights (1995) *Rwanda: Death Despair and Defiance*, African Rights London

Afshar, H and D Eade eds (2004) *Development, Women, and War -Feminist Perspectives*, Oxfam Publications, Oxford

Ali, D and K Gelsdorf (2012) *Risk-averse to risk-willing: learning from the 2011 Somalia cash response*, in Maxwell et al (2012)

ALNAP (2012) *The State of the Humanitarian System 2012*, ODI London

Anderson, M B (1999) *Do No Harm –how aid can support peace –or war*, Lynne Rienner Colorado

Anderson, M, D Brown and I Jean (2012) *Time to Listen –hearing people on the receiving end of international aid*, CDA Collaborative Learning Projects, Cambridge MA USA

Anten, L, I Briscoe and M Mezzera (2012) *The Political Economy of State-building in situations of fragility and conflict: from analysis to strategy*, Conflict Research Unit, Netherlands Institute of International Relations 'Clingendael', January 2012

Appaiah, P (2003) *Hindutva –Ideology and Politics*, Deep and Deep Publications, New Delhi

Barnett, M (2013) *Empire of Humanity –A History of Humanitarianism*, Cornell Univeristy Press

Bennett, J, S Pantuliano, W Fenton, A Vaux, C Barnett and E Brusset (2010) *A Multi-donor evaluation of support to conflict prevention and peacebuilding activities in Southern Sudan 2005-2010,* ITAD Ltd UK

Berdal, M and D Malone (2000) *Greed and Grievance —economic agendas in civil wars,* Lynne Rienner

Bhatt, Ela R (2006) We *are Poor but so Many —the story of self-employed women in India,* Oxford University Press

Bhatt, Ela R (2015) *Anubandh —building hundred mile communities,* Navajivan Publishing House, Ahmedabad

Bhattarai, Baburam (2003) *The Nature of Underdevelopment and regional structure of Nepal —an economic analysis,* Adroit Publishers, Delhi

Birdsall, N and H Kharas (2014) *The Quality of Official Development Assistance —Third Edition,* Brookings/Center for Global Development

Black, Maggie (1992) *A Cause for our Times —Oxfam: the first 50 years,* Oxfam/ Oxford University Press

Black, M (2007) *The No-nonsense Guide to International Development,* New Internationalist Publications

Bolton, G (2007) *Aid and Other Dirty Business,* Ebury Press

Buchanan-Smith, M and S Davies (1995) *Famine Early Warning Systems and Response: The Missing Link,* IT Publications, London

Bugnion, F (2003) *The International Committee of the Red Cross and the Protection of War Victims,* ICRC/Mamillan

Calderisi, R (2006) *The Trouble with Africa —why foreign aid isn't working,* Yale University Press

Carothers, T and D de Gramont (2013) *Development Aid Confronts Politics, -the almost revolution,* Carnegie Endowment for International Peace

Chambers, R (2005) *Ideas for Development,* London: Earthscan

Coghlan, B et al (2007) *Mortality in the Democratic Republic of Congo: An Ongoing Crisis,* IRC

Collaborative Learning Projects (2006) *Has Peacebuilding Made a Difference in Kosovo?,* CDA/CARE

Collier, P (2007) *The Bottom Billion —why the poorest countries are failing and what can be done about it,* Oxford University Press

Collier, P (2009) *Wars, Guns and Votes –democracy in dangerous places*, The Bodley Head

Commission for Africa (2005) *Our Common Interest: Report of the Commission for Africa*, London: Penguin Books

Commission on Human Security (2003) *Human Security Now*, Commission on Human Security, New York

Crowell, D (2003) *The SEWA Movement and rural development*, Sage Publications

Dalrymple, W (2013) *Return of a King –the battle for Afghanistan 1839-42*, Bloomsbury

Darcy, J and C-A Hofmann (2003) *According to Need? Needs assessment and decision- making in the humanitarian sector*, HPG Report 15, ODI London

Dayal, M (2001) *Towards Securer Lives –SEWA's Social-Security Programme*, Ravi Dayal/Longman India

Deaton, A (2013) *The Great Escape –health, wealth and the origins of inequality*, Princeton University Press

De Haan, Arjan (2009) *How the Aid Industry Works –an introduction to international development*, Kumarian Press

De Waal, A (1997) *Famine Crimes: Politics and the Disaster Relief Industry in Africa*, Oxford: James Currey

De Waal, A (2009) *Fixing the Political Marketplace: How we can make peace without functioning state institutions?* Fifteenth Christian Michelsen Lecture, Bergen 15 October 2009

De Waal (2015) *Getting Away with Murder: The SPLA and its American Lobbies*, in de Waal Ed (2015)

De Waal, A (ed) (2015) *Advocacy in Conflict –Critical Perspectives on Transnational Activism*, Zed Books, London

De Waal (2015a) *The Real Politics of the Horn of Africa –money, war and the business of power*, Polity Press

DFID (2002) *Conducting Conflict Assessments –Guidance Notes*, DFID London

DFID (2004) *The Rough Guide to a Better World –and how you can make a difference*, DFID

DFID (2006) *Preventing Violent Conflict,* DFID London

DFID (2009) *Political Economy Analysis —How To Note,* DFID London

Disaster Mitigation Institute (DMI), Humanitarian Initiatives and Mango UK (2001) *Independent Evaluation: The DEC Response to the Earthquake in Gujarat,* London: DEC.

Dreze, J and A Sen (2013) *An Uncertain Glory —India and its Contradictions,* Allen Lane

Duffield, M (2001) *Global Governance and the New Wars,-the merging of development and security,* Zed Books London

Duffield, M (2007) *Development, Security and Unending War —governing the world of peoples,* Polity Press Cambridge

Easterly, W (2006) *The White Man's Burden: Why the West's efforts to aid the rest have done so much ill and so little good* Oxford University Press

Elworthy, S and G Rifkind (undated) *Making Terrorism History,* Random House Books (Kindle)

Ghani, A and C Lockhart (2008) *Fixing Failed States —a framework for rebuilding a fractured world,* Oxford University Press

Gill, P (1970) *Drops in the Ocean —the work of Oxfam 1960-70,* Macdonald Unit 75 London

Gill, P (2010) *Famine and Foreigners: Ethiopia since Live Aid,* Oxford University Press

Gill, P (2016) *Today We Drop Bombs —Tomorrow We Build Bridges —how foreign aid became a casualty of war,* Zed Books London

Glennie, J (2008) *The Trouble with Aid —why less could mean more for Africa,* Zed Books

Glover, J (1999) *Humanity —a moral history of the Twentieth Century,* Jonathan Cape

Goodhand, J (2006) *Aiding Peace? The Role of NGOs in Armed Conflict,* ITDG

Gourevitch, P (1998) *We wish to inform you that tomorrow we will be killed with our families, -stories from Rwanda,* Picador

Green, D (2008) *From Poverty to Power –how effective citizens and effective states can change the world,* Practical Action/Oxfam: new edition dated 2012

Green, D (2016) *How Change Happens,* Oxford University Press

Hallegatte, Stephane; Vogt-Schilb, Adrien; Bangalore, Mook; Rozenberg, Julie. (2017) *Unbreakable : Building the Resilience of the Poor in the Face of Natural Disasters. Climate Change and Development;* Washington, DC: World Bank. © World Bank. https://openknowledge.worldbank. org/handle/10986/25335 License: CC BY 3.0 IGO

Hamilton, L M (2015) *Florence Nightingale –a life inspired,* Wyatt North

Hancock, Graham (1989) *Lords of Poverty,* Macmillan London

Harrell-Bond, B (1986) *Imposing Aid: Emergency Assistance to Refugees,* Oxford University Press, Oxford

Harriott, A (2000) *Police and Crime Control in Jamaica –problems of reforming ex-colonial constabularies,* University of the West Indies Press

Hartmann, B and J Boyce (1979) *Needless Hunger: Voices from a Bangladesh Village,* San Francisco: Institute for Development Policy

Hogan, T (2012) *Beyond Good Intentions –A journey into the realities of international aid,* Seal Press

HPG/Tufts/King's College London (2016) *Planning from the Future – Is the Humanitarian System Fit for Purpose?* final report at www. planningfromthefuture.org

International Federation of Red Cross and Red Crescent Societies (IFRC) (1991) *Code of Conduct for the International Red Cross and Red Crescent Movement and NGOs in Disaster Relief* at www.ifrc.org

IFRC (2005) World Disaster Report –focus on information in disasters, IFRC Geneva

Ignatieff, M (1998) *The Warrior's Honor –ethnic war and the modern conscience,* Chatto and Windus

Inter Agency Standing Committee (2015) Inter Agency Humanitarian Evaluation of the Response to the Crisis in South Sudan, March 2016 https://interagencystandingcommittee.org/evaluations/content/ south-sudan-iahe

Jackson, T and D Eade (1982) *Against the Grain: The Dilemma of Project Food Aid,* Oxfam Oxford

Jalil, Tariq (2014) *Islam Plain and Simple —Women, Terrorism, and Other Controversial Topics,* Quinn Press, Santa Monica USA (Kindle)

Johnson, Douglas H (2003) *The Root Causes of Sudan's Civil Wars,* The International African Institute

Keen, D (1994) *The Benefits of Famine: A Political Economy of Famine and Relief in Southwestern Sudan 1983-9,* Princeton University Press

Lappe F M, J Collins and D Kinley (1975) *Aid As Obstacle —twenty questions about our Foreign Aid and the Hungry,* San Francisco: Institute for Food and Development Policy

Lockwood, M (2005) *The State They're in: An Agenda for International Action on Poverty in Africa,* ITDG

Majid, N and S McDowell (2012) *Hidden dimensions of the Somali famine,* in Maxwell et al (2012)

Manor, J (ed) (2007) *Aid That Works —Successful development in fragile states,* World Bank Washington

Marriage, Z (2006) *Not breaking the rules, Not Playing the Game — international assistance to countries at war,* Hurst & Co London

Maxwell D and M Fitzpatrick (2012) *The Somalia famine: context, causes and* complications in Maxwell et al (2012)

Maxwell, D, N Haan, K Gelsdorf and D Dawe (2012) *The 2011-2012 Famine in Somalia: Introduction to the Special Edition,* Global Food Security 1 (2012) 1-4

Moyo, D (2009) *Dead Aid —why aid is not working and how there is another way for Africa,* Allen Lane

Mulley, C (2009) *The Woman who saved the children: A biography of Eglantyne Jebb, founder of Save the Children,* Oneworld publications, London

OECD-DAC (2007) *Principles for Good International Engagement in Fragile States & Situations,* OECD Paris

OECD-DAC (2000) *DAC Criteria for Evaluating Development Assistance,* OECD Paris

Overseas Development Institute (ODI) and Center for Global Development (2015) *Doing Cash Differently: How Cash Transfers can Transform Humanitarian Aid* —report of the High Level Panel on Humanitarian Aid, ODI London

Paffenholz, T and L Reychler (2007) *Aid for Peace —A Guide to Planning and Evaluation for Conflict Zones*, Nomos

Pinker, S (2011) *The Better Angels of our Nature —the decline of violence in history and its causes*, Allen Lane

Polman, L (2010) *War Games*, Viking Books

Povey, E R (2004) *Women in Afghanistan: passive victims of the borga or social participants?* Afshar and Eade eds (2004)

Practical Action, Save the Children and CfBT (2011) *State-Building, Peace-Building and Service Delivery in Fragile and Conflict-Affected States: Literature Review -Final Report* GSDRC website

Pye, E (1942) *Food Conditions in Europe —A Statement on the Effect of War and the Blockade on People in German-controlled Countries*, London: Famine Relief Committee

Rashid, A (2008) *Descent into Chaos —Pakistan, Afghanistan and the Threat to Global Security*, Penguin Books

Relief and Rehabilitation Network (1994) *Code of Conduct for the International Red Cross and Red Crescent Movement and NGOs in Disaster Relief*, Network Paper 7, ODI London

Riddell, R C (2007) *Does Foreign Aid Really Work?* Oxford University Press

Rieff, D (2002) *A Bed for the Night: Humanitarianism in Crisis*, London: Vintage

Robertson, G (1999) *Crimes Against Humanity —the struggle for global justice*, Allen Lane/ Penguin

Roepstorff, K (2016) *India as Humanitarian Actor: Convergences and Divergences with DAC Donor Principles and Practices* in Sezgin and Dijkzeul Eds (2016)

Rose, K (1992) *Where Women Are Leaders —the SEWA Movement in India*, Zed Books

Sachs, J (2005) *The End of Poverty,* New York: Penguin Press

Save the Children and Oxfam (2012) *A Dangerous Delay: the cost of late response to the 2011 drought in Somalia,* Joint Agency Briefing Paper, January 2012

Schuller, M (2012) *Haiti's Bitter Harvest –Humanitarian Aid in the 'Republic of NGOs',* in Donini, A ed (2012) *The Golden Fleece –Manipulation and Independence in Humanitarian Action,* Kumarian press, Boulder and London

Sen, A (1981) *Poverty and Famines: An Essay on Entitlement and deprivation,* Oxford University Press, Oxford and New York

Sen, A (1999) *Development as Freedom,* Oxford University Press, Oxford and New York

Sen, A (2005) *The Argumentative Indian –writings on Indian Culture, History and Identity,* Penguin Books

Sen, A (2006) *Identity and Violence –the illusion of destiny,* Allen Lane, London

SEWA (2002) *Shantipath –Our Road to Restoring Peace,* at www.sewa. org

Sezgin, Z and D Dijkzeul Eds (2016) *The New Humanitarians in International Practice – emerging actors and contested principles,* Routledge London and New York

Slim, H (2007) *Killing Civilians –method, madness and morality in war,* Hurst and Company, London

Slim, H (2012) *IASC Real-time evaluation of the humanitarian response to the Horn of Africa Crisis in Somalia, Ethiopia and Kenya,* IASC

Smillie, I and L Minear (2004) *The Charity of Nations: Humanitarian Action in a Calculating World,* Bloomfield: Kumarian Press

Smith, A and T Vaux (2003) *Education, Conflict and Development,* Issues Paper for DFID London

Sogge, D (2002) *Give and Take: What's the Matter with Foreign Aid?* London: Zed Books

Soros, G (1998) *The Crisis of Global Capitalism –open society endangered,* Little, Brown and Company

Stewart, R and G Knaus (2011) *Can Intervention Work?* W W Norton and Company Inc, New York and London

Telford, J and J Cosgrave (2006) *Joint evaluation of the international response to the Indian Ocean tsunami: Synthesis Report,* Tsunami Evaluation Coalition

Terry, F (2002) *Condemned to repeat – the paradox of humanitarian action,* Cornell University Press

UN (2015) *The Millennium Development Goals Report* http://www.un.org/millenniumgoals/2015_MDG_Report/pdf/MDG%202015%20 rev%20(Jul y%20I).pdf

UNDP (2010) *UNDP Contribution to Disaster Prevention and Recovery,* UNDP New York

UN General Assembly (2012) *Accelerating Progress Towards the Millennium Development Goals – Annual Report of the Secretary General*

UN General Assembly (2016) *One Humanity: Shared Responsibility – Report of the UN Secretary General to the World Humanitarian Summit* https://consultations.worldhumanitariansummit. org/bitcache/e4988Ica33e3740b5f37162857c edc92c7cIe354?vid=569I03&disposition=inline&op=view

Uvin, P (1998) *Aiding Violence, the development enterprise in Rwanda,* West Hartford CT: Kumarian Press

Varadarajan, S (Ed) (2002) *Gujarat – the making of a tragedy,* Penguin Books India

Varshney, A (2002) *Ethnic Conflict and Civic Life, -Hindus and Muslims in India,* Yale University Press

Vaux, T (2000) *Through the Looking Glass – programmatic, contextual and systemic considerations relating to WFP food aid responses in Ethiopia and Kenya,* unpublished report for Oxfam

Vaux, T (2001) *The Selfish Altruist – relief work in famine and war,* Earthscan London

Vaux, T. (2002) *Disaster and Vulnerability,* Ahmedabad: Disaster Mitigation Institute/Self Employed Women's Association.

Vaux, T. and Lund, F. (2003a) 'Working women and security: Self-Employed Women's Association's response to crisis', Journal of Human Development, 4(2): 265-287.

Vaux, T. and Lund, F. (2003b) 'Human Security of Working Women: Response to Crisis', in L.C. Chen et al. (eds) Human Insecurity in a Global World, Cambridge: Harvard University Press. pp. 137-162

Vaux, T (2005) 'Beyond Relief – Review of a human securities approach to the Gujarat earthquake', Experience Learning Series, 32, Ahmedabad: All India Disaster Mitigation Institute.

Vaux, T and E Visman (2005) Service Delivery in Countries Emerging from Conflict, CICS Bradford

Vaux, T, M Bhatt, A Bhattacharjee, M Lipner, J McCluskey, A Niak and F Stevenson (2005) Independent Evaluation of the DEC Tsunami Crisis Response, Valid International

Vaux, T with A Bewa and P Sampson (2007) Aid and Conflict in the Democratic Republic of Congo, DFID http://www.humansecurity.org.uk/downloads/DRC_SCA.pdf

Vaux, T, S Pantuliano and S Srinivasan (2008) Stability and Development in the Three Areas, unpublished report for DFID

Vaux, T (2009) Aid and Fragility –aid effectiveness in fragile and conflict-affected states, unpublished paper for ActionAid and CARE UK

Vaux, T (2009) Work-focused Responses to Disasters: India's Self Employed Women's Association, in E. Enarson and P. Chakarabarti (eds) Women, Gender and Disaster, India: Sage. pp. 212-223

Vaux, T et al (2010) Evaluation of Oxfam's DFID Programme Partnership Agreement, November 2010 (unpublished report for DFID)

Vaux, T (2015) Inter Agency Humanitarian Evaluation of the Response to Conflict in South Sudan, May 2015 (unpublished report for OCHA)

Vaux, T (2016) Traditional and Non-Traditional Humanitarian Actors in Disaster Response in India in Sezgin and Dijkzeul Eds (2016)

Walker, P and D Maxwell (2009) Shaping the Humanitarian World, Routledge

Weissman, F (2004) In the Shadow of 'Just Wars' –violence, politics and humanitarian action, Medecins Sans Frontieres (Translation published by Hurst)

Whittell, R and M Eshwarappa (2010) Dodgy Development –films and interviews challenging British aid in India, Corporate Watch London

World Bank (2009) *Problem-driven governance and political economy analysis –good practice framework,* World Bank, Washington

World Bank (2011) *Political Economy Assessments at Sector and Project Levels,* World Bank, Washington

World Bank (2011a) *World Development Report 2011 –Conflict, Security and Development,* World Bank, Washington

World Bank (2014) *World Development Report 2014 - Risk and Opportunity, managing risk for development,* Washington DC: World Bank.

World Bank (2015) *Global Monitoring Report 2015/2016* Washington DC: World Bank

World Bank (2016) *Poverty and Shared Prosperity 2016 –taking on inequality* Washington DC: World Bank

Wrong, M (2009) *It's our turn to eat,-the story of a Kenyan whistleblower,* Fourth Estate London

Yunus, M (1998) *Banker to the Poor –the story of the Grameen Bank,* Aurum Press

Made in the USA
Columbia, SC
13 February 2018